China and Israel

*Chinese, Jews; Beijing, Jerusalem
(1890–2018)*

Jewish Identities in Post-Modern Society

Series Editor:
Roberta Rosenberg Farber (Yeshiva University, New York)

ACADEMIC
STUDIES
PRESS

China and Israel

*Chinese, Jews; Beijing, Jerusalem
(1890–2018)*

ARON SHAI

BOSTON
2019

Library of Congress Cataloging-in-Publication Data

Names: Shai, Aron, author.

Title: China and Israel : Chinese, Jews; Beijing, Jerusalem (1890-2018) / Aron Shai. Other titles: Sin ṿe-Yiśra'el. English

Description: Boston : Academic Studies Press, 2019. | Series: Jewish identities in post-modern society | Includes bibliographical references and index. | Identifiers: LCCN 2018054902 (print) | LCCN 2018057750 (ebook) | ISBN 9781618118967 (ebook) | ISBN 9781618118943 (hard-cover) | ISBN 9781618118950 (pbk.)

Subjects: LCSH: Israel–Foreign relations–China. | China–Foreign relations–Israel. | Israelis–China. | Jews–China.

Classification: LCC DS119.8.C5 (ebook) | LCC DS119.8.C5 S5313 2019 (print) | DDC 303.48/256940510904–dc23

LC record available at https://lccn.loc.gov/2018054902

© Academic Studies Press, 2019

ISBN 978-1-618118-94-3 (hardcover)

ISBN 978-1-618118-96-7 (electronic)

ISBN 978-1-618118-95-0 (paperback)

Book design by Lapiz Digital Services.

Cover illustration by Avi Katz, reproduced by permission.

Published by Academic Studies Press

28 Montfern Avenue

Brighton, MA 02135, USA

press@academicstudiespress.com

www.academicstudiespress.com

In memory of Geoffrey Hudson and
Richard Storry, my mentors at Oxford

Contents

Preface

My Road to China

This book, which has been many years in the making, is a collage composed of numerous and varied perspectives on the Israel–China saga.

In August 2007, I was due to fly to the United States to begin a semester sabbatical at New York University, but unfortunately, my long-awaited journey was briefly delayed by illness. I was hospitalized for several days at Sha'arei Zedek Hospital in Jerusalem, where for generations some members of my family had been healed while others, unfortunately, had drawn their final breaths. I felt that finally I had been granted a forced break that allowed for introspection and reflection or, to use Aristotle's term, contemplation. During my stay in the hospital, I reached some conclusions and made a number of decisions. Perhaps, I thought, there was a positive side to my situation. I recalled the story in the ancient Jewish texts about Rabbi Eliezer ben Hyrcanos, whose brothers sent him to plow on the side of a mountain. When his cow fell down and was maimed, Rabbi Eliezer declared, "It was fortunate for me that my cow was maimed." Indeed, his misfortune resulted in a positive outcome, as he then immersed himself in the world of Torah learning, and the great men of the nation came to sit before him.[1] In a parallel Chinese legend, the saying *Sàiwēngshīmǎ*[2] also hints at how bad luck can be reversed. In this case, an old man's warhorse runs away across the Mongolian border,

---

1   In another version of this story, the hero is Abba Yudan, a wealthy man who fell on hard times. While he was plowing the reduced field that he had left, the earth split beneath him. His cow fell into the crevasse and broke her leg. When he bent down to lift the cow up, he discovered a huge treasure beneath her. "It proved fortunate for me that my cow's leg was broken," he declared, as his wealth was restored.

2   塞翁失马 Pinyin: Sàiwēngshīmǎ.

but the horse eventually returns with a rare and valuable colt at its side, and so the man is rewarded. In my case, the unexpected hospital stay pushed me to complete this book. My relationship with China began in the United States in 1963. After completing my military service in the Israeli Defense Forces (IDF), I had originally planned to return to Kibbutz Hatzerim, where I had intended to make my home. Instead, I went off to northern California, where I attended a small college in San Mateo. As part of the program, I heard a lecture by a veteran of the Japanese theater of the Second World War about American involvement in Asia. At the time, John F. Kennedy was president, and after the failure of his attack on the Bay of Pigs in Cuba, he plunged his country into disastrous intervention in Vietnam, initially by sending American "advisors" to the South Vietnamese Army. Thus, the United States returned to the Asian arena in full swing. Its large-scale involvement had begun with the Spanish–American war in the final years of the nineteenth century. During this conflict, the United States became entangled in the Philippines due to the misguided decisions made by American statesmen under the leadership of President William McKinley.

In the lectures I heard, I enjoyed learning about the faulty decision-making process that led the United States to sink unintentionally into the quagmire of East Asia. The chain of events intrigued me. Sometimes policy-makers, both American and other, are themselves shaped rather than shapers—they are dragged into whirlpools of disaster, rather than leading the way to a desirable solution. A thorough study of American involvement in the Philippines reveals that President McKinley was unable to navigate the developments that unfolded, and it was a group of jingoistic navy officials who caused the surprising, unplanned annexation of the Philippines by US imperial power. Following the acquisition of the Philippines, American interest in China grew, as did US obligations in Asia and the Pacific. Eventually, these became even more important than American obligations toward European nations. For this reason, during the Second World War, Asian considerations were stronger and more dominant than European issues. The need to defeat Japan was more urgent than the need to overthrow Germany. Due to Judeo-centric and Eurocentric attitudes, the Israeli (and European) reader will sometimes find it difficult to understand the full scope of Asian importance in World War II. But if we reflect on the wars that followed World War II, we find that throughout these conflicts as well, Asian issues were central factors in US policy. The Korean and Vietnamese wars dragged the United States into the Asian imbroglio. Ever since, the United States has been forced to view the Asian factor as a crucial component of its foreign and defense policies. This is certainly true when we examine North Korean–American tensions almost seventy years after the 1950 to 1953 war.

The rise of the new China, and particularly the success of the Open Door Policy since the 1980s, have drawn much attention to Asia. China incontrovertibly proved its economic abilities, and therefore drew the United States back into the Asian arena and into harsh competition between the two countries.

In my student days, I deliberated the question of what was the best way for proper implementation of equality and justice, both on the local level in Israel and on the international level. In those days of the Cold War, Third World countries faced two models or ideals: the Soviet Communist model and the so-called "free" American model. Although these were early days, I had already concluded that neither of these models was appropriate for practical application to the Asian world, the Middle Eastern nations, or even to Africa and South America. A regime of dictatorship ruled in Russia, and despite the ideological and sociological lip service it paid to the principles of justice and equality, it was fundamentally harsh and unsympathetic to the desires and aspirations of individuals. On the international level, the Communist regime showed no consideration for the small countries in the bloc that it controlled, or for their citizens. But I also thought that the American model seemed hopeless, as its internal mechanisms were completely lacking in compassion. The US system demonstrated no sensitivity toward citizens who lacked financial means, and public health care was limited. In fact, as I saw it, the individual was left abandoned to his fate. At times, the minimal international assistance that the United States gave other countries seemed designed for the mere glorification of Washington and advancement of American consumer interests. By contrast, the nascent People's Republic of China appeared naïve and full of goodwill toward the Third World. In Africa, for example, China's envoys, like their Israeli colleagues, excelled in empathizing with the locals. As opposed to the Western emissaries, they did not isolate themselves in luxurious neighborhoods but rather went to live alongside the local populations that they were helping. Possibly, my attitude also shared this naïve optimism. Historian Ya'akov Talmon might have identified it as "that spark of political messianism that infects the Jews."

My relationship with China thus developed behind an ideological lens. As a socialist (today I can say old-school socialist with updates mandated by time), I believed that Beijing, not Moscow or Washington, would be the harbinger of a new and challenging vision for the Third World nations. My imagination was captured by leaders such as Zhou Enlai—an experienced diplomat, an intelligent man of action, refined and principled. I thought he seemed like a friendly man (recently published works, particularly the study by Jung Chang and Jon Halliday,[3] describe him as Mao's spineless puppet and a low-level opportunist). At any rate, this was before the Cultural Revolution in China, a time of sober national reflection after the failure of Mao's Great Leap Forward, that foolish attempt to achieve utopian, eschatological socialism in the here and now. China's behavior was moderate. At times, it seemed that China was finally joining the international community and positioning itself firmly on a pragmatic trajectory that was recognizable to all.

In retrospect, had I joined thinkers such as Gottfried Liebnitz, Louis Le Comte, Etienne Silhouette, Jean-Baptiste Duhold, and Voltaire—in other words, all those who followed Francois Quesnay, who promoted the "Chinese dream" of almost unchecked admiration for China?

To me, Israel before the Six Day War, or the "First Republic" as I usually call it, was not only my beloved homeland but also a nascent utopia, the fulfillment of Isaiah's vision of peace and harmony that would reign at the end of days. As I saw it, thorough knowledge of China could advance that dream. In 1964, when I was a young man visiting Belgrade, capital of the former Yugoslavia, I attempted to visit the Chinese embassy to obtain firsthand public relations material about current events there. I had also finally resolved to learn Chinese. But the visit was a failure—the authorities wouldn't permit me to enter the building or speak to anyone. In those days after the Great Leap Forward and before the Cultural Revolution, the Chinese were a locked box, a long way from the friendliness that I had naïvely imagined in my youth. At the Hebrew University at Givat Ram in Jerusalem, I continued my academic studies and began to learn Chinese in a small group with a handful of other students.

In those days I envisioned a rapprochement between China and Israel, as there were similar characteristics in their ethos, such as their attitudes toward tradition and to the family unit. To me, China and Israel were

---

3   Mao: The Unknown Story.

more than just another pair of nations about which academics could write dissertations that were far removed from the reality of international relations. The two countries bore important messages that I believed were worth promoting. Eventually, my research and teaching on the topic of China–Israel relations convinced me of the depth of historical and cultural similarity between them.

When the Six Day War broke out, I found myself facing a new dilemma. On one hand, many Israelis were swept up in patriotic fervor following the return to historic regions that we had studied from afar and that we longed for atavistically, in theory as the heritage of our ancient forefathers. I fought in Jerusalem, and I heard the cries of jubilation at the liberation of the Western Wall, where I was one of the first to visit, as well as Rachel's Tomb and other historical sites. The excitement conquered my imagination. Still, I realized all too quickly that over the long term, domination of the "New Territories," as they were called then, would drag the Zionist enterprise into dire straits.

How could I apply my thoughts about the new China, where the Great Cultural Revolution had begun a year earlier in 1966, to the new situation in Israel? Were there lessons from China's experience that Israel could adopt?

In contrast to my deliberations over these dilemmas, another student in my Chinese language class, a kibbutz member who was older than I was, expressed confidence in his views and saved himself the soul-searching. He was a radical who admired Mao, and he was certain that the Cultural Revolution would bring salvation to the entire world. In our conversations he always expressed himself unambiguously. Like me, he was also drafted into service in the IDF during the Six Day War. After the war was over, he told me that he had participated in the occupation of Gaza, but "I couldn't aim my gun at the so-called enemies, so I shot up at the sky." He told me that on the eve of the war, during the waiting period before attack, he had written a personal letter to Chinese leader Mao Zedong, warning against Israeli aggression and rising Israeli imperialism. He was deeply disappointed that he never received a reply, particularly since he had asked Mao to intervene and prevent Israel from entering the war. We had many discussions about the Cultural Revolution, which was then in its early days. Despite the evidence of extreme violence and intolerance, he remained firm to his position—this was the only way to achieve liberation of the proletariat and bring about revolution. Eventually he was disappointed and asserted,

"Mao isn't Maoist enough." This statement reminded me of an old story about Charlie Chaplin, who sneaked into a competition of Charlie Chaplin impersonators but never even reached the finals.

After completing my BA in history and philosophy at the Hebrew University, I continued for my master's degree. I took all the courses that were related to China, including courses by Professor Zvi Schiffrin, who later was awarded the Israel Prize. At the time there was no East Asian Studies Department anywhere in Israel, and the classes on the "Far East" were offered sporadically and in various departments. After completing my MA, I received a scholarship to Oxford University, where I continued to pursue my interest in China. Two professors made a particular impression on me and encouraged me throughout my studies. Richard Storry was an expert on Japan who had fought in World War II on the Burmese and Indian fronts, and who was investigating Japanese prisoners of war. Geoffrey Hudson focused on China, and was known for his work on Chinese and world politics before 1800. My doctorate was on Sino–British relations during the Sino–Japanese War in the 1930s. I focused on the Western powers' conciliatory attitude toward Japan, comparing it to a similar attitude adopted by other European countries toward Italy and Germany. My central argument was that the Western powers had sacrificed their principles and made concessions to Japan out of weakness and fear. Although there was no East Asian equivalent of the Munich Agreement, the Western powers appeased Japan in a roundabout manner, gradually, and despite a rising tide of principles that the Western powers professed to uphold.

While at Oxford, I received an offer of employment from Professor Zvi Yavetz, one of the founders of Tel Aviv University and mythological head of the Department of History, who was visiting England for several days for his academic work. His worldview was overwhelmingly Eurocentric, as was that of the other senior professors, as well as the younger members of the department. To them, Europe was the cradle of human civilization, and thus its history represented the history of the entire world. Of course, they were aware of Russia (mainly the Moscow aristocracy, Peter the Great and his ilk), the United States, and even Latin America, Africa, and the Middle East (for which our university set aside its own distinct, impressive department), but the feeling was that in the final analysis, Europe was the focal point of the world.

Undoubtedly, the history department at Tel Aviv University was worthy of admiration. Its reputation was widespread, not just in Israel but in academic circles across the ocean. Six of its members were awarded the Israel Prize. It boasted a large number of tenured positions and offered a broad variety of courses, majors, and tracks. The ancient world, medieval period, and early modern history were perhaps the jewels in the crown, but modern history of the nineteenth and twentieth centuries were also points of pride. Yavetz was completely unwilling to adopt my suggestion that I teach the history of China and East Asia, not even as a fraction of my teaching hours. But at the time, in the early 1970s, I was one of the few people in Israel who had studied modern Chinese history, in addition to my focus on England and imperialism. Yavetz didn't believe in the importance of the non-European regions and insisted that I had to learn German and focus on Germany. Eventually I did manage to teach on China, practically underground, as part of a survey course entitled "China—From Empire to Republic." The course covered international events and internal developments in China from the Opium War until Mao's successors. It was not until the 1990s that I managed to convince the dean of the faculty and the university president of the demand for this subject. Finally, I was able to initiate the opening of the Department of East Asian Studies at Tel Aviv University, and it was as if a dam had burst—students flocked to the departmental office to register. Twenty years later, the number of students surpassed seven hundred, and ours became the largest academic department in the Faculty of Humanities of Tel Aviv University, and the largest in Israel.

My first visit to China was in September 1989, three months after the events in Tiananmen Square, eventually known in the West as the Tiananmen Massacre. To me it felt like a return visit, as I had been following events in the country for many years through its maps, stories, books, and economic developments. A feeling of *déjà vu* accompanied me throughout my trip, as if my eyes had seen every corner there in a previous reincarnation. I arrived as academic leader of a small group of students, and we toured the distant land for a month, during which we heard comprehensive lectures on a host of issues related to China. The experience was particularly meaningful for me, since China had long been my heart's desire. My decades-old dream was finally realized.

But even then, I was disappointed to note many telltale cracks appearing in Chinese society. Thirteen years after Mao's death and the formal end of the Cultural Revolution, I observed economic gaps and their social consequences in Chinese society, which had extracted itself from the revolutionary and cultural chaos that had led to almost complete equality. After that point, I observed beggars on the streets of Beijing alongside villagers in worn rags, while beside them strolled members of the new, affluent middle class. As I was an idealist who supported the ideal of equality, I felt drawn to probing the issue of Chinese socialism. Was China exhibiting a retreat from the principles that I admired, and that had attracted me to it in the first place? Would China's opening to the world at large and the international commercial market mean that in the future I would see enormous skyscraper hotels with restaurants revolving in their towers, alongside slums like the ones I observed in Beijing? At a time that neighborhoods still had public toilets, since private homes had no bathrooms, luxury high-rises sprouted simultaneously across the street.

My idealistic, utopian image of China as the model state was also shaken by my first encounter with the security forces. When our group arrived at Tiananmen Square, the "Gate of Heavenly Peace," soldiers stopped us and did not permit us to enter. Since we were very close to the incident in the Square, both geographically and chronologically, I was very interested in the details of events during the first days of June that year. I soon realized that people who had been present in the Square didn't know exactly what had happened either. The statistics about victims in the Square varied widely. At Heathrow Airport, while on our way to Beijing, I had bought a book that described the Tiananmen Massacre in harsh words and grisly photos. This was a mass market book, published quickly and without thorough research, but of the type that makes a powerful first impression. When I showed it to one of the guides that accompanied us in China, he turned white. He was petrified. He stared silently at the photos, and although he himself had been present at the Tiananmen Square during the events, it seemed to me that he was discovering new, shocking information. He suggested to me in a friendly manner that I hide the book and not show it to anyone else.

During one of our first tours of the Forbidden City, a formal delegation arrived at the famous site. Unidentified guards firmly pushed aside the ordinary tourists, both locals and foreigners. Our own tour guide implored us to leave the site immediately. In my diary, I wrote that everywhere, the fear of authority was palpable.

The most important milestone of progress in the establishment of relations between China and Israel was the opening of the Chinese embassy in Tel Aviv in 1992. I was in contact with several of its representatives, particularly Ms. Zhang Xiao-an, the deputy ambassador. At the same time, I had contact with the representatives of Taiwan stationed in Tel Aviv at what was known as the "Taipei Cultural and Economic Office." Of course, navigating between these two entities wasn't easy, as the Chinese embassy was very wary of Israelis who had any contact with the Taiwanese office. A rumor even went around that the Chinese were spying on the receptions given by the Taiwanese to find out which Israelis were consorting with the enemy. Throughout my dealings with the Chinese, I was surprised by the embassy's efficiency of operation. Its staff was well-informed of what was going on in Israel and even in the East Asian Studies Department at Tel Aviv University, including activities and names of lecturers. In one case, an embassy attaché phoned me and asked, or rather demanded, that we cancel a planned lecture on the Falun Gong movement.[4] I explained to him the meaning of academic freedom in Israel, but he was not convinced. He simply insisted that we cancel the lecture. Over the years they interfered in other events as well, such as their attempt to remove an exhibit of Falun Gong supporters in the entrance to the main library.

I also had close contact with the Taiwanese representatives in Israel, and they invited me to visit their country. When I was researching my biography of Zhang Xueliang, I requested their assistance in arranging a meeting with him in Hawaii. They tried their best to comply, but returned to me in disappointment. The general was almost one hundred years old, ill, and could not receive me. Shortly afterward, he died, and my dream of a meeting evaporated.[5]

After the establishment of diplomatic relations between Israel and China, much discussion ensued on the background of each culture, Chinese

---

4   Falun Gong (法轮功) or Falun Dafa (法轮大法). This spiritual movement was founded in 1992 by Li Hongzhi. It focuses on meditation and slow qigong exercises (physical movements based on spiritual principles), and emphasizes moral development as well. Since the late 1990s, when the number of Falun Gong practitioners reached tens of millions, the Chinese Communist Party has energetically worked to discourage this movement, and in 1999 the Chinese authorities under Jiang Zemin declared it an illegal practice. Much evidence (although it is disputed) shows that this categorization led to the violent suppression, imprisonment and torture of Falun Gong members, and even harvesting of their organs for international trafficking.

5   General Zhang Xueliang, nicknamed the "Young Marshal," was a Manchurian Chinese. Born in 1901, he ruled under the nationalist regime of Chiang Kai-shek and plotted with the communists to organize the kidnapping of his commander. For this, he was placed under house arrest for over fifty years. My book *Zhang Xueliang: The General Who Never Fought*, discusses his life against the background of the history of modern China.

and Jewish, in an attempt to identify their shared foundation and unifying factors.

David Libai had participated in the same tour of China in 1989 as I did, and he was later appointed Minister of Justice in Yitzhak Rabin's government. Before his first formal trip to China, he asked me to write his chief address. It was a great pleasure for me to write this address; for me, this was an opportunity to point out shared aspects of the two nations. When discussing these two celebrated, ancient peoples located at the two extremes of the Asian continent, we noted that China's inhabitants had lived in their country continuously, but the Jews did not have the privilege of remaining in their homeland for long. In fact, after the destruction of the Second Temple, the Jews' national existence in their homeland ended for hundreds of years. Thus the story of the Jewish people's return to their land and reestablishment of a national home is an experience unfamiliar to the Chinese.

Around 1850 BCE, during the rule of the quasi-mythological Xia dynasty, the first to earn mention in the records of Chinese historians, the Jewish forefather Abraham made his way from Ur of the Chaldees in Mesopotamia to the Land of Israel. His descendants experienced several exiles from their land. Still, the similarities between these two peoples overcome their differences. The written language, which is the focus for the development of every human culture and for preservation of the values accumulated over generations, was preserved in both the Jewish and Chinese cultures. This is a rare core that no other nation in the world (except for Greece) has enjoyed for such a long history. In most of the world, languages have undergone processes of disruption and distortion.

Both cultures nurture the family unit, with rituals and ceremonies providing a firm foundation for cultural continuity. It would be superfluous to expand on the importance of the Bible and the significance of the Oral Torah in Judaism, and the same is true for the special importance of the writings of the Chinese philosophers—Confucius, Lao Tzu, and their successors. Both cultures place a high value on learning, introspection, and study of the secrets of the universe and of human existence. Neither sanctified the military ethic, and violent combat was spurned. A Chinese proverb emphasizes that just as one does not forge nails from quality metal, so one does not mold soldiers from fine men.[6] We find similar expression of

---

6   好鐵不當釘; 好兒不當兵 Pinyin: Hǎo tiě bùdāng dīng; hǎo er bùdāng bīng.

the ideal of peace and tranquility in the prophecies of Isaiah,[7] and in the writings of Chinese philosophers such as Mencius. Confucius emphasized the values of family, honoring one's parents, tradition, and ceremony, values that Jews have held dear for millennia. Several decades ago, a book of Confucius' analects was translated into Hebrew, and it received much attention in Israel.[8]

Although every generation has a desire to rebel, change, and improve, both cultures have preserved their traditional principles. When Confucius was asked to give one word that would serve as a guideline for life, he answered, "Reciprocity," and expanded, using almost the same phrase as Hillel the Elder: "Do unto others as you would have them do to you."

In the hundreds of lectures that I have given on China throughout my academic career, I felt that despite my fifty years of studying the culture, history, and economy of this distant land, I was never able to completely break down the barrier between my "Israeliness" and complete internalization of "Chineseness." Although I believed in my ability to understand in an academic context the historical processes that affected China, I was repeatedly astonished at the wonders and surprises presented by this country.

Furthermore, I eventually realized that there was a wide gap between the Judeo-Christian ethos and the cultural tenets of East Asia and China, a gap that was very difficult to bridge. The European worldview is dichotomous and has distinct categories: good and bad, pure and impure, male and female, light and dark, yes and no. This decisiveness parallels the Israeli mentality and language, appearing in expressions such as "Are you coming or not?"; "Do you agree or disagree?"; "Do you accept this or not?"; "Are you communist or capitalist? Religious or secular?" But this approach does not fit the Chinese view of life. Chinese culture was inspired by a philosophical and ethical system that is thousands of years old and is based on the concept of *yin* and *yang*. *Yin* means negative, darkness, the cloudy or northern side of the mountain, while *yang* represents the positive, light,

---

7 It will come to pass at the end of days.... They will beat their swords into plowshares, and their spears into pruning hooks. Nation will not lift up sword against nation; neither will they learn war any more" (Isaiah 2:2–4).

8 In the introduction to their translation, which was published in 1960, Daniel Lesley and Amatzia Porat wrote that because the classic was written during the period of Ezra and Nehemiah (early Second Temple period), they decided to use biblical style in their translation, to match the general ideas found in Judaism as well. In Amira Katz's 2006 translation of Confucius' analects, she uses modern Hebrew, mainly in order to render his ideas accessible to the younger generation.

and the abundance of the sun's warmth. But although these forces may seem to be working against each other, in fact they are interrelated and interdependent, like Siamese twins. They represent the unity of opposites. Further, they nurture each other. Pairs in nature, such as light and dark, warmth and cold, and even life and death express the concept of *yin/yang*, which forms the foundation of China's philosophy as well as its science, medicine, and military arts.

I believe that this sophisticated spectrum, which enfolds opposites in a single embrace, holds the key to understanding China. It is the only way we can understand, for example, the Open Door Policy that China has adopted in the modern era, which permits a rare coexistence between the free economic market and a police state controlled by the Communist Party. I do not have space here to pursue this philosophical issue, but I will offer an instructive example, which Henry Kissinger presents in his book on China.[9]

Kissinger emphasizes the diplomatic and strategic implications of this thesis. In his view, the Chinese are experts in realpolitik. Their strategic approach is completely different from that practiced in the West. History has taught them that not every problem has a solution. In opposition to the accepted belief in the West (including many sectors in Israel), the belief in the ability to achieve complete domination over events—whether a crisis, dispute, or any other definitive historical event—is merely an illusion. The actions resulting from this illusion can disrupt the world's harmony. Security, or even complete satisfaction, cannot be found in our world. Rather, it is the roundabout, sophisticated path, which sometimes focuses on wearing down the opponent, that provides the desired relative advantage.

This concept finds ample expression in the difference or contrast between two games that are representative of the two cultures: chess, and the Chinese *wei qi* or *go* (围棋), in which the object is to surround the most territory. As opposed to chess, in which the winner is usually the player who has completely destroyed his opponent by pursuing the king and removing it, the Chinese game has no clear, definitive goal that marks the end or the winner. Instead, the game ends when the players have no more interest or desire to continue. At this point, the players count the points on the squares of the game board, which represent the territory that each one

---

9   Kissinger, *On China*, 23–25.

has captured. The winner is whoever earns the most points. The uninitiated observer of the board after a game between skilled players cannot immediately determine the winner in a decisive manner.

While chess emphasizes the conclusive battle, *go* focuses on a battle of attrition in which the participant works calmly to achieve a relative advantage. In chess the pieces are readily observable, identifiable, and constantly prepared for action, while in the Chinese game the player must correctly evaluate and consider not only the pieces present on the board but also the reserves available to his opponent, which he can throw into the ring. Mao Zedong's military theory drew on similar ancient Chinese philosophies, and thus it largely relied on the concept of indirect warfare through the use of "empty" terrain, bypass techniques, and flexible strategy.

Structure and Contents

While this book differs from my previous research works, it resembles the two historical novels and the biography of Zhang Xueliang that I published. In the novels I attempted to breathe life into the characters and make the reading experience as captivating as possible, alongside careful presentation of the historical framework. The biography, which was published in Hebrew, English, and Chinese, is an exact factual depiction of the man and the state, but it also has a narrative element.[10]

This book rests on three foundations. The first is historical-political, and analyzes the bilateral relationship between the two countries—Israel and China. As is accepted in academia, it relies on primary and secondary documents, insofar as these were available to me while writing this book. In

---

10 My academic works in English: *Origins of the War in the East: Britain, China, Japan 1937–1939*, London: Croom Helm, 1976; *Britain and China 1941–1947: Imperial Momentum*, London: Macmillan, St. Antony's College, Oxford and St. Martin's Press, New York, 1984; *The Fate of British and French Firms in China 1949–1954: Imperialism Imprisoned*, Houndmills, Basingstoke: Macmillan in association with St. Antony's College, Oxford, 1996; *Zhang Xueliang: The General Who Never Fought*, Houndmills, Basingstoke: Macmillan, 2012; *BenHazar, Son to a Stranger*, Jerusalem: Gefen Publishing House, 2009. In Hebrew: *From the Opium War to Mao's Successors: China in the International Sphere, 1840–1990*, Tel Aviv: Zmora-Bitan, 1990; *China in the Twentieth Century*, Tel Aviv: Ministry of Defense Publishing Department, Broadcast University, 1998; Novels (in Hebrew): *Benhazar*, Tel Aviv: Am Oved, 1990; *She Called Him Mano*, Tel Aviv: Zmora-Bitan, 1997; *Zhang Xueliang: The General Who Never Fought*, Or Yehuda: Zmora-Bitan, 2008.

Israel I used material from the national archives[11] and secondary material written by my fellow researchers and myself.[12] In addition, I conducted interviews with Israelis who were instrumental in forming the relationship between Israel and China.

The second foundation is the story of several central figures who are woven throughout the story of China's relationship with the Jews before the establishment of the State of Israel, and with Israelis after the state was founded. For example, I summarize the fascinating story of Moshe Cohen, known as Morris ("Two Gun") Cohen, who according to several versions of the story, was Sun Yat-sen's assistant. I also relate the unique and little-known story of Dr. Jacob Rosenfeld, which begins between the two world wars in Vienna and ends in Tel Aviv, three years after Israel's independence. In the interim, he spent a decade in China.[13] I also relate the colorful, positive, but also disappointing experiences of major Israeli businessmen and their companies in recent years. This foundation offers a glimpse into the personal aspect and into the world of the Israeli companies that do business with China.

The third foundation is a personal one, and it is mainly expressed in this introduction and in the last chapter. It comprises my sketches and musings as an academic. Beginning in the early 1960s, I conducted a consistent observation of events in China and the transformations that it underwent, recorded them, and lectured on them. Thus this book contains over fifty years of insight on China and the Chinese.

This tripartite foundation is reflected in the structure of the book, which enables readers to examine various themes in the order that they prefer. The book is based on testimonials, documents, letters, interviews, and current studies, and on insights that I have collected over the course of the past fifty years.

In Chinese the surname is written before the given name. Sometimes different versions are given for the same name, in accordance with the

---

11 Gallia Lindenstrauss wrote an unpublished study of Israel-Chinese relations from 1950–1992 (Jerusalem, 1994), under my direction. See pages 92–106 of her study. Appendices 2–12 are reprinted documents from the archives of the Israel Ministry of Defense. References to this archive refer to these appendices.

12 See, for example, Yegar, The Long Road to Asia [Hebrew]; Goldstein (ed.), China and Israel; Shen (ed.), China and Anti-Terrorism; and Shai, Sino–Israeli Relations.

13 These chapters are mainly based on two books that document comprehensive research on these individuals. On Moshe Cohen: Daniel S. Levy, Two-Gun Cohen: A Biography, and on Jacob Rosenfeld: Gerd Kaminski, General Luo Genannt Langnase [in German].

accepted form in different regions of China and its environs. Transliteration of well-known place names such as Beijing, Guangzhou, or Shandong are non-hyphenated. Historically, romanization was not always uniform, since various spelling systems were used according to the period, place, or local custom, which often caused variety in the original spellings. At any rate, the index in the back of the book enables rapid identification of the pinyin spelling used here.

* * *

It was natural that aside from my involvement in general history and East Asian Studies, I would also focus on Israel–China relations and consider describing and analyzing this issue in a book. But this book would never have reached publication without the professional assistance of my research assistants at Tel Aviv University, especially Rinat Shachar, Avital Rom, Roni Deshe and Or Biron, outstanding graduates of the East Asian Studies Department, who have assisted me in my work in recent years. Or Biron accompanied me to interviews and also provided great assistance in editing sections of the book and offering helpful suggestions. I offer my sincere thanks to all of you. I would also like to thank Mrs. Jessica Setbon, who so professionally translated this study into English while providing her helpful insights.

As Shaul N. Eisenberg Professor of East Asian Affairs, I have benefited from the assistance of Mrs. Lea Nobuko-Eisenberg and the support of her daughter Emily and son-in-law Horacio Furman, true friends of the East Asian Studies Department at Tel Aviv University. Unfortunately, this limited space does not permit me to list the names of the interviewees (they are mentioned in the text of the book and the bibliography), friends, colleagues, and all those who encouraged me along the path to publication of this book. Last in order but first in importance, I thank my wife Puah, my lifelong companion whose assistance and constructive criticism is worth far more than its weight in gold.

Introduction

Jewish Communities in China

The history of relations between China and Israel is intertwined with the particular history of the Jews in China in various eras. A relationship between Jews and Chinese existed centuries before the establishment of the two modern states in the mid-twentieth century. China, the empire that was frequently split by foreign occupation and internal warfare, and ancient Israel, from which the Jews were exiled and scattered across the globe, encountered each other at a single meeting point—the Jews who built their homes in the land of the Chinese.

The Kaifeng Community

The first Jews to reach China were merchants who travelled on the Silk Road, which led from Europe into the heart of the "Middle Kingdom" (as the Chinese called it). They first arrived in the ninth century, during the Tang dynasty, and put down roots in many locations throughout China. They made a particularly deep and long-lasting impression in the city of Kaifeng. According to the available evidence, the Jewish community of Kaifeng existed for eight hundred years, from the eleventh century until the early twentieth century. Most of the information on Kaifeng Jewry comes from primary sources that were preserved, such as stone inscriptions, Jewish community documents, and documents recorded by Christian missionaries (first Jesuit and later Protestant). The number of Jews in the Kaifeng community today is unknown, as it is unclear whether those who consider themselves descendants of the ancient community are indeed Jews.

Community members suffered troubles and crises, from natural disasters and political problems (such as invasion of the city by Taiping rebels in 1857) to assimilation into the cultures of the surrounding communities. This process of "sinification" was gradual and unavoidable. According to reports of Jewish and Christian visitors to the city during the second half of the nineteenth century, the only deterrents to this process were the multiple reconstructions of the Pure Truth Temple, a synagogue that was repeatedly destroyed and then reconstructed until it was finally razed for the last time in 1852.[14]

Apparently, the Kaifeng Jews originally came from India and Persia. The first evidence of their existence comes from two written records, one in Hebrew, the other in Persian, that describe Jewish merchants in East Turkestan (today's Xinjiang region) on their way to China.[15] The Jews reached Kaifeng, then the capital of the Northern Song dynasty. In those days, Kaifeng was an impressive urban settlement with over one million inhabitants and an important center of commerce and transportation. The city hosted many communities, including Muslim, Persian, and Nestorian. But the Jews did not live under Chinese rule for long. In 1127 Kaifeng was invaded by the Jurchen, and about 150 years later it fell to the Mongols. During this period, the Kaifeng Jews are mentioned in the writings of the Venetian traveler Marco Polo. Chinese sources from the same period document that the authorities forbade both Muslims and Jews to circumcise their sons, slaughter certain animals, and marry relatives.[16] On the other hand, some assert that the Mongol regime was friendly to Muslims and Jews, and that Jews participated in government institutions as economic advisors and tax-collectors.

During the Ming dynasty (1368–1644), the ethnic Chinese reestablished their rule over the kingdom. During that era, the Jesuits began to visit China. The well-known Jesuit priest Matteo Ricci met with representatives of the Kaifeng Jewish community, and through him word reached Europe regarding the existence of a Jewish community in China.

At first, the authorities tried to impose a process of sinification on the Jews by mandating practices such as intermarriage with Chinese (the Han people). But this idea was rapidly abandoned. Still, even without the authorities' coercion, over time the Kaifeng Jews integrated and assimilated

---

14 Urbach, "The Kaifeng Jews: Between Revival and Obliteration," 38–53.
15 Herbert, "Der Weg nach Osten" [German], 36.
16 Leslie, "Integration, Assimilation and Survival," 50.

into Chinese culture. They adopted Chinese family names and even sat for the imperial exams, a system for selecting and recruiting government clerks through rigorous examinations.[17] Adopting Chinese family names led to assimilation of the Chinese family dynasty model and was also an outward sign of this process. This practice created a linear family line, headed by an ancestral, mythical forefather who was considered founder of the dynasty and was accorded appropriate honor. Thus the Jewish families of Kaifeng followed the traditional Chinese practice of hanging pictures of the dynastic forefathers on the walls. The significance of this was integration into the Chinese ethos, and from here it was only a short step for Jewish men to adopt the Chinese practice of marrying several wives, including Chinese women.

During the Manchurian Qing dynasty (1644–1911), the Jews in Kaifeng continued to preserve their traditions and customs on the one hand, and on the other, to assimilate into the Chinese environment. For example, in the seventeenth century they adopted the Chinese custom of burying the dead in family plots.[18] Yet the Jews continued to observe some of the Jewish *mitzvot*, or religious laws. This situation continued until the late nineteenth and early twentieth century. By the nineteenth century, according to Protestant missionaries, the members of the Kaifeng Jewish community had the same outward appearance as the Chinese among whom they lived.

Judaism as a Popular Religion

The Chinese viewed Judaism as a popular religion, just one more of the host of such religions that had existed in China throughout its history. These creeds combined a wide variety of beliefs and streams of thought that originated in Confucianism, Daoism, and the Chinese form of Buddhism.[19] The Chinese defined Judaism as a religion or a separate religious group that had a religious leader (*jiaozhu* 教主) and a temple for its worshippers. The Chinese used the term *jing* (经) for the community's sacred texts—the same term used to describe the Chinese classics.

---

17 Eber, *Sinim ve-yehudim: mifgashim bein tarbuyot* [*Chinese and Jews: Intercultural Encounters*] [Hebrew], 21

18 Ibid., 22.

19 Irene Eber thinks that the identity of Judaism as one of many sects did not harm it, but rather enabled its preservation for centuries, since the community existed as a separate group. See Eber, *Chinese and Jews*, 51.

The Chinese called Judaism "the sect of those who pick out tendons" (a reference to Jewish dietary practices); "the sect of those who teach Torah"; and "Muslims who wear the blue cap."[20] The Jews, however, used other names to refer to themselves, such as "followers of the Torah."[21] The term (犹太人) which is used today is a relatively late term that apparently originated in the nineteenth century and was probably chosen as proper transliteration of the word *Judah*.

The Jews of Kaifeng followed rabbinic practice, as opposed to Karaite. However, Jesuit missionaries who reached Kaifeng noted that the Jewish community possessed no copies of the Babylonian or Jerusalem Talmud. Any such texts had apparently been lost over time. The chief rabbi and community leader was called *wuseda*, the Chinese pronunciation of the *usted*, which in Persian means rabbi or lord. Rabbis of lower status also served the community, most from families named Li and Ai.[22]

The Kaifeng synagogue was an important center of community life. It was erected in 1163 by Rabbi Levi and remodeled and reconstructed at least ten times.[23] One of these reconstructions took place in 1279. A stone inscription found at the site notes that the synagogue was located "southeast of the produce market street and its perimeter was 35 jang in length (about 106 meters)."[24] In 1642, the synagogue was destroyed in a flood and refurbished with the financial assistance of a senior official named Zhao Yingcheng (1619–57).[25] In 1663, the synagogue was reconstructed, and it housed thirteen Torah scrolls written with black ink on parchment made of sheep or goat skin. These scrolls were repaired by members of the Jewish community after the flood of 1642. Seven of them were restored and are still preserved today. Possibly, the other scrolls also survived, but their location is unknown, and we may assume that they are in the possession of various collectors.[26] The synagogue continued its activity and was remodeled many times, but finally destroyed in 1852 after floods so severe that they caused the Yellow River to diverge from its course.

Kaifeng Jewry gradually adopted Confucian principles, an expression of their assimilation into the local population, but the Jews preserved Jewish

---

20 *tiaojinjiao* 挑筋教, *jiaojingjiao* 教经教, *lanmaohuihui* 蓝帽回回.
21 *jiaozhong* 教众 or *jiaoren* 教人.
22 Pollak, *Mandarins, Jews, and Missionaries*, 298.
23 Xu Xin, "On the Religious Life of the Kaifeng Jewish Community," 131.
24 Shatzman Steinhardt, "The Synagogue at Kaifeng," 7.
25 Leslie, "Integration, Assimilation and Survival," 51.
26 Pollak, "The Manuscripts and Artifacts," 83–85.

theological concepts and ethical values. An example of this syncretism between Judaism and Confucianism appears in a stone inscription from 1489, which explicitly states that Judaism and Confucianism have shared values, and that the difference between them is mainly in the texts. The Jews observed certain Jewish ceremonies very carefully, and most observed the rituals and laws of the Sabbath, Passover, Yom Kippur, Tisha b'Av, and other holidays. They also observed Jewish burial rites, mourning customs, and maintained their belief in one God.

During the eighteenth and nineteenth centuries, the Jews assimilated into their environment, and their physical appearance grew to resemble that of the Chinese. Sometime around the turn of the twentieth century or slightly afterward, the connection was lost between the Jewish community in China and Jewish communities in other locations around the world (as an exception, a certain connection was created with the members of the Jewish Sefardi community in Shanghai). The Chinese Jews no longer considered themselves as a separate or foreign group, but rather as one tile in the mosaic of communities and sects in China.

Eventually, the unique character of the Kaifeng Jewish community faded, and members of the community completely blended into their environment and underwent deep processes of sinification. There is no evidence that Christian missionaries (Jesuit or Protestant) ever succeeded in converting any of the Jews in China.

The Harbin Community

Jews from Russia and Eastern Europe reached the border of China and the city of Harbin, which developed into a major metropolis following construction of the Chinese Eastern Railway, which began in 1898 as a branch of the Trans-Siberian Railway. The Manchurian government granted Russia the rights to lay a railway line in Manchuria (Dongbei 东北), and a branch of the railroad also extended to Dalian, the southern port city in the region. Travel was now made easier for European passengers and immigrants, including many Jews. The first Jews came to Harbin from Siberia or the western regions of Russia, fleeing from pogroms, expulsions, and restrictions passed against them there.[27]

In 1903, the Jewish community built a synagogue in the city. One year later, hundreds of Jews arrived in Harbin following pogroms in southern

---

27 Kaufman, *Yehadut Harbin asher be-libi* [Harbin Jewry in my heart] [Hebrew], 12–13.

Russia. The Russo–Japanese War (1904–5) provided additional momentum for the growth of the Jewish population of the city. Some Jewish soldiers in the Russian czar's army abandoned their units and remained behind in Harbin. After the war, a number of these Jews settled in the city instead of returning to their homes in Russia.[28] One of the Jewish soldiers who stayed in Harbin was Joseph Trumpeldor.[29] He passed through the city with his troop while returning from wartime imprisonment in Japan and was promoted there to the rank of *unteroffizier*, thus apparently becoming the first Jewish officer in the Russian army.[30]

In 1914, after the First World War broke out, a third wave of Jews came to Harbin. Like their predecessors, these Jews enjoyed freedom and fair treatment from the local residents and the authorities. In 1920 the Jewish community of Harbin numbered some thirteen thousand individuals. In the following years, it grew to reach twenty-five thousand. The fourth wave of Jewish immigrants arrived during the Bolshevik Revolution and after the First World War. After this, some Jews moved out from Harbin to other Chinese cities, such as Dalian, Mukden, Tianjin, and Shanghai.

Despite the difficult situation in China after the fall of the Qing dynasty, the Harbin Jewish community continued to blossom. The Jews dealt in commerce, trades, and agriculture, and they even established financial institutions (such as "The Jewish People's Bank"), educational and medical organizations, and print media.[31] The Jewish community reached its peak from 1914 to 1931, when the Chinese still held control of the town, before the Japanese occupation. Among the organizations created then was HEDO (Harbinskoe Evreiskoe Duhovnoe Obshestvo—Harbin Jewish Religious Community), which assisted in the establishment of other community institutions and aided refugees. HEDO offered lodging for the needy, medical aid, academic scholarships, and other assistance. The financial resources for the community organizations came mostly from a tax on the community members based on their income. During the years surveyed until the end of World War II in 1945, the community had two

---

28 Eber, *Chinese and Jews*, 34.
29 Laskov, *Trumpeldor: Sipur hayav* [Trumpeldor: A biography] [Hebrew], 30.
30 Prof. Dan Ben-Canaan, who lived in Harbin and became an expert on the Jews of the city, relates that there are several versions of the story of Trumpeldor's stay in the city. According to old Russian sources, he remained there for two years, but there is no other evidence of this. At any rate, he apparently stayed there for longer than a tourist passing through.
31 Eber, Chinese and Jews, 34–35.

leaders: Chief Rabbi Aharon Moshe Kisilov and Dr. Avraham Kaufman, a physician and director of a hospital for the indigent.

The Jews established a commercial guild and a local trade exchange for currency and merchandise, mainly soybeans and furs. Among the well-known and wealthy residents were the three Skidelsky brothers (including David Solomon), Gregory Krol, and Issac Susskin.

Religious, Cultural, and Social Institutions

Several Ashkenazi synagogues functioned in Harbin. Their members also founded community organizations such as the burial society (*hevra kadisha*), Zionist Federation, Keren Kayemet Le-Israel (Jewish National Fund), and the local newspaper *Yevreyskaya Zhizn*.[32] The city had a Jewish library, and in 1920 an elementary school or Talmud Torah was established. This school taught Bible and Jewish philosophy as well as secular subjects including geography, mathematics, history, and Russian language.

Charity organizations included a women's organization (DEBO), a local branch of WIZO, the Ezra Charitable Society, a soup kitchen (which opened its doors to non-Jews as well—Russians and Chinese), an old age home and a cemetery (1903), a clinic called "Mishmeret Holim" (1920), a Jewish hospital (1938), and a special clinic for the disabled and chronically ill (1942). In the Harbin Jewish cemetery, 583 gravestones are still standing, with inscriptions in Russian and Yiddish. In 1958 the cemetery was moved outside the center of town. In 1992, after the establishment of diplomatic relations between Israel and China, it was refurbished at the request of the Association of Former Residents of China in Israel. Rabbi Aharon Shmulevitz Kisilov, who served as the community's rabbi, is buried there, as is Yosef Olmert, grandfather of former Prime Minister Ehud Olmert.[33]

---

32 Kaufman, *Yehadut Harbin Asher Be-Libi*, 31–34.

33 Lev-Ari, "Kehillat Harbin" [The Harbin community] [Hebrew]. In terms of Zionist politics, this well-to-do community supported the Revisionist ideology. It produced several prominent members of Israeli society, such as Mordechai Olmert and Yosef Tekoa, Israel's former ambassador to the UN. Several became fighters in the Irgun (Etzel). The grandfather of Israel's former Prime Minister Ehud Olmert settled in Harbin, and Ehud's parents, Bella and Mordechai, were born there. Mordechai was active in the Revisionist movement in the city. In contrast to most of the other Jewish youth, who attended Russian high schools, he attended a Chinese high school, and so he knew Chinese. Bella and Mordechai moved to Israel in 1930. Others who were born and grew up in Harbin include the parents of Member of Knesset Efraim "Effi" Eitam; the father of poet Dalia Ravikovitz; Prof. Haim Tadmor—father of David Tadmor,

Zionist youth movements also opened branches in Harbin, beginning with Ze'irei Zion and Hashomer Ha-Tza'ir in the early twentieth century, then Maccabi and Beitar in 1929. The latest also became the largest and most influential of the youth movements, and eventually remained the only one. At first, anti-Zionist movements were also present in Harbin, such as the Labor Bund and the Volkspartei, but over the years the overwhelming majority of Harbin Jews joined the Zionist groups, including Revisionists, General Zionists, and Mizrachi. The community maintained a strong connection with Mandate Palestine and imported merchandise including food and newspapers.

Harbin Jews Following the Japanese Occupation

In September 1931, the Kwantung Army, an expeditionary group of the Imperial Japanese Army, invaded Manchuria, and the situation of the Harbin Jewish community began to deteriorate. Many of its members abandoned the city and moved south to other Chinese cities that were not yet occupied, while others emigrated overseas.

To serve their imperialist purposes, the Japanese developed industry and infrastructure in greater Manchuria, including Harbin. But they imposed a harsh military regime that was aggressive and cruel to the Chinese. By contrast, the Jewish and Russian minorities enjoyed considerate treatment. The Jews adapted to the new reality, and some even cooperated with the occupiers. Others were accused of maintaining contact with the Soviet Union and were sent to prison. In general, despite pressure from Nazi Germany on its Japanese ally to replicate the Nuremberg Laws and persecute the Jews in the areas under their control, the Japanese authorities avoided extreme actions. Instead of targeting the Jews in Harbin, the Japanese remained largely unaffected by antisemitism and instead professed great admiration toward Jews. Another reason for the Japanese attitude was that as the occupier, they considered all of the non-Chinese to be foreigners, members of the same community without distinction.

---

former director general of the Israel Antitrust Authority; and Ya'akov Lanir, a member of the Irgun and later a senior official in the Israel Security Agency (Shabak). In June 2004 Olmert visited the city in his then role of deputy prime minister, and recited the Kaddish at his grandfather's grave together with his brother Amram. Following his visit, the cemetery erected a special gravestone in his honor.

Meshual Meir Meshayoff, an Ashkenazi Jew who visited East Asia from 1934 to 1935 as a rabbinic envoy, reported that the Harbin Jewish community was in miserable condition.[34] In an article appearing in *Ha'Aretz* on January 21, 1936, under the dramatic headline "The Destruction of Harbin," Meshayoff wrote that the city was virtually empty of Jews, and that the situation of the synagogues and the Jewish school had deteriorated unrecognizably. Out of twenty thousand Jews living in the city before the Japanese invasion, only some six thousand remained. Meshayoff noted the Russian antisemitism that affected the city and documented the decline in the Jews' situation during the five years of Japanese occupation. As a traditional Jew, the envoy from the Land of Israel expressed his opinion that modernization was the cause of the community's troubles. In his view, the Jews of Harbin were satisfied with teaching their children a smidgen of Jewish tradition when they reached bar and bat mitzvah age. For this reason, he asserted, Jewish identity had evaporated, in a process similar to that taking place in the United States. He wrote: "Ever since the Japanese occupation, a trend has begun of banishing the Jews from the field of commerce…. A secret boycott against the Jewish merchants has sprung up here. Further, the occupation regime is trying to transfer industry to Japanese cities, and in this manner the Chinese are also disinherited…. The Jews suffer for this, as their livelihood came from the wider Chinese market."[35] The sale of the railway by the Russians to Manchukuo, the puppet state created by Japan in Manchuria, and departure of thousands of Russians who had managed it also damaged Jewish life. In the field of real estate, the Japanese occupiers considered themselves exempt from rent payments, and this hurt Jews whose incomes were either directly or indirectly dependent on rent. "This is the situation of the Harbin Jews," Meshayoff concluded, "in the political sense—despair and mortal danger."[36]

After Japan's collapse and defeat in 1945, the Soviet Red Army ruled in Harbin and throughout Manchuria and lent its support to the establishment of the People's Republic of China under the Communist Party. Undoubtedly, the Japanese invasion, the Soviet occupation, and the Chinese civil war that broke out in Manchuria from the end of World War II until the rise of the revolutionary regime in 1949 all led to the decline of Harbin and, eventually, the end of Jewish life there. The Chinese Jews emigrated

---

34 Meshayoff, *Sefer Ha-Zichronot* [Memoir] [Hebrew], n.d., private publication, 86–116.
35 Ibid., 107.
36 Ibid.

to other countries. Many went to Israel after its establishment in 1948. In 1963, the Jewish community organizations in Harbin officially closed, and some twenty years later, the last Jew living in Harbin died. The old synagogue was converted into an activity center for parents and children, and the Jewish high school now houses a school for Korean immigrant students. The commercial college that was founded by Avraham Kaufman became an institute for technological and scientific research, and the Jewish hospital now operates as a small ophthalmological clinic.

The Baghdadi Sephardic Community in Shanghai

The first Jews to reach Shanghai were citizens of the British Empire who originally came from Baghdad and went East after the Opium War. The war ended in 1842 with the Treaty of Nanjing, which the British imposed on the Chinese and which gave preferential rights to foreigners. In traveling to Shanghai, the Jews followed in the wake of British merchants, including opium traders. The Jews often served as intermediaries for international commerce, mainly between British-controlled India and China, as well as the countries adjoining it.[37] At its height, the number of Jews in the Shanghai community, which was called "She'erit Israel," reached one thousand.

The driving force behind the existence of the Shanghai community was the wide variety of business opportunities open to the Jewish entrepreneur following the Treaty of Nanjing. Like other coastal cities in China, Shanghai was open to everyone. British citizens and later citizens of other countries were permitted to trade freely with China and its vast lands. New concession neighborhoods were built adjoining Shanghai, and eventually some of these combined into an international quarter (this did not include the French Concession, which remained independent). These neighborhoods were designated for the foreigners, who enjoyed extraterritorial protection. Although they lived in China, the legal system and other institutions of daily life were European in every way. The autonomous French Concession was located next to the international quarter, and later, an autonomous Japanese quarter was also established.[38] The Jews lived in the international quarters.

---

37 Meyer, *From the Rivers of Babylon to the Whangpoo*, 11.
38 Meyer, "The Sephardi Jewish Community," 349–350.

One of the prominent Jewish families in the city was the Sassoons. Elias Sassoon (1820–80) was apparently the first Jew to arrive in Shanghai. He was sent from Bombay by his father David (1792–1854) to manage the family business, David Sassoon & Sons. Elias was followed by his seven brothers, and by the late 1850s, some twenty Jews employed by the Sassoon family were living in Shanghai. Estimates place the Jewish population at 175 by 1895.

At first, the family business was based on opium and textiles. Later, the range of business grew to include metals, dried fruit, tea, gold, cotton, and silk. Within a few years, the Sassoon family expanded its business to include all the cities on the Chinese coast: Hong Kong, Guangzhou, Tianjin, Hongkou, Yantai (formerly Zhifu), and Ningbo, to name only a few. In 1867, Elias Sassoon founded his own company, E.D. Sassoon & Co., which operated a branch in Bombay. Elias's company mainly dealt in finance and real estate, rapidly becoming larger and more important than his father's. Envoy Meshual Meir Meshayoff also visited Shanghai. In his memoirs, he mentions the Sassoon family's property and influence in the Baghdad community.

Another prominent figure from that period was Benjamin David Benjamin, who became one of the wealthiest individuals in Shanghai. Originally from Bombay, he went to work for Elias Sassoon's company and extended his dealings to banking and the local stock market. Benjamin purchased large shares in the banking corporations of Hong Kong and Shanghai, but in the 1890s his businesses began to fail and he left only a limited imprint on the city.[39]

Another Baghdadi Jew who had enormous influence on the Jewish community and on the entire city was Silas (Salah) Aaron Hardoon (1851–1931), who began his career as an employee of David Sassoon in Bombay. He went to Shanghai as a low-level debt collector and rose in the ranks to become a partner and manager in Elias's company. Hardoon had finely honed business instincts, and over time he accumulated massive capital, mainly from real estate deals. Slowly he became one of the wealthiest merchants in all of East Asia. His worth was then estimated at 150 million dollars. Hardoon also served on committees in the French Concession and gained political influence. As opposed to other Chinese Jews, he did not distance himself from Chinese religion and culture. On the contrary, he

---

39 Meyer, *From the Rivers of Babylon to the Whangpoo*, 16–17.

welcomed them, even taking on the practice of Buddhist customs.[40] His Euro-Asian wife, Luo Jialing, had a strong influence on his way of life, and she encouraged him to contribute generously to the Chinese community and heritage, in addition to assisting the Jewish community. In 1927, he contributed three hundred thousand dollars toward the construction of the Sephardic synagogue in Shanghai, Beit Aharon, and to other Jewish institutions, including schools and the Zionist movement Keren Ha-Yesod.

Silas and his wife did not have their own children, but they adopted ten Chinese children. When Hardoon died in 1931, his wealth and property was divided among Jewish institutions and individuals, and Chinese and Buddhist ones.

Institutions of the Baghdadi Jewish Community in Shanghai

The Shanghai Jewish Communal Association (SJCA) was founded in 1909. Its main projects included managing the financial interests of the community, maintaining the Jewish cemetery, opening a new burial ground, and managing charity organizations. In addition, the organization supervised kosher slaughter and collected information about community members: births, marriages, divorces, and deaths. It also administered a school that taught Judaism, Hebrew, Jewish history and theology, and a few secular subjects. However, the wealthy patrons of the community preferred to send their children to the elite British schools, and the Jewish school gradually declined.[41]

In 1933, Noel Jacobs led the community in establishing the Jewish section of the Shanghai volunteer military force (Shanghai Volunteer Corps—SVC). The SVC was established to protect the international quarter from rebels' attacks and oppression from the Chinese military.

The Shanghai Jewish Youth Association (SJYA) was founded in 1937 by Horace Kadoorie, another wealthy Jew. The purpose of this association was to provide professional training and leisure-time activities for the Jewish youth, particularly those from poor families.

The Shanghai Zionist Association (SZA) was founded in 1903. Sir Eli Kadoorie served as its president and hosted in his home many representatives

---

40 For example, printing the Chinese Buddhist canon for worldwide distribution.
41 Meyer, *From the Rivers of Babylon to the Whangpoo*, 367. Regarding the activities of the Jewish National Fund in China during this period, see Frustig, "The Activity of the Jewish National Fund in China between WWI and WWII," MA thesis.

who supported the Zionist dream. But Kadoorie later rescinded his support for the association after Keren Ha-Yesod rejected the idea of establishing a grandiose garden city in the Land of Israel as a memorial for his wife Leora. The SZA's greatest achievement was obtaining a declaration from three countries—China, Japan, and Siam—that supported the Jews' right to establish a national home in the Land of Israel. The Baghdadi Jews also encouraged introductory tours of the Land of Israel and imported merchandise from there to China.

In 1898 two synagogues served the community: Beit El and She'erit Israel. A third synagogue, Ohel Rachel, was built in 1921 with the financial assistance of Sir Jacob Sassoon and his brother Sir Edward Sassoon. As mentioned, Silas Hardoon funded a fourth synagogue, Beit Aharon.

Although the Baghdadi community was the smallest of the three Jewish communities in Shanghai, it was the strongest and most influential. Baghdadi community members were educated in the British imperialist tradition, while the Jews of Russian and European (Ashkenazi) background maintained their own ethos. While the Baghdadi community fiercely upheld its Sephardic-British identity (its members seldom intermarried with members of the Ashkenazi communities), it supported the other Jewish communities and cooperated with them in the social welfare and educational institutions that it had founded, despite the difference in character.[42] Baghdadi Jews also developed connections with the remaining Jews of Kaifeng. They hosted Kaifeng representatives in their homes, as they considered them authentic Sephardi Jews, and offered them assistance in the field of education and in reconstructing their synagogue. In doing so, they violated the decree prohibiting British subjects from having contact with the local Chinese.

Although Meshayoff observed and recorded details of Jewish life in Shanghai, he bemoaned the "stamp of assimilation" on the Jews, as he considered them influenced by the Reform movement in London. He mourned the fact that many Jews married "White" Russians, who were renowned for their beauty. Although these brides converted, he called them "cash converts," accusing them of remaining faithful to their original religion and having a negative influence on their children. In addition, "there are many Jewish girls who have reached marriageable age and due to competition with the beautiful Russian girls, they have no one to marry and so they

---

42 Ibid., 360.

marry the orange-skinned Chinese."[43] Regarding the White Russians, he wrote that they pined for the halcyon days of czarist Russia, "as is the custom of Jewish men." He commented that the Russian Jews kept "war flags from Old Russia" in their committee meeting room. These flags had escaped capture by the enemy and were kept "under permanent guard, until they can be returned to their former position and glory." However, he also noted the Beitar nationalist spirit that prevailed among the Jews and the influence of the Land of Israel on this Jewish community.

The Russian Jewish Community in Shanghai

The first Russian Jew to reach Shanghai was apparently a man named Haimovitch, who settled there in 1878. Other Jews followed him, including representatives of the major tea corporation W. Wissotsky and Company. The small Russian–Jewish community formed in Shanghai following two waves of immigration from Russia in the early twentieth century. The first wave arrived in the early decades in the wake of the pogroms against the Jews and the Bolshevik Revolution of 1917. The second wave arrived in the 1930s from Manchuria, when the political situation there became unstable and the economic position of the Jews declined. This community was known as Ohel Moshe, after the synagogue of that name. It was constructed in 1907 and named after community leader Moshe Greenberg. At its height, in the 1930s, the community numbered some six thousand members. As opposed to the wealthy Baghdadi community, the Russian Jews were of simple means. Most settled in the Hongkou neighborhood, while those of improved economic status went to live in the French Concession.[44]

In 1925, Rabbi Meir became leader of the community. He was an Ashkenazi Jew, a Lubavitcher Chassid who earned the esteem of the Baghdadi community as well. Like their co-religionists in the Baghdadi community, in 1923 members of the Russian community also helped found the Jewish brigade of the international Shanghai Volunteer Corps. The Jewish brigade numbered 120 members.

In 1941, when Ohel Moshe synagogue became too small to contain the entire community, a new, modern synagogue was constructed in the French Concession. Called the New Synagogue, it seated one thousand

---

43 Meshayoff, *Memoirs*, 108.
44 Eber, *Chinese and Jews*, 8.

congregants. The synagogue sponsored a rich cultural program, with activities held in Russian.

The Russian Jewish community in Shanghai founded its own newspaper, called *Our Life*. Other newspapers published in the international and French concessions included the English monthly *The Monitor* (1931); Bnei Brith organization's *The Zionist Review* (1932), also in English; the Revisionist movement journal *The Jewish Voice* (1935); *and The Tagar* (1946) of the Po'alei Zion movement.

The community also established a Hebrew welfare society and a shelter that provided lodgings for some fifty needy Jews. They collected donations and supplied food, medical care, clothing, and other necessities. The Russian Jews preferred foreign schools, such as the French college or the private British school.[45]

Other organizations included the Ezra charity fund that granted loans to business people, the burial society, a scholarship fund, a clinic, and a hospital established by Bnei Brith. Religious services were organized and provided by another local organization known as *Jüdische Gemeind* or *Einheitsgemeinde* ("Comprehensive Community Association").

After World War II, members of the Russian Jewish community began to leave Shanghai, mainly due to the tense situation during the civil war in China between the Nationalist army (Guomindang) and the rebel Communists. Most emigrated to the United States, Australia, South Africa, and Israel.

The European Refugee Community in Shanghai

The third strand in the Jewish fabric of Shanghai was the community of European refugees who reached the city at the end of the 1930s, searching for refuge from the antisemitic attacks of the Nazis and their supporters. They mainly came from Germany after the *Kristallnacht* pogroms in 1938 and from Austria after its annexation by Germany (the *Anschluss*). Most of these Jews were poor, and they settled in Hongkou, a suburb that also had many Japanese inhabitants. The refugee community was the largest of the Jewish groups and at its peak numbered around twenty thousand members. While the other two communities considered Shanghai their permanent residence, for the recently arrived refugees it was a temporary stopover,

---

45 Krasno, "History of Russian Jews in Shanghai," 335–336.

a haven on a rainy day. Some referred to it as a *Wartesaal*, or waiting room, and in tough times, a mousetrap. They dreamed of eventually reaching the United States.[46]

Still, the temporary shelter that this community enjoyed in Shanghai was miraculous to them. Indeed, in those harrowing days for European Jewry, Shanghai may have been difficult to reach, but it was the only location that permitted entry to Jewish refugees without visas. The Chinese authorities were under pressure, as parts of northern China, including Shanghai, were under Japanese occupation beginning in the summer of 1937 and were not under the authority of any recognized sovereignty. Even so, the Chinese proved to be enlightened hosts. Even more importantly, the economically flourishing section of Shanghai was very much an international city and thus remained free of harsh regulations on many issues, including immigration. In fact, as opposed to the ethos that developed after the opening of diplomatic relations between Israel and China in 1992, it was the Japanese rather than the Chinese authorities who de facto permitted the entry of Jews into China.[47]

Beginning in August 1939, the Japanese limited Jewish immigration to Shanghai, although they did not stop it altogether. They did so under pressure from the other Axis powers, but also from the Jewish community in the city, which feared the strained economic situation that had developed there. Ironically, while powerful, "enlightened" nations such as Britain and the United States locked their gates and their hearts against Jewish refugees, it was this far-flung, foreign city that granted a safe haven to this persecuted people, and all while under the control of a nation aligned with Nazi Germany. In December 1938, a committee that convened in Tokyo decided to permit the entry of Jews to Shanghai.[48] The first Jews who arrived were members of the Steiner family from Austria, who had reached the city in August 1938. Most of the German Jews who came to Shanghai arrived after *Kristallnacht*, in November of that year. Several hundred more came from Poland and Czechoslovakia. Recently unearthed documents in Chinese state archives reveal that in 1939, the Chinese proposed a national plan to take in large numbers of European Jews, believing this was a morally imperative act. The idea was to settle persecuted European Jews in the southwestern Yunnan province, close to the Burmese border. When the initiative

---

46 Eber, *Chinese and Jews*, 30; Sigmund and Hirschberg, *From Berlin to Shanghai*, 37, 39.
47 "Introduction, by Guy Meron." In Sigmund and Hirschberg, *From Berlin to Shanghai*, 18.
48 Kranzler, "Jewish Refugee Community," 402–3.

was drafted, the Chinese government was in the midst of a humiliating withdrawal inland, retreating from the Japanese forces charging west. The plan was never implemented, but it reflects the Chinese establishment's sympathy for the Jews and its willingness to help them in their time of need. Broader, more pragmatic considerations also stood behind this initiative.

Despite the differences in character, the established communities in the city, particularly the Baghdadis, assisted the European refugees and eased the hardships of absorption and integration. Naturally, this process was not easy for the newcomers. They suffered from language barriers and had to adapt to the climate and the tropical diseases that affected the area. In addition, the refugees faced economic barriers, and only a few succeeded in running businesses and achieved a decent standard of living.[49] Some tried their hand at importing products from Europe or established small businesses such as cafes, restaurants, and stores in the German and Austrian style. They created a "Little Vienna" in the heart of the Chinese city. Some refugees were involved in building new structures, and the Bauhaus style was visible in some areas.

Newspaper businesses were successful, and a broad Jewish-German communications network developed, including German-language radio broadcasts. Alongside work, community members developed their own cultural life. They founded libraries and sponsored shows and concerts. The local theater produced a number of dramas.[50]

Decline of the Shanghai Communities

Until war broke out in the Pacific theater after the Japanese attacked the US naval base at Pearl Harbor, the situation of the Jewish communities in Shanghai was relatively stable. The new situation created in Shanghai in those days was an example of Jewish solidarity. The older communities in the city and its environs collected money for aid. The American Jewish community; the international American Jewish Joint Distribution Committee; the Hebrew Immigrant Aid Society (HIAS); Jewish Colonization Association (ICA, later merged with HIAS to form HICEM); Jewish Labor Committee; and Vaad Ha-Haztalah organization all stepped up to help.[51] This was the only way to provide the necessary assistance and

---

49 Sigmund and Hirschberg, *From Berlin to Shanghai*, 21–24.
50 Eber, *Chinese and Jews*, 32.
51 Kranzler, "Jewish Refugee Community," 405.

expand the institutions of welfare, education, and health. Despite the aid, from that point on the community gradually declined. The leaders of the Baghdadi community were subjects of the British Empire, which was at war with Japan. They were interned and forced to cease extending their assistance to the new communities and the needy. Furthermore, because Shanghai was then cut off from the United States, donations from overseas also ended. In February 1943 the authorities imposed additional restrictions, and the Jews no longer enjoyed freedom of movement as in the past. In May, the authorities delineated an area that was eventually known as "the Shanghai Ghetto," and Jewish refugees who had recently arrived from Europe were forced to relocate there. This decree was not applied to the two established communities, and this ghetto also differed from its counterparts in Europe as despite the restrictions, the suffering there did not cause mass deaths among the inhabitants from starvation and disease. The neighborhood was not fenced in, and the Jews were permitted to go out to work. The Japanese security forces were relatively fair in their treatment of the residents, and the community organizations mostly operated as usual and without limitations. Ironically, the incident that most harmed the Jews was when the Americans accidentally bombed part of the ghetto in July 1945. Thirty-one Jews were killed and 250 injured, and several hundred Chinese were injured as well.

As mentioned, after the war the Jews began to emigrate from Shanghai to countries overseas, mainly the United States, Israel (ten thousand went there), and Hong Kong. When the Communists took control of China in 1949, only fifteen hundred Jews remained in the city. By the early fifties, almost all the Jews had left China, and only a handful remained.

In some cases, the young State of Israel permitted entry to Jews from China who had criminal backgrounds, although according to the Law of Return, they could have been refused. Such was the case of a certain Jewish resident of China who was a thief and pickpocket. This man, who was in his forties and married to a Christian, submitted a request to immigrate to Israel in 1949. Due to his criminal background, the authorities rejected his application. But in the early 1950s, all the foreign workers were fired at his place of employment, and the Israelis decided to permit him entry. In another case, a young metalworker from Tianjin was convicted of murdering his Chinese partner. He was sentenced to death, but the sentence was converted to life imprisonment. After four years in prison, the Chinese authorities announced that if the Israeli officials would permit him entry, they would release him. The Israelis complied, and the man was allowed to immigrate.[52]

Years later, Israel officially recognized the historical significance of Shanghai for the Jews during the Second World War. During celebrations for the sixtieth anniversary of Israel's independence, the Israeli consulate in Shanghai invested a significant sum in initiatives designed to express the gratitude of the state and the entire Jewish world to the long-time inhabitants of the Hongkou quarter, who had received and hosted the Jewish refugees in their neighborhood during the 1930s and 1940s.[53] In June 2007 and January 2008, the Israelis remodeled an old age home and senior citizens' activity center in the former ghetto neighborhood, providing air conditioning and heating units, sports facilities, musical instruments, and libraries. The jewel in the crown of this initiative was the establishment of a computerized database with information on twenty thousand Jews who found shelter in Shanghai during the war, as well as details of the older Jewish communities in the city.[54]

The Israeli consulate also helped the authorities establish the Jewish Refugee Museum inside Ohel Moshe synagogue, which was refurbished in 2007. It also commemorated the status of Righteous Among the Nations granted to He Fengshan, who served as China's consul-general in Vienna from 1938 to 1940. This diplomat issued entry permits to Shanghai for Jews fleeing Vienna, endangering himself and his family in order to save hundreds, perhaps thousands of Jews from the Nazis' clutches. In March 2002 a ceremony in his memory was held for the first time on Chinese ground, led by his daughter, Manli He.[55]

The Hong Kong Community

During the second half of the nineteenth century, Hong Kong grew into an important commercial city of the British Empire. As they had

---

52 Joshua N. Shai's files, "List of Special Cases," Immigration and Citizenship Services (n.d., ca. 1954).

53 Uri Guttman, Israel's Consul General in Shanghai, in a letter to Avner Shalev, chairman of Yad Vashem, March 4, 2008.

54 "Unique database commemorating the Jews of Shanghai arouses a wave of global reactions," data from a source in the Israeli consulate of Shanghai, June 2008.

55 Goldstein, "China Honors Its Holocaust Rescuer"; "He Fengshan," Yad Vashem website: http://www.yadvashem.org/yv/he/righteous/stories/ho.asp?WT.mc_id=wiki, retrieved in September 2013; Feng-Shan Ho, *My Forty Years as a Diplomat*.

Shanghai, Baghdadi Jewish traders reached Hong Kong as well, and the two communities maintained a close connection. Later, Ashkenazi Jews also came to the British colony, and estimates at the beginning of World War II place the number at seventy-five families. The Ohel Leah synagogue that served the community members was founded in 1902 with a donation from Sir Jacob Sassoon. A community social center was built seven years later, funded by Sir Elie Kadoorie.

Today, with Hong Kong once again under Chinese rule as an autonomous administrative unit, some five thousand Jews live there, including Israelis. Most are merchants and businessmen. The Hong Kong Jewish community center holds a wide variety of social activities, and the city also has kosher restaurants, a Jewish school, and other community services.

Other Jewish Communities in China

In addition to the Jewish communities in Kaifeng, Harbin, Shanghai, and Hong Kong, a number of communities existed elsewhere in China, most of Russian origin. During the Japanese occupation, these Jews often suffered harassment and persecution; they were even suspected of spying for the Soviet Union. One such community was in Inner Mongolia. The first Jews went there as soldiers in the czar's army in the late nineteenth century. Most lived in Hailar and Manchuli, and they maintained close ties with the Harbin community. Synagogues were established in these two cities just before the First World War. Schools and other community organizations were also founded. Estimates place the number of Jews in these cities at 130 on the eve of World War II. Some Jews lived in Hulun Buir, but they left after the Japanese occupation. In Liaoning Province, Jews lived in the cities of Dalian and Mukden (today Shenyang). There as well, as in Inner Mongolia, the pioneers of the community were Russian-Jewish soldiers, and they were followed by merchants. At its height, the Dalian community numbered 180 residents, with a smaller community in Mukden.

Tianjin, near Beijing, hosted a relatively large Jewish community that numbered some thirty-five hundred members at its apex in the 1930s. Russian Jews came to this city as early as the 1860s and 1870s. Most were merchants, and after them, Jewish soldiers from the czar's army arrived. The community was officially founded in 1904. After the October Revolution, the number of Jews expanded. In 1925 the community founded a Jewish school, and in 1937 a publishing company that printed a newspaper in

Russian and English. Most of the Jews in the city enjoyed a high standard of living.

Jews of German origin settled in Qingdao on the coast of the Yellow Sea. They reached this city in the late nineteenth century when the Germans took control of this part of China. Most were merchants and bankers. A second wave of Jews came to Qingdao from Russia after the Revolution. A synagogue was built, and in 1920 a Jewish organization was established to support the economic, cultural, and religious life of the community. Before World War II, about two hundred Jews lived there.

As opposed to what we might expect, the number of Jews in Beijing was small, and no organized Jewish community existed. No synagogue was ever built there. We do know of several Jewish intellectuals who taught in the city's universities in the early twentieth century, including Rudolph Leventhal (1904–96), who studied the Jews of Kaifeng. In 1938, some 120 Jews lived in Beijing.[56]

Today China is host to a community of Israelis who went to China and continue to travel there for long periods for work, business, or studies. The largest Israeli community is in Shanghai, although some Israelis live in other cities. Jews from the United States and other countries have also made their permanent homes in China. Thus the winding path of history has led to a new situation of Jewish communities of mixed origin that are fundamentally different from those of the past. In their own way, they preserve a tradition of prayer, mainly on the holidays. They also enjoy the assistance and support of Chabad houses, which are scattered widely throughout the country.

---

56 Fang, *History of the Jews*, 270–275.

Chapter One

1948 to 1955—The Early Years of Trial and Error

This chapter covers the first seven years of China–Israel relations and describes the attempts made to establish connections between Israel, which became an independent state in May 1948, and China, which underwent revolution and transformation in October 1949. Between these two dates, Israel pursued relations with Nationalist China under the control of Chiang Kai-shek and his Nationalist Party, the Guomindang. This state rapidly initiated contact with Jerusalem. However, this relationship lasted only slightly over a year, as in 1949, China was taken over by the new Communist regime under the leadership of Mao Zedong, and the mating dance between the two countries began again. Almost half a century would pass before a positive result finally crystallized in January 1992 when diplomatic ties between Jerusalem and Beijing were initiated.

This chapter focuses on analysis of "the missed opportunity"—referring to the failure to institutionalize Israel–China relations in the early 1950s. Before addressing this issue, we must examine several major historical processes, if only in outline form. These include the late nineteenth-century transition of the Jewish and Chinese nationalist movements from the proto-nationalist stage to full-fledged modern nationalism and the role of the two world wars and the inter-war period in consolidating these movements and defining their character.

The Jewish and Chinese peoples are among the oldest communities in the world. Both have survived to this day, donned modern garb, and overcome inestimable challenges. The national movements engendered by these two peoples have sprouted into the shoots of new nations. We observe many lines of similarity between these movements: in the events and processes they experienced as well as the ideologies that shaped them from their initial consolidation up to the twenty-first century and the current age. The Chinese national movement crystallized and reached its apex with the activity of Sun Yat-sen, who is considered the father of the modern Chinese nation. The Jewish national movement, known as Zionism, underwent a similar process, although with some differences, led by visionary Theodor Herzl. These two individuals belonged to the same generation (although Herzl died twenty years before Sun), and their momentous activity began in the last decade of the nineteenth century.

During that period, Herzl experienced outbreaks of antisemitism in Europe. As a journalist, he witnessed the sentencing in the Dreyfus trial in Paris. Herzl became convinced that the Jews must abandon the Diaspora and establish a sovereign, independent Jewish state. The publication of his programmatic book *The Jewish State* and his extensive political and diplomatic activity led to the convening of the First Zionist Congress in Basel in 1897. This meeting became the first milestone in the creation of the national Jewish movement known as Zionism. Along the way, the proto-nationalist ideologies were abandoned. A clear and well-documented line led from Herzl's Zionism to the fulfillment of his vision—the establishment of the State of Israel in 1948.

During that same decade, Chinese republican revolutionary Sun Yat-sen was also acting tirelessly. For example, he established the Revive China Society (*xing zhong hui*), which eventually worked in cooperation with other revolutionary movements. In 1905, the United League (*tong meng hui* 同盟会) was founded in Japan, becoming the nucleus of the modern Chinese nationalist movement in the late nineteenth and early twentieth century.

Under the Guomindang regime, the Republic of China established contact with the fledgling Jewish state. Bolstered by China's support of Zionism, these connections continued after the establishment of the State of Israel in 1948. On April 24, 1920, over twenty years earlier, Sun Yat-sen wrote a letter to Nissim Elias Benjamin Ezra, founder of the Shanghai Zionist Association, expressing identification with the Zionist movement:

> Chinese nationalism disappeared when China was conquered by the Manchu foreigners. But China was not the only country that was conquered. The Jewish people also lost their homeland . . . . Although their country was destroyed, the Jewish people have continued to exist to this day . . . . The Zionist movement is one of the greatest movements of the present

time. All lovers of democracy cannot help but wholeheartedly support and enthusiastically welcome the movement to restore your wonderful and historic nation, which has contributed so much to the civilization of the world and which rightfully deserves an honorable place in the family of nations.[57]

Undoubtedly, the First World War represented a momentous and common landmark for aspiring nationalist movements around the world. Through this war, nationalist leaders in various states hoped to attain their goals, sometimes by aiding the Allied powers. In the case of the Jewish national movement, Britain's granting of the Balfour Declaration may be viewed in the broader context of British attempts to wrest Palestine from Turkish hands, and British expectations of assistance from the Jewish community then residing in Palestine. Indeed, entities in the Jewish community of Palestine, as well as in the Jewish Diaspora, attempted to help Britain achieve its objectives in the war, as far as they were able. The establishment of the Jewish Brigade and the Zion Mule Corps (designed to provide logistical support during the war) were important milestones in fulfilling these aspirations.

In China the declaration of war by the two governments existing simultaneously in the South and North came relatively late, in 1917. China sent over one hundred thousand recruits to labor in the killing fields of France (it also sent logistical assistance to the Allied armies), an act intended to generate political credit for China. The hope was that in the diplomatic processes to come after the war, the world powers would reward China for its assistance. In 1919, however, following the Treaty of Versailles, the Chinese were bitterly disappointed: the Allies did not free China from the Japanese burden, and fear of the Land of the Rising Sun meant that the Allies were ungrateful toward the Chinese.

The issue of the compensation that the two nationalist movements received (or did not receive) for their services is a separate subject and one that we will not pursue here in length. But when examining the internal developments within these movements, we cannot ignore the First World War and the connections that these movements created with the Allied Powers.

Chinese disappointment in the Allies' disregard for their demands and expectations led to the emergence of the May Fourth Movement. Among

---

57 Goldstein, "The Republic of China and Israel," 3.

other aims, it acted to protest against the Allies and aided in formulating the new Chinese nationalism. As for the Jewish national movement, the Balfour Declaration and the establishment of the British Mandate in Palestine represented fundamental stages in the road to strengthening the Jewish community there and the eventual establishment of an independent state.

The period between the two world wars—the 1920s and 1930s—was of vital significance to the continued development of the two national movements. The Jewish settlement in Palestine enjoyed relatively robust economic development during the 1920s under the Mandate government. Paradoxically, clashes with the Arab national movement also aided in strengthening the Zionist movement (1929 riots, the Arab Rebellion of 1936–39). In addition, persecution of the Jews in the 1930s paralleled the Nazis' rise to power. While the Nazi movement intensified in power and influence and led to the decimation of European Jewry, the world gradually realized that the Jews needed their own shelter.

In China, the growth of the national movement during the 1920s took place alongside intensification of internal tensions between the two factions within it. Another impetus for growth was the anti-imperialist initiative that was articulated in the Northern Expedition for the unification of China, a goal which was attained on October 10, 1928. The nationalist movement weakened during the 1930s due to the Manchurian Incident in 1931, Japan's aggressiveness, and the war of defense that China was forced to wage against its militaristic neighbor.

It seems, then, that both nationalist movements benefited from the tough challenges they faced at home and abroad. We cannot truly understand the establishment of the State of Israel without considering the roles of the Second World War and the Holocaust. The accepted assumption is that if the international community had not been shocked by the decimation of European Jewry, the United Nations would never have enabled the establishment of the Jewish state. In the case of China as well, to understand the rise of nationalism under the Communist Party, we must look to the need that intensified during the war for a social and economic platform and an anti-Japanese national agenda. Certainly, the development in China of a national ethos of war against Japan, and the active and organized resistance to Japanese aggression that reached its peak in the Nanjing Massacre of 1937 represented necessary conditions for the rise of the new China under the Communist Party.

These concepts have received much recognition and attention in recent years. An increasing number of researchers draw parallels between the history of the Zionist movement in the twentieth century and that of the Chinese nationalist movement. Professor Xu Xin, director of the Institute for Jewish and Israel Studies at Nanjing University, has written extensively on Holocaust studies in China. During the war and in the post-war period under Mao's regime, China mostly suffered from ignorance regarding the Holocaust; at best, the topic was not given appropriate weight.[58] However, after the 1980s when China opened to the West, the Chinese began to take an interest in Jewish studies in general, and particularly the study of the Holocaust. They have written and continue to write books, give courses, and hold seminars on this topic. Unsurprisingly, Xu Xin has also identified the resemblance between the Holocaust and the butchery committed by the Japanese at Nanjing. He further emphasizes that Germany accepted full responsibility for the acts of the Nazi regime and was even willing to apologize and pay reparations, while Japan's approach, under a host of governments, has been much more severe and uncompromising. The Japanese are still unwilling to accept full responsibility for the Nanjing Massacre. Xu Xin expresses great admiration for the Jews and their success at building a new society from the low point of the destruction they suffered. In this context, he highlights philosophical and ethical interest in the Holocaust regarding the issue of human nature—good or bad—which forms the core of Chinese philosophy.[59]

Another common denominator between the two peoples from a historical viewpoint is the socialist ideological basis that was a fundamental ethos in both countries. Both China and Israel began their paths as socialist states, albeit in different shades. Over the years, however, this ethos has largely dissipated in both, and they have become states that chiefly raise the banner of the free market.

On November 29, 1947, the UN General Assembly authorized the Partition Plan, paving the way for the establishment of the State of Israel, which declared its independence on May 14, 1948. Nationalist China under Chiang Kai-shek continued to maintain diplomatic contact with Zionist activists and was one of the ten countries that abstained from casting a

---

58 In the spirit of Soviet communism, emphasis was placed on the damage caused by fascism as the ultimate form of capitalism that led to the murder of millions, and not on the massacre itself or the identity of those killed.

59 Xu Xin, *Holocaust Education in China.*

ballot in this historic vote. In the final analysis, China's abstention aided in creating the majority necessary for authorizing the establishment of two states in the British Mandate of Palestine (two-thirds). Despite the abstaining vote, the media in Nationalist China joyfully welcomed Israel, the new state of the Jewish people returning to their homeland.[60]

As noted, the vast majority of the Jews who were living in the various communities throughout China emigrated between 1948 and 1949, to Israel and elsewhere. The several hundred Jews who remained in China were involved in local and international commerce. After 1950 the new government prevented emigration from China, especially for individuals with international business ties.[61] In 1956 David Marshall, an Iraqi Jew who attained prominence as Singapore's first Chief Minister, visited China for two months as the guest of Chinese Prime Minister Zhou Enlai. He took this opportunity to push the request of some four hundred Russian Jews to leave China.

Mutual Recognition and Establishment of Diplomatic Relations

In late February 1949, Nationalist China's UN representative contacted Abba Eban, Israel's ambassador to the United States. China indicated that it would be willing to grant official recognition to Israel after the fledgling state gained admission to the UN. Israel was duly accepted to the UN as its fifty-ninth member on May 11 of that year. Nationalist China, however, did not last much longer. On October 1, 1949, Beijing declared the establishment of the People's Republic of China under the leadership of Mao Zedong and the Communist Party. One hundred days later, on January 9, 1950, Israel took a surprising and daring step: it decided to recognize the new regime in China, thus becoming the first state in the Middle East and the seventh in the Western bloc to do so. The decision to send the telegram recognizing China was made following extensive discussions among officials in Israel's Ministry of Foreign Affairs, despite their fear of a furious reaction on the part of the Americans. Ya'akov Shimoni, director-general of the Asian department at the Israel Foreign Ministry from 1949 to 1952, proposed a consultation with Washington before taking this step. But Foreign Minister Moshe Sharett decided not to do so—and moreover, he did not

---

60 Pan, *China and Israel.*
61 Shai, *The Fate of British and French Firms in China.*

even inform Abba Eban.[62] Finally, Israel sent the message of recognition to Zhou Enlai in Moscow, where the Chinese premier was visiting along with Mao Zedong. It was indeed unusual for Israel to act against the American position at the height of the Cold War, when even the Arab nations avoided such a step. At that point, Israel's relations with Nationalist China (Taiwan) were limited to low-level, informal contact of a cultural and commercial character alone.

After its establishment and for the next two years, the State of Israel adopted a policy of non-identification. The reason for this was that in the post-World War II period, many Jews were still scattered throughout the globe, mainly in population centers in the two main blocs, the United States and the Soviet Union. Diplomatic policy and public opinion in Israel dictated that the state must remain politically neutral, as only in this manner could it create extensive connections on both sides of the international political barrier and overcome political isolation in the international arena due to the Israeli–Arab conflict. Here we must recall that the non-identification policy was also important for local appeasement, as the parties that arose in Israel represented a broad political spectrum: from a clear pro-Western stance to almost total identification with the Soviet bloc.[63] Still, it was clear that the balance of powers would not remain this way forever. "The one hundred million dollars we received from the Export Bank in 1949 at Truman's orders saved the Jewish community in Israel," related Ze'ev Sufott, Israel's first ambassador to Beijing. "The money had been in British hands. We were completely dependent on the West, but at that stage the Americans did not intervene and did not say a word."[64]

Documents from the Chinese archives reveal that during that period, China was keeping close tabs on processes in other countries as they began to recognize its new regime. A document from January 1950 sent by the Beijing Foreign Ministry to the Chinese Embassy in the Soviet Union poses the question: has the Israeli government sent a formal letter documenting its recognition of the popular regime in Beijing? The letter went on to ask the embassy to confirm as soon as such recognition arrived.[65] During those months, Mao and the central figures of the Chinese leadership were visiting

---

62 Interview with Dr. Ze'ev Sufott, September 6, 2004, Jerusalem. All interviews cited were conducted by this author, unless otherwise noted.

63 Shai, "The Israeli Communist Party and the PRC," 84.

64 Interview with Ze'ev Sufott.

65 Archives of the Chinese Ministry of Foreign Affairs, January 29, 1950.

Moscow. Mao had gone there to visit Stalin and receive his instructions for the next steps, which is why most of the diplomatic correspondence was channeled through Moscow.

Accordingly, on January 9, 1950, the State of Israel declared its formal recognition of the People's Republic of China in a telegram sent by Foreign Minister Moshe Sharett to Premier Zhou Enlai. Of course, this meant that Israel recognized the Communist government in Beijing as the only legitimate government, and that from then on it ceased to recognize Chiang Kai-shek's exiled government in Taiwan. The Chinese documents reveal that immediately following the declaration of a new regime in China, the two capitals began to correspond on the topic of recognition.[66] On January 16, 1950, one week after Israel sent the telegram, Zhou Enlai reacted to the announcement with a formal declaration in accordance with the diplomatic protocol then in practice. A careful examination of the drafts written for Zhou's telegram shows that corrections were made to the original. For example, several warm words were added, and one of the Chinese expressions was changed, since it might have been interpreted as addressing an individual low down in the diplomatic hierarchy. Another addition was personal—several expressions responding in a friendly tone to the heartfelt congratulations Moshe Sharett had sent to the country and to Zhou himself.[67] However, Zhou did not relate to China's intentions or political stance and basically left the Israeli initiative one-sided. Formally, the regime in Beijing had no reason to grant recognition to the government in Jerusalem, as the State of Israel was already an established and recognized fact in the eyes of the international community and China itself (under the previous regime). We therefore have reason to question whether Israel should have expected any reward for its recognition of China.

Later that month, the Chinese Foreign Ministry forwarded to Moscow other telegrams relating to the establishment of ties with various states and governments, with an emphasis on diplomatic recognition. These countries included Denmark, Afghanistan, Finland, Sweden, Vietnam, and Switzerland. In these telegrams, the ministry requested instructions on this issue from Mao himself.[68]

---

66 Archives of the Israel Ministry of Foreign Affairs, file 2391/32, in Yemima Rosenthal, ed., *Documents on the Foreign Policy of the State of Israel, 1949–1951* (Jerusalem: National Archives, 1980, 1988, 1991).

67 Archives of the Chinese Ministry of Foreign Affairs, January 14, 1950; January 16, 1950.

68 Ibid., January 1950.

Several months later, on June 20, 1950, Israeli and Chinese diplomats met in Moscow for the first time.[69] The Chinese Ministry of Foreign Affairs asked their embassy in Moscow to take the pulse of the Israeli ambassador and investigate his government's intentions regarding an exchange of diplomats.[70]

In response to these feelers, in June 1950 the State of Israel reached a decision on the principle of establishing diplomatic relations with China, and the two countries seemed to be on a path toward a new and promising future. But publication of the news had to be postponed, because June 25 brought a dramatic development onto the international scene that changed the makeup of foreign relations throughout the world: the forces of Communist North Korea crossed the 38th parallel, and the Korean War broke out.

On July 2, 1950, the Israeli government convened to discuss its response to the war and determined that it would adopt the UN decision on this issue. This decision, initiated by the United States, called for all organization members to act to thwart North Korean aggression. The winds blowing from New York immediately prompted the question of Israel's position on the tension between the blocs. While Moshe Sharett and other government leaders called for granting only political and diplomatic support to the South Korean regime, Ben Gurion went further and proposed sending Israeli soldiers to fight alongside UN forces.[71] His proposal was rejected by the other statesmen. Instead, Israel demonstrated its solidarity and support for the war effort by sending medical assistance and food supplies to the UN forces in Korea.

But Israel had not forgotten China. Israel's leaders decided to inform the Beijing government that in principle, the Israeli government was interested in continuing the process of establishing diplomatic relations with China. This message was sent through the Israeli ambassador in Sweden to his Chinese counterpart in late November 1950. But relations between the two countries lacked a suitable foundation, and only a few messages were sent between the two sides. After that, silence reigned until the war ended in July 1953.

The above events, beginning with Israel's joining the UN coalition in Korea, signaled the end of Israel's non-identification policy. After that

---

69 Shai, "Israeli Communist Party and PRC," 84.
70 Archives of the Chinese Ministry of Foreign Affairs, May 31, 1950; June 27, 1950.
71 Brecher, *Israel, the Korean War and China*, 31.

point, Israel attached itself to the United States bloc. Israel found itself in the thick of the global conflict—the Cold War in Asia.

Israel Recognizes the People's Republic of China

What considerations prompted the Israeli government to form ties with the new China? Just before January 1950, when the State of Israel had decided to recognize the People's Republic, China was boycotted by most nations of the world, first and foremost the United States. The Israel of that time was very different in character from the Israel of the twenty-first century. It was characterized by a unique, moderate form of socialism and a balanced policy of non-identification. The principle that guided it during that period was the attempt to obtain support from world powers and other states in the advancement of its own interests.[72]

When the State of Israel was established, great hopes blossomed that the majority of Jews around the world would abandon the Diaspora and immigrate to the *Altneuland*, the "Old New Land," as Herzl called it. Members of the Jewish communities of China, including refugees from White Russia, central Europe, and other regions, were also looking forward to exchanging their temporary shelter for a permanent home. To many, the Land of Israel, where the new Jewish state was founded, was an attractive alternative. But Western developed countries also called out to the Jews in China—the United States, Australia, New Zealand, and others. From the official Israeli standpoint, the number one priority was to obtain the good-will of the Chinese authorities: at first Nationalist, and later Communist. Israel's government assumed that this was the only way to ensure that the Chinese would permit the Jews to leave China and immigrate to Israel.

While the State of Israel aspired to achieve cooperation with states in both the Eastern and Western blocs, official documents reveal that the establishments in Great Britain, the United States and other Western countries were suspicious of the new society that was developing in Israel and its hegemonic ethos. This society supported not only equal rights, but also socialist and social-democratic ideologies. This suspicion was made possible in the atmosphere of the Cold War and stemmed from a liberal ethos that feared leftist economics. Further, the Arab regimes were clearly

---

72 Bialer, "Ben Gurion and the Question of Israel's International Orientation, 1948–1956."

anti-communist, and thus the Western states might consider them more reliable and worthy assets.[73]

From Jerusalem's viewpoint, Israeli recognition of the new government in Beijing was considered natural and appropriate, and it earned the approbation of Eastern bloc countries. But from a Western perspective, it was a defiant gesture. Although Britain was also one of the first countries to recognize China, this step could be accepted with understanding and tolerance, since it was motivated by economic considerations. High-capital British concerns operating in China anticipated enormous profits or, at the very least, to maintain the value of their decades-old investments. These companies faced the imminent danger of extinction, and if London ignored or provoked the new regime, these interests might be immediately harmed. At least the British had no ideological basis for backing socialism.

When David Ben Gurion was asked about Israel's motivations for recognizing the People's Republic so early, he emphasized that the Communists had seized control and held it, and that the nations of the world had to recognize this fact. He also stressed the legitimate right of the new China to be accepted as a legitimate member of the international community and to be treated accordingly.[74]

When the Korean War broke out, however, Israel took the first significant step of distancing itself from the non-identification policy it had previously adopted. When the State of Israel decided to assist the UN forces in stopping North Korean hostility, this precipitated a turning point in the budding relationship between Jerusalem and Beijing. The war shuffled the deck and relegated to the sidelines the issue of ties between the two nations in their new formats. From then on, this issue became part of a broader, global arena.

Yet despite its decision to end non-identification, Israel continued its previous policy toward China. For example, on September 19, 1950, the Israeli representation at the UN General Assembly voted to grant China's seat to the People's Republic and remove it from Nationalist China in Taiwan. In this process, Israel de facto joined the bloc of fifteen nations that acted to grant full legitimacy to the Communist regime. Foreign Minister Moshe Sharett explicitly declared that although Israel's concept of democracy was far from Beijing's, it would still be an error to ignore the political

---

73 Shai, "China and Israel," 149–150.
74 Brecher, *Israel, the Korean War and China*, 31.

reality in China and permit the previous regime, which had lost control of the subcontinent, to receive a seat in the international organization.[75] From then on, the issue of the Chinese seat at the UN arose almost every year at the General Assembly and symbolized the development or suspension of relations between one country or another and China.

In 1954 the Israeli delegation to the UN did not support Beijing's position, but in all the other votes, Jerusalem systematically protected the legitimate right of the People's Republic for continued existence as well as the right to China's designated seat in the General Assembly and the Security Council. This was the Israeli government's official policy, not just the position of ideological and political circles working assiduously to advance China's interests, such as the Israeli Communist Party or the Committee for Justice and Peace in the Holy Land.[76] In so doing, Israel adopted a political stance that was very similar to nations such as India, which clearly distinguished between support for US policy in the Korean Peninsula and preference for the People's Republic over Taiwan in other international arenas. The Israel delegation's vote in 1954 was an exception, and in early 1955 the State of Israel even apologized to the Chinese government for it. Israel explained that casting its vote along with the United States and its allies had been unintentional, and that the error was corrected as requested.[77] In 1965 Israel changed its tactics on this issue.

Israel's process vis-à-vis the People's Republic contained the trace of an *a priori* strategic step that represented out-of-the-box thinking. Ministry of Foreign Affairs documents clearly reveal that this step resulted from a comprehensive international outlook that belied Israel's traditional Eurocentric approach. Forging ties with China was considered a means of strengthening the international status of the young state. The Israel of the fifties was attempting to recruit the support of any potential partner, whether these were the Soviet Union, India, the United States, or China.[78] China was then a

---

75 Shai, "Strange Bedfellows," 150.

76 As we learn, for example, from a letter sent by the Committee on September 9, 1954 to Moshe Sharett and the Israeli delegation at the UN General Assembly, calling to support the acceptance of the People's Republic into the UN. Yad Tabenkin Archives, section 15, Israel Bar Yehuda series, file 26d.

77 In a conversation between David Hacohen and Yao Zhongming, Archives of the Chinese Ministry of Foreign Affairs, January 26, 1955.

78 Experts appearing on "The China Connection," a program on China produced for the Voice of Israel radio station in 1975, including Prof. Shlomo Avineri (Foreign Ministry director in 1976–1977) and Dr. Meron Medzini; individuals who influenced the

closed state that was not understood and even lagging behind, but to Israel's Foreign Ministry, it offered the possibility of a positive connection with other Asian countries, and this prompted the government to act in a creative and even groundbreaking manner. Thus in contrast to the Eurocentric approach that characterized Israel's statesmen throughout most of its history, during this period a pluralistic conception reigned, which placed Asia and its future importance in an appropriate position.

At that time, David Hacohen, who had resigned from his positions in the Histadrut (Labor Federation) and the Knesset, expressed interest in appointment as the first Israeli envoy to Burma. He explained that his appointment would enable implementation of ties with the new states in Asia that had yet to initiate contact with Israel, and in most cases, did not recognize it at all. Hacohen said that although he could have chosen a more attractive diplomatic position in a more comfortable location such as Rome or Paris, he viewed distant Burma as a potential bridge to the other Asian states. At that time, Burma was slightly more open than the other Asian countries and had socialist tendencies. Hacohen's approach reflected a refreshing Israeli view, which aimed at partnership not only with the West against the background of expectations of economic achievements, but also with the East, based on its potential and familiar ideology.

Before formally appointing Hacohen in December 1953, Moshe Sharett paid a visit to Burma, followed by Hacohen himself. Their hosts expressed an honest interest in establishing diplomatic ties with Jerusalem, and their expectation of a mutual relationship. Hacohen defined this in his unique way: "They wanted a real ambassador, not just someone to drink whiskey with."[79] He argued that relations with Burma strengthened his awareness and thirst for similar ties with China. Following in Hacohen's footsteps, other foreign ministry bureaucrats visited Burma, including Walter Eitan, director general; and Daniel Levin, head of the Asian department, who opened the road to China toward the end of the Korean War. Levin asked the Israeli ambassadors in several European capitals—Stockholm, Prague, Warsaw, Bucharest, and Sofia—to put out feelers with their Chinese counterparts regarding their countries' stance toward Israel. The Chinese ambassadors

---

decision-making process during that period, such as Abba Eban (Israeli ambassador to the US), David Hacohen (Israeli envoy in Burma), Ya'akov Shimoni (director of Asian affairs at the Foreign Ministry), and members of the Israeli delegation to China—Meir De-Shalit and Yosef Zarchin.

79 "The China Connection," Hacohen.

replied unanimously that their government was definitely ready to discuss establishment of formal ties with Israel, but they left the diplomatic ball in the Israeli court.

Initial Ties

On December 31, 1953, the Chinese ambassador to Burma, Yao Zhongming, sent a telegram under the heading, "Israel interested in establishing commercial relations with us," in which he reported on his talks with Hacohen. He related that Hacohen was interested in forming commercial ties with China, either directly or indirectly, through Burma. The principal Israeli commodity under discussion was fertilizer, but Yao reported that Hacohen also offered to supply other products. China's formal response came two weeks later and was decidedly enthusiastic. The two sides thus expressed interest in bilateral trade. Hacohen supplied a list of products that Israel could export, including fruits and vegetables, both fresh and preserved; textiles; electronics; medicines and vaccines; cosmetics; fertilizer and phosphates; cement; glass; agricultural technology; and even vehicles. Hacohen was active in Koor, a Histadrut company, and he was well aware of the Israeli market's potential and its products. He also proposed the idea of sending a commercial delegation to China. For their part, the Chinese emphasized their enthusiasm for his initiative, and Ambassador Yao was asked by his superiors to probe this issue further.[80]

In another document, Yao noted that Israel was a small country and that establishing friendly ties with it would be significant for both sides. He reported that Israel was about to establish relations with Thailand and Japan, and that it hoped to host representatives from China. He also stated that the United States, due to its official anti-China position, had recommended to the Israeli government that it refrain from sending a commercial delegation to China. According to Yao's version of events, the Israeli prime minister insisted that this was an internal Israeli matter and that it was inappropriate for Washington to become involved. As for the commercial issue, Yao emphasized that although Israel was a small country, it had advanced industry and professional engineers. Hacohen explained that Israel would adapt its production to China's needs, and that they would sign a trade

---

80 Archives of the Chinese Ministry of Foreign Affairs, December 31, 1953.

agreement valid for six years. Yao added that Israel could serve as a bridge between manufacturers in Western Europe and the Chinese consumer.[81]

The personal ties between Hacohen and Yao gradually tightened. Each played a central role in strengthening the relationship between the two countries, largely thanks to the status and importance that they held in their countries. Yao consistently gave positive descriptions of Israel, listing its advantages and pointing out the benefits it served to reap from connections with China.

On April 7, 1954, Yao sent another telegram describing Israel's intention of sending a commercial delegation to China. The list of addressees was long, including the top echelon of the Communist Party and even Chairman Mao. Yao also reported that the Israeli representative had paid him a visit, but that he had acted in accordance with the instructions of his office. He wrote that Hacohen had asked to know why China had not yet replied to the issue of hosting the Israeli delegation. Yao was keen for this to take place as soon as possible, during the Geneva Conference on the future of the Korean Peninsula or even beforehand. "This will be a winning blow against the United States," Yao asserted in attempting to persuade his superiors. "As everyone knows, Israel is a pro-American state. Holding negotiations between Israel and China will be another nail in the US coffin. They hope to receive a reply soon and begin negotiations right away . . . . The reason for Israel's enthusiasm . . . is the decline of its relations with the countries of the Arab bloc."[82] Yao thought that Israel was planning to use the delegation to break through the isolation which it was then experiencing. He concluded that he would continue to act in accordance with his office's instructions. He would postpone the response to Israel until the end of the Geneva Conference and decide according to the conditions that would then prevail.

What were the Chinese government's considerations for establishing ties with Israel? From the telegram the Chinese ambassador in Burma sent, stating that close ties with Israel would be "a nail in the US coffin," and that Israel feared isolation against the Arab states, it seems that the Chinese were analyzing Israel's advantages as a state with an advanced socialist regime that expressed interest in establishing relations with China despite its relations with the United States. Although the State of Israel was not

---

81 Ibid., January 26, 1955.
82 Ibid., April 7, 1954.

considered important in size, its location in the Middle East and political advantages granted it special importance. In 1950, it was clear that Beijing had no chance of establishing diplomatic ties with the Arab regimes: Farouk's Egypt, Faisal's Iraq, Saudi Arabia under Ibn Saud, conservative Syria under Hashim al-Atassi and Adib Shishkali, and Jordan under King Abdullah. From Beijing's perspective, then, Israel remained the only ray of light in the Middle East.[83]

Ya'akov Shimoni, director of the Asian section at the Israel Foreign Ministry, thought that Israel was important to the Chinese, and that China wanted Israel's recognition and reciprocal ties. He asserted that the Communists were then interested in establishing relations with as many countries as possible. The fact that Israel became one of the first to recognize China in the non-communist world was to its benefit. Still, it was clear that the Chinese hesitated to cross a certain line, such as opening an official representation in Israel, which was boycotted by so many countries.[84]

Another motive for strengthening ties with Israel was economic interest. After the Korean War, the leaders in Beijing concluded that they must try to expand ties with countries around the world. The comprehensive boycott that the Americans imposed on China weighed heavily on its economy, and so the Chinese attempted to find ways to overcome or circumvent the boycott. Although their efforts were mainly focused on Asia, the Chinese also looked toward other destinations. The new State of Israel made an impression on policy-makers in China with its power of invention, rapid development, the reparations agreement it signed with West Germany in 1952, and most of all the ties it had formed with the United States and Western countries. The Chinese thought that contact with Israel would make it easier for them to purchase merchandise and products from the United States and Germany, even indirectly by means of the Trans-Siberian Railroad through the Soviet Union.[85]

Documents from the Chinese Foreign Ministry indicate this intention. The importance of this issue is evident in the address list for telegrams on this topic, which included senior party and state officials—Zhou Enlai, Liu Shaoqi, and Deng Xiaoping—and sometimes even Mao himself.

We thus see that in 1954 the establishment of ties between Israel and China still seemed possible. On September 23, Zhou Enlai, then the prime

---

83 "The China Connection," Mezdini.
84 Ibid., Shimoni.
85 "The China Connection," Mezdini.

minister of China, informed the first convocation of the People's Congress that contacts between Beijing and Jerusalem were taking place. His declaration came as a surprise, as he did so without informing Israel in advance.[86] US Secretary of Defense John Foster Dulles, a rabid anti-communist, protested angrily against this development and pressured Israel to cancel all diplomatic initiatives for strengthening ties with China. This pressure was designed to send a clear message to Beijing that Israel was dependent on the United States.[87] Around April 1955, the embryonic relations between the two countries cooled, and subsequently China ceased making positive suggestions on the issue of Israel.

Parallel to negotiations with Beijing, Jerusalem held talks that strengthened ties with three other countries: Burma, Russia, and India. The connections formed between these three countries and Israel contributed to advancing Israel's relationship with China, although they were not sufficient to establish formal connections.

Burma, Russia, and India Help Initiate Contact

The Asian section of the Israel Foreign Ministry was created in 1949. Ya'akov Shimoni, who served as director until 1952, documented the Ministry's Asian orientation during those years and the increasing interest in the region.[88]

In late 1953, following the Korean War, Israel opened a representation in Rangoon. As mentioned, this enabled ties between the Chinese ambassador and his Israeli counterpart, David Hacohen. The Israeli representative believed that his presence in Rangoon would help in normalizing Israel's relations with Asian countries and advancing trade with China in particular.[89] Hacohen placed great importance on the commercial and economic connection with China, as well as on disseminating information to the Asian peoples on issues of Judaism, the Arab–Israeli conflict, and Israel's place in the global arena. The connection between Chinese ambassador Yao and Hacohen was based on Beijing's directive to avoid initiating contact and only react to Israeli overtures. At the same time, Yao was instructed

---

86 Ibid., Shimoni.
87 For more on Israel's position between the two blocs, see Bialer, *Between East and West*.
88 "The China Connection," Shimoni.
89 Hacohen, *Burma Diary*.

to continue to put out tentative but polite feelers toward his Egyptian colleague in Rangoon.[90]

When Zhou Enlai arrived in Rangoon for a visit, Zhou invited Hacohen to meet with him. At the reception that the Chinese held in Hacohen's honor, he was the only Western representative. After the reception, Zhou called him in for a personal conversation. According to Hacohen, at this meeting Zhou expressed satisfaction regarding the developing ties between the two countries and invited Hacohen to visit China as its official guest. Although the topic of formal relations between the countries was not raised, Hacohen read between the lines of Beijing's escalating interest in such ties.[91] Throughout this process, Hacohen demonstrated sincere enthusiasm regarding the establishment of relations with China. Despite the obstacles, he continued to believe in the sincere will of the Chinese to create ties with Israel. His excitement infected his colleagues in the Foreign Ministry, the Knesset, and even in the Histadrut.[92] His hopes were realized when an Israeli delegation finally visited China in late January 1955.

Ya'akov Shimoni replaced Hacohen in Burma, presenting a picture that was less glowing and optimistic than Hacohen's. He noted that as part of his position, he had to fulfill the promises that Hacohen had made out of "his enthusiasm and personal charm," but that not all of these had official backing. Some of the promises were far-reaching but had negative consequences on future developments.[93] At any rate, Burma served as a central axis in diplomatic communications on the issue of Israel–China relations.

The intense exchange of telegrams between Yao and the Beijing Foreign Ministry during December 1953 indicated the relative frequency of the meetings and discussions held between himself and Hacohen. Yao repeatedly emphasized to his government that Hacohen was interested in trade issues between the two countries, whether through Burma or directly.[94] Inspired by the discussions on commercial contact, the political feelers also grew in significance. Hacohen anticipated that discussions in the diplomatic field would be based on agreements on the commercial issue.

---

90 Archives of the Chinese Ministry of Foreign Affairs, telegram of December 8, 1953 sent by Yao to his government.
91 "The China Connection," Hacohen.
92 Shai, "Strange Bedfellows," 151.
93 "The China Connection," Shimoni.
94 See, for example, Archives of the Chinese Ministry of Foreign Affairs, December 8, 1953.

Until the rupture between Israel and China, Burma remained an important junction for contact between the two countries. Burma also served as a focal point for diplomatic communication during the Israeli trade delegation's visit to China in early 1955. From the Chinese viewpoint, connections between the two countries should be formed in two stages. The first stage ripened to the point of sending the Israeli delegation. The second stage, which was never implemented, focused on testing the waters toward the signing of a diplomatic agreement and establishment of full formal relations. According to Chinese government directives, the planned steps were meant to be steered by the Burma representations of both countries.[95]

But even before the Israeli representation in Burma was opened, the Chinese and Israeli embassies in Moscow acted to manage initial contacts. In May 1950, the Chinese Foreign Ministry asked its ambassador to Moscow, Wang Jiaxiang, to check with his Afghani and Israeli colleagues as to whether their countries planned to send a diplomatic representative to Beijing. Wang requested clear instructions regarding the reply that he should give to his fellow ambassadors if they should ask any questions about China. In September 1951, he reported on his conversation with the Israeli ambassador in Moscow, noting that the Israel Foreign Ministry had decided that due to financial considerations, Israel would not send a representative of any diplomatic rank to China. For the time being, the diplomatic topics between the two countries would be discussed through their Moscow ambassadors.[96] We must assume that the Israeli government's considerations were related to the Korean War, which was being waged at the time, and to fear of an adverse American reaction to overly close ties between Jerusalem and Beijing.

After Burma, which was the first forerunner in the strengthening of ties with Asian countries, the Israeli foreign minister began to seek out other potential partnerships on the Asian continent. China was not necessarily the focus, and David Hacohen noted that the briefs he received before commencing his position did not mark China as a clear diplomatic goal. The countries that were targeted were Burma and India. Regarding the latter, Israel intended to transform what was called "our miserable consulate in Bombay" into a vehicle for a serious upgrade of diplomatic relations. He further stated that it was the contact with the Chinese ambassador in

---

95   Archives of the Chinese Ministry of Foreign Affairs, February 26, 1955.
96   Ibid., May 31, 1950, September 10, 1951.

Burma that pushed China to the top of Israel's list of Asian countries with which ties should be established.

As India was the first preferred target for Israeli ties with Asian states, it served as a test case for the trend in Israeli relations toward China. We recall that in 1963, Ben Gurion forecast that China and India would become the most powerful states in the world, and so Israel should prioritize creating ties with them.

The problem from the Indian government's point of view was the need to avoid alienating its Muslim citizens, or even the need to placate them, mainly due to the Kashmir problem. In those days, Abba Eban was holding talks regarding the establishment of relations with India through Madam Vijaya Lakshmi Pandit, Prime Minister Nehru's sister. He revealed that although she was initially optimistic, she was rapidly forced to admit to obstacles in her path—mainly referring to the veto that a Muslim minister had cast on the initiative. Pandit thus thought that Israel would have to settle for India's recognition without progressing to the opening of embassies.

The Israeli Commercial Delegation to China

In January 1955, Israel sent a commercial delegation to China, which represented a partial success for David Hacohen in Burma. Some nine months earlier, in March 1954, the Chinese Foreign Ministry had sent a telegram to Ambassador Yao in Burma, expressing its agreement in principle to receiving and hosting a delegation from Israel. However, the Ministry also noted that it had to consider the possibility of angering Egypt and other Arab countries, as these "object to the American imperialist power establishing defense organizations and military allies in the Middle East." Thus the timing for sending the delegation was not ideal. The Chinese Foreign Ministry proposed postponing the commercial negotiations with Israel and indicated that in addition, "the amount of merchandise available at the moment on both sides is small." In other words, the Chinese assumed that warmer relations with Israel could harm their overall political interests, while their incentive was minimal. The Ministry further noted that a final decision regarding the delegation would be made only after the conclusion of the Geneva Conference discussions in July 1954. At that point, they assumed, the saga of the Korean War would be ended. During this interval, China also planned to conclude the establishment of diplomatic relations with Egypt. Still, the Chinese Foreign Ministry instructed its ambassador to remain ambiguous in discussions with his Israeli colleague. The ambassador was also requested to avoid creating the impression that the Chinese government was completely uninterested in relations with Israel. Apparently, then, the Chinese were trying to keep two balls in the air at once—Israeli and Egyptian-Arab.

Accordingly, several months after the conclusion of the Geneva Conference, Zhou Enlai proposed that his government host an Israeli trade delegation. However, he also emphasized that the discussions with the delegation had to focus on commercial issues alone. The delegation could not address the subject of diplomatic ties, and this topic would be postponed to "the next stage." At the same time, he noted the Arab connection, stating that diplomatic ties with Israel could represent a barrier to the establishment of relations with Arab states.[97]

During October and November 1954, an intensive exchange of telegrams flew between the Chinese embassy in Burma and the high echelons in Beijing. The Chinese diplomats who were active on the Israeli issue included Ambassador Yao and the ministry official responsible for this area. Their higher-ups instructed them to act in a cautious manner that would work to cool Hacohen's enthusiasm regarding the trade delegation. This directive was intended on the one hand to maintain the contact that had already been established, but on the other, to avoid using relatively warm words such as "invitation" and "guests." Again, the discussions were limited to trade between the countries. Yao was supposed to discuss diplomatic issues with Hacohen only at the initiative of his counterpart. If Hacohen raised the topic, Yao was expected to deliver the message that the matter would be addressed only after the delegation arrived in Beijing. Yao was asked to obtain as much information as possible about the members of the mission, their party affiliations, and the topics they intended to raise during the visit. In addition, he was instructed to demonstrate familiarity with Israel's foreign policy.

A message that Yao received on November 17, 1954 clearly addressed the question of the identity of the delegation's members. In addition, Yao was instructed to follow the content of the speech that Foreign Minister Moshe Sharett planned to give in the Knesset on foreign policy. China's two-pronged tactic was also expressed in a telegram on December 7, which again argued that Israel had only a limited quantity of merchandise to

---

97   Archives of the Chinese Ministry of Foreign Affairs, March 25, 1954; August 29, 1954.

export to China and raised doubt regarding the logic of the planned visit. Still, the telegram did express agreement regarding the delegation's visit and even regarding contact between the countries, on certain conditions. It also indicated the quantity of sulfates that Israel could export to China.[98]

After the two countries finally decided that the visit would take place, Hacohen pressed to set a date. He noted that Moshe Sharett hoped that a reciprocal visit of a Chinese delegation in Israel would also take place: "Because trade missions are the first step in building relations in other areas, we do not want China to be isolated from the rest of the world, and we hope that China can create ties with all countries," he wrote. During the Israeli delegation's visit, the members presented a formal invitation for a visit by a Chinese trade mission to Israel with the goal of signing a commercial treaty.[99]

Yao interpreted Hacohen's eagerness to push the process as a reaction to the delay in the Chinese response to setting a date for the Israeli delegation's visit. Hacohen apparently thought that China's foot-dragging was connected to the Israel delegation's exceptional vote against China's bid for membership, cast at the Ninth General Assembly of the United Nations in 1954. According to Yao, Hacohen suspected that China might change its policy toward Israel and the delegation's visit. According to this version of events, Sharett and Hacohen emphasized China's isolation in the world with the intention of encouraging it to give a positive reply regarding the Israeli visit.

As for a reciprocal visit by a Chinese delegation, the Chinese Foreign Ministry suggested that Ambassador Yao express the Chinese prime minister's hope that after the visit of the Israeli delegation, China would send its own delegation to Israel. In December, the Chinese Foreign Ministry sent instructions to the Burmese embassy that the Israeli delegation was expected "to exchange opinions and ideas with the Chinese side regarding the possibilities for trade between the countries. It will not discuss specific commercial issues and will not sign trade agreements."[100] At the end of the month, the agenda for the visit was decided. Again Beijing showed interest in the composition of the delegation and its members. Chinese officials also expressed amazement at the wide variety of languages that the Israelis spoke, at their efforts to learn about China before joining the mission,

---

98 Ibid., October–December 1954.
99 Ibid., December 8, 1954; "The China Connection," Zarchin.
100 Ibid., December 8, 1954; December 24, 1954; December 31, 1954.

and at their backgrounds and experience in diplomacy and international relations.

The Chinese proposed that the delegation travel to Hong Kong and enter China through Shenzhen. Accordingly, on January 26, 1955, the six members of the Israeli delegation finally stepped on Chinese soil and arrived in Guangzhou.[101]

Excitement was high on the Israeli side. Abba Eban was usually described as having warned Israel against excessive overtures to China, for fear of the American reaction. But two decades after the visit, in a radio program entitled "The China Connection," he asserted that he had supported the initiative and even tried to give the delegation a political mission as well. Indeed, in early January 1955, two weeks before the visit, he sent the following in a telegram to Israel's Foreign Ministry: "Relations with China are likely to strengthen Israel's international status, and therefore must not be postponed. I believe that the United States will accept the act and perhaps even benefit from it. Israel has the ability to soften the negative American reaction. I do not think that the Americans will be preoccupied with this now, despite their objection. We must rely on the Netherlands' attempt. I was told by the Dutch that establishing relations [with China] did not harm Dutch–US relations in the long-term. Considering this precedent, I regret that we are going there only to clarify the commercial relationship and not the diplomatic one as well."[102] Ze'ev Sufott described Eban's statement as part of the transformation he underwent, his "change of skin" that began in the fall of 1954.[103]

On the Chinese side, instructions were given to schedule the first three weeks of the visit for tours of China's regions and one week for trade negotiations. An itinerary and directives were sent to districts and branches by the Chinese Foreign Ministry, the Office of Foreign Trade, and the Central Government Committee for Directing International Activities. The instructions covered the sleeping arrangements for the delegation and their transportation between cities and sites. Directives were given regarding the tax exemption granted to the guests, the mode of escort, and organization of the reception and departure ceremonies in each city. The ceremonies were planned to be warm but not wasteful.[104]

---

101 See, for example, ibid., January 26, 1955.
102 "The China Connection," Eban.
103 Interviews with Sufott.
104 Archives of the Chinese Ministry of Foreign Affairs, February 4, 1955.

The delegation traveled from Guangzhou to Beijing, Tianjin, Shenyang (Mukden), and Anshan.[105] The Israelis visited industrial factories, steel and textile mills, and several villages in the region of Manchuria (Dongbei). Although the Chinese were unused to receiving foreign delegations, they were practical and efficient.

On February 21, the delegation left China the same way it had entered. The talks held with officials of the Ministry of Foreign Trade, led by Deputy Minister Lei Renmin, were signed in a memorandum that was devoid of written commitments and unusual statements[106] and mainly consisted of declarations of good intent.

Although the delegation made no breakthroughs, the visit was important in principle, and in addition, two members of the delegation carried out negotiations with Chinese companies. These were Yosef Zarchin of the Ministry of Industry and Trade and Moshe Bejerano, representing the Israel Association of Commerce and Manufacturers. They discovered that to conclude the agreements, they would have to work with quasi-official European agents (Italian or Dutch) located in Beijing. These agents usually acted through private companies in their countries of origin, which had connections with Israel. Thus the Chinese were able to purchase Israeli merchandise in an indirect manner.[107]

The Chinese ambassador to Burma remained an optimistic proponent of relations with Israel. He noted that Moshe Sharett permitted delegation members David Hacohen and Daniel Levin to discuss topics outside the commercial arena that were directly related to the establishment of diplomatic relations. He added that the two had hoped to meet with Zhou Enlai,[108] but such a meeting never took place. Several days after the conclusion of the visit, a confidential telegram was sent to the Chinese envoys in Burma, India, and Indonesia. The telegram reported that during the visit,

---

105 The delegation included: David Hacohen and his wife; Daniel Levin, director of the Asian section in the Israel Foreign Ministry; Meir De-Shalit, a senior official in the Ministry and in the Prime Minister's office; Moshe Bejerano, the Israeli economic attaché in Moscow, as representative of the Israel Association of Commerce and Manufacturers; and Yosef Zarchin, director of the export department in the Ministry of Industry and Trade.

106 Yegar, *The Long Journey to Asia*, 245.

107 "The China Connection," Zarchin; Archives of the Chinese Ministry of Foreign Affairs, February 26, 1955.

108 Archives of the Chinese Ministry of Foreign Affairs, January 26, 1955.

general discussions had been held on the establishment of diplomatic and commercial relations between China and Israel.

Such discussions did take place between Hacohen and Levin on the Israeli side, and on the Chinese side, Deputy Foreign Minister Zhang Hanfu and the foreign minister's assistant, Chen Jiakang. Chen also held an additional meeting with Levin, who asked to know where China stood on relations with Israel and whether the Israelis could expect the opening of embassies in both countries within a defined time limit. Chen's response was vague. He avoided Levin's direct questions and merely repeated the mantra of a "two-stage plan" of trade first and diplomacy later, meaning that the Chinese would begin with informal contact. In other words, China would make decisions on weighty formal issues only after the Afro-Asian conference in Bandung. Only then would China be able to discuss a reciprocal visit of a Chinese mission to Israel, establishment of formal diplomatic ties, and other significant matters.[109]

The Chinese Foreign Ministry reported that the Israeli delegation members were satisfied with their visit.[110] But there was at least one member who was not. Meir De-Shalit of the Israeli Foreign Ministry, who had served as mission secretary, expressed doubt as to the future of relations between the two countries. He stated his hope that one day the Chinese would show their cards and decide the argument he was waging with David Hacohen. Indeed, delegation members were divided in their opinions on the success of their mission: in opposition to De-Shalit's view, David Hacohen took an optimistic stance. De-Shalit could not ignore the minor incidents that took place during the visit and which he thought indicated a lack of appropriate seriousness on the part of the Chinese regarding establishing diplomatic ties with Israel. For example, delegation members were interested in meeting with ministers in the Chinese government but were not granted this privilege, although David Hacohen had met with Prime Minister Zhou Enlai in Burma at the latter's invitation. Further, De-Shalit related that delegation members had brought a translation of Mao's writings into Hebrew as a gift. They had hoped to deliver it to Zhou personally, shake his hand, and take a photo with him, as per accepted protocol. But the Chinese did not permit this, asserting that the prime minister was busy and that his assistants would deliver the books to him later. De-Shalit

---

109 Ibid., February 26, 1955.
110 Ibid.

related that when the topic of exchanging envoys between countries arose during their visit to Shanghai, the Chinese escorts showed no reaction at all and instead merely stared at the Israelis in astonishment.[111]

In the final analysis, De-Shalit's assessments were revealed to be justified, since immediately following the Bandung conference, the embryonic relations between Beijing and Jerusalem deteriorated. This time, it was the Chinese side that presented obstacles.

A Missed Historical Opportunity?

The goal of the conference of Asian and African nations held in Bandung, Indonesia was to advance economic and cultural cooperation between these states. Israel, Korea, and Taiwan were boycotted and not invited to participate. Although the principles espoused by the participants were non-identification and non-involvement of one nation in the affairs of others, many participants voiced condemnations of Israel, alongside encouragement and support for the position of the Arab states. Furthermore, during the conference, the participants made a unanimous decision calling for Israel to withdraw to the partition borders drawn by the UN in 1947. Only India and Burma requested an addition to the text of the decision, which stated that all conference decisions had to be carried out peacefully. China remained neutral on this issue. In the years following the conference, the strengthening of solidarity between Asian and African countries led China to tighten its ties with the Arab states, particularly Egypt. This rapidly led to the termination of the developing relationship between China and Israel.

What was the real turning point in China's policy toward Israel? When exactly did the window of opportunity close for establishing full diplomatic relations between the two nations? Was the Bandung Conference the main stumbling block?

Some believe that even in December 1954, as hinted above, a significant retreat had begun in the process of reinforcing the China–Israel relationship. At this time, a preparatory meeting for the Bandung Conference was held in Bogor, Indonesia. At this gathering, U Nu, leader of the Burmese delegation, tried unsuccessfully to ensure Israel's participation in the conference. But the Arab position, mainly presented by Egypt, ruled the roost,

---

111 "The China Connection," De-Shalit.

and Israel was not invited.[112] After this low point, however, the Israeli trade delegation visited China in January and February 1955—in between the Bogor meeting and the Bandung Conference. Still, a cooling of ties between the countries was recognizable in November and December 1954, and it is possible that the delegation's visit changed nothing.

Some eighteen months after the Bandung Conference, during the Sinai Campaign (or the Suez War) of 1956 and following, Israel cooperated with the two declining colonial powers Great Britain and France, while China adopted a clear anti-Israeli stance, accusing Israel of serving as an imperialist tool. From that point, relations between the two countries entered a long period of deep freeze, as we will explain below.

The hypothetical historiographic question that repeatedly arises is, if Israel had acted with greater daring and imagination before ties between the two countries began to deteriorate, would this have produced better results? The issues of Israeli hesitation at accepting the Chinese initiative to establish ties and whether the Israeli government made a historical error are thorny topics that inspire diverse reactions.

David Hacohen, who had sounded the optimistic note on the issue, consistently criticized the behavior of the Israeli government and the Foreign Ministry under Sharett, mainly from 1954 to 1955. According to Hacohen, the diplomatic lines that Israel drew in the matter of relations with China were exaggerated—while countries such as Great Britain, Holland, and Norway, who were in similar positions, showed no hesitation in tightening ties with China! When Sharett asked him about continuing in his position in Burma, Hacohen pressured his superior to appoint him as representative in China despite his longing to return to Israel and the challenges of adapting to the foreign culture and difficult language.

Hacohen was unsparing in his criticism of Sharett's colleagues, the government ministers who influenced his decision on China. He asserted that just before the Bandung Conference, he had succeeded in convincing Sharett that his position on China was correct, but Sharett disappointed him in the end. He blamed Sharett's refusal on "two ministers who decided a lot in Mapai": Pinchas Lavon and Zalman Aran. Hacohen argued that Israel could have used reparations money from Germany to advance cooperation with China, but his suggestion was not accepted. He also warned that delaying the diplomatic process with Beijing would mean the evaporation of all

---

112 Sufott, "Chinese Policy Toward Israel, 1950–1992," 583–585.

previous efforts in this area, but to no avail.[113] Unfortunately, his prediction was fulfilled.

Other targets of Hacohen's barbs were Abba Eban, then Israel's ambassador to the United States; Reuven Shiloah, who had resigned from directorship of the Mossad and then served as political envoy in Israel's embassy in the United States; and Teddy Kolleck, Ben Gurion's representative in Washington. Throughout the period under analysis, these three served as the American advocates who warned against what they considered a misadventure. The three feared that Israel's policy of non-identification would do unprecedented harm to Israel's relationship with the United States. Hacohen accused the ambassador's assistants of blindly following "minor clerks in the US State Department" and succumbing to the Cold War atmosphere that reigned on the American streets and within Jewish communities.[114] In the end, the thesis upheld by these three won out and after a stormy debate in the cabinet, it was accepted, and Israel gave up a measure of its diplomatic freedom.

Against Hacohen's arguments that a historic opportunity had been missed, Abba Eban asserted that the signing of bilateral agreements with Beijing in 1954 could have been a terrible mistake. Washington might have interpreted this as a hostile act, and it might have damaged US economic and moral support for Israel. Was the "dubious indulgence of establishing an Israeli embassy in China" so valuable? Ben Gurion's stance on the matter was not far from Eban's.

Eban also argued that although he criticized the steps recommended by Hacohen, in 1955 Washington's stance was softened, and this was the opportunity to be daring and follow in the steps of Holland and Norway in establishing relations with China. As mentioned above, he emphasized this approach twenty years after the events, noting that he had even tried to convince members of the government and Foreign Ministry to adopt a new position. If there was indeed a "missed opportunity," it was in 1955 and not 1954.[115]

In his book *A China Diary* and in interviews, Ze'ev Sufott, Israel's first ambassador to China, bolstered and defended Eban's position.[116] In his opinion, Eban was unfairly blamed for the failure. In fact, Eban had

---

113 Yegar, *The Long Road to Asia*, 249–251.
114 "The China Connection," Hacohen.
115 "The China Connection," Eban.
116 Telephone interview with Sufott, December 10, 2013.

supported initiating ties with China and believed that this would fortify Israel's international position. He thought that there was no reason to limit the Israeli trade delegation's mandate to the commercial field.[117] But apparently, Suffott's claims were inexact, as delegation members were given the opportunity to discuss diplomatic issues with the Chinese. Sufott related only to the delegation's official mandate and seems not to have been aware of this green light, which was given in strictest confidence.

Israeli Prime Minister Golda Meir wrote in her autobiography that Israel made every effort in this regard, and that it was the Chinese who failed to respond to Israel's initiative and even demonstrated contempt for Israel's desire to create ties.[118] Ya'akov Shimoni also supported Eban's approach. He actually blamed Moshe Sharett and the conservative position he adopted. But he argued that even if Sharett's approach was in error, it was hardly a mistake of historical proportions, because in April 1955 China changed its tune, so that any positive development would have been buried at any rate.[119]

In retrospect, it seems that the debate on the "missed opportunity" between Hacohen's camp and Eban's was reduced to disagreement on the size of the window of opportunity—in other words, the question of when a chance had existed of saving Israel–China relations, which were fragile from the outset. Here was no deep question of principle, as we sometimes get the impression.

Beginning in 1955, China's acquaintance deepened with Arab states, where weighty political changes were taking place. Egypt became a republic, actively searching for contact with Third World nations that would strengthen its international status; Great Britain abandoned the Middle East; and the struggle began for control of the Suez Canal. The ideological and political map was fundamentally different from that identified during the establishment of revolutionary China and Israel's revival. In Beijing, the new regime grew anxious that Egypt had not yet granted it recognition. Egypt was the cornerstone in the fabric of potential relations with the Arab world and one of the pillars of the non-identifying bloc. Egypt had already recognized Burma and was considering sending an economic delegation to Taiwan. To China, endangering the relations(or lack thereof) with Israel did not seem such a heavy sacrifice when compared to the political profit

---

117 Sufott, *A China Diary*.
118 Yegar, *The Long Road to Asia*, 253–254.
119 "The China Connection," Shimoni.

it served to gain in the Afro-Asian sphere. Further, the Chinese wondered, would Israel be an appropriate supplier of products to China?

As already noted, in January and February of 1955 the enthusiasm of the Chinese toward relations with Israel had cooled. Members of the trade delegation were unable to cash the "open check" granted to them by Moshe Sharett. Holding the positions of prime minister and foreign minister simultaneously, Sharett had permitted them to discuss diplomatic and political issues in addition to economic and trade affairs.

After the delegation's return to Israel, Daniel Levin worked to preserve his tenuous relationship with Chen Jiakang, assistant to the Chinese foreign minister, but his efforts were to no avail. His attempts to interest his colleague in the history and culture of the Jewish people did not bear fruit. He pushed the Chinese to give a response by the end of the summer regarding the progress of Israel–China relations. However, Chinese Foreign Ministry documents reveal that while he was occupied with this, glorifying China's role and even emphasizing that Beijing alone would be the one to determine the level of representation for the two countries, the initial enthusiasm of the Chinese had waned. They no longer intended to relate to the Israeli initiatives on a practical level. Chen was the sole official who still retained authority to engage in secret talks with Jerusalem, but he had no real room to maneuver. He was merely authorized to repeat that in principle, without stating a date, China would establish relations with Israel. Yosef Avidar, Israel's ambassador to the Soviet Union, and his colleagues in Burma and Finland were left without a response when they made inquiries about this issue.[120] Avidar even made a personal visit to China in 1955, but it led nowhere. In fact, Chinese documents show that his arrival actually embarrassed Beijing, which feared the possibility that the Israeli diplomat's visit might overlap with a visit by Nasser.[121] Although Avidar met with Zhang Hanfu, China's deputy foreign minister, the meeting was fruitless.

The Chinese were well aware of the Israeli enthusiasm to create ties, but among themselves, they emphasized that in light of the Bandung Conference, they must "freeze the matter temporarily." This was due to the diplomatic process with the Arab states, as the Chinese anticipated the initiation of ties with them. Accordingly, a delegation comprised of representatives from Syria, Lebanon, and Jordan was received in Beijing.

---

120 Archives of the Chinese Ministry of Foreign Affairs, July 17, 1955; August 11, 1955; September 2, 1955.

121 Ibid., June 2, 1955.

Abba Eban and other Israelis who worked on this matter thought that in the final analysis, the question of bilateral relations with China was purely academic. The argument was that even if suitable relations with China had developed and representations had opened in both countries, as soon as the Six Day War broke out Beijing would have recalled its envoys from Israel, as did all of the Communist bloc states except for Romania. The counterargument to this is that China was likely to copy the behavior pattern of Romania under Ceaușescu, not automatically to follow the line dictated by Moscow. In fact, after the break with the Soviet Union, China often tried to demonstrate its independence. If active diplomatic relations had existed between Israel and China between 1954 and 1967, and strong cooperation in the fields of agriculture, technology, and military had been an established fact (as indeed occurred after 1992), mutual understanding and esteem between the sides might have led to a mere temporary severing of relations (as happened with the Soviet Union). In such a case, the relationship infrastructure already established between the two states would have enabled future cooperation. We may also assume that in its efforts to prove its autonomy from Russia, the ideological mother figure, China would have adopted an approach similar to Romania's and thus rid itself of any responsibility toward Moscow. In this manner, China might have left its Israeli representation open and operating.

Policy-makers in Jerusalem had difficulty admitting a "missed opportunity" or distress at committing a significant error during the attempt to create an appropriate texture of relations with China. Their natural tendency was to place the blame for the failure of the diplomatic process on the consolidation of the Third World, particularly the Afro-Asian bloc that boycotted Israel. Indeed, Israel's relations with African countries also collapsed due to the Six Day War. It was easier to cite Ben Gurion's words that Israel had no natural ally in the international arena,[122] and that Israel was hard-put to find a common denominator with other countries.[123]

---

122 "The China Connection," Avineri.
123 Statements made on July 5, 1955, Archives of the Prime Minister's Office, 7/5565/C.

Chapter Two

Moshe and Ya'akov—Two Jews in China

We cannot begin our story of China–Israel relations without a quick peek into the lives of two exceptional Jewish individuals: Moshe (Morris "Two-Gun") Cohen and Jacob Rosenfeld. These men were not deeply involved in the organized Jewish community life of China, nor were they part of the formal fabric of relations between the two old-new nations. However, these figures were uniquely colorful, and each made a significant mark, if not on the formal history of modern China, then in stories that were passed down orally over decades and sometimes recorded in writing. Their personalities appeared every so often in local anecdotes, like marginal players or silent extras in an underground performance. In some mysterious, perhaps figurative way, they recalled their biblical namesakes, Moses and Jacob. Undoubtedly, these trailblazers possessed unusual talents that enabled them to push their way onto the back benches of the stage of Chinese history.

Moshe (Morris) Cohen

Moshe (Morris) Avraham Cohen was born in Poland in 1887 to a large religious family.[124] When Morris (called Moishe) was a young boy, the family

---

124 For over four decades, researchers of Moshe Cohen's story relied on the 1954 account by Charles Drage, *Two-Gun Cohen*, written at Cohen's initiative. Finally, in 1997, an educated, balanced book of the same name was published by Daniel Levy. Levy's is an impressive biography based on many years of extensive research. As Levy showed, most of what was previously written about Cohen was simply incorrect. In the 1920s, when Cohen was known to the authorities and had drawn the attention of various journalists, he was able to mold his life story according to his own agenda, and convinced many of the truth of his version. But was Cohen really as central as he portrayed himself? Was he really one of the leading forces in Chinese history? After years of study, Levy's answer

immigrated to England and settled there. In London he rapidly proved to be the black sheep of the family. Despite his strict religious upbringing, he preferred to roam the streets rather than sit in the *cheder* (religious school) and made friends with non-Jewish toughs, joining them in fistfights and street battles, petty crime, and pickpocketing. Eventually he was sent to an institution for underage criminals. As a last resort, his father sent him off to Western Canada to work on a farm of a family friend. But even there, Moshe continued his pranks, gaining a reputation as a card sharp, swindler, skirt-chaser, and gunman. His career at the farm lasted for about a year, and then he began to wander around the towns of Western Canada. He made his living by picking pockets, gambling, and various and sundry shady jobs, including street barker and front man for a circus. He often landed in jail for the frauds that had become his way of life. In Saskatchewan, so the story goes, he physically prevented an armed robbery of a Chinese restaurant where he was dining. For a European to come to the aid of a Chinese person was then considered a rare act of generosity. In appreciation, the grateful restaurant owner introduced Cohen to his friends, and Cohen developed special ties with members of the Chinese community. The Chinese told the young Jewish adventurer about the secret Tong Meng Hui organization (Sun Yat-sen's revolutionary group) and even accepted him as a member.

Eventually, Cohen secured his economic future when he became involved in real estate. His skill at smooth talk, which had aided him in many swindles, also proved useful in deals that were above the table. At age twenty-two, he was able to purchase a new home for his parents in a respectable neighborhood in England.

Moshe operated in the local Chinese community in Canada until the First World War began. Canada's economic situation rapidly deteriorated. Employment opportunities were nil and many had no other option but to volunteer for the army. The real estate office where Moshe worked closed. For this reason, or perhaps even out of a sense of patriotism toward the England of his childhood, he volunteered for the Canadian military forces.

---

is negative: "I had to ignore everything that Drage wrote," he emphasized, and asserted that "His book is historical fiction" (263–264). For example, Cohen's statement that he had met Sun Yat-sen in Canada while the Chinese leader was collecting donations for his movement had to be fictional, as Cohen was sitting behind bars at the time. Cohen also falsely claimed that he was wounded on the European front during World War I, and lied about his military rank. In order of publication, the books on Cohen are: Drage, *Two-Gun Cohen*; Portman and Kipfer, *Shadow over China*; Levy, *Two-Gun Cohen*.

But even as a soldier, Moshe did not abandon his opportunistic ways. Along with other soldiers, even those under his command as a sergeant, he got in trouble with the police and was arrested several times for the use of rude language and illegal consumption of alcohol. In court he always managed to wangle his way out of punishment.[125] In 1917 Cohen's regiment was transferred to the Corps of Canadian Railway Troops and sent to Europe, where they joined another regiment. Cohen took advantage of the trip to pay a visit to his family in England, during which he enjoyed the services of a local prostitute. After returning to his regiment, he discovered that the price for his weekend entertainment was steep—he was infected with gonorrhea and could not join his troops at the front. He was also stripped of his sergeant's stripes. Eventually, however, his rank was returned to him, and thanks to his connections with the Chinese, he was sent to work with a Chinese military support force of over 170 laborers. He declared that he was the only person who knew how to deal with the Chinese. The language barrier, the Europeans' sense of superiority toward the Asians, and the cultural differences could often lead to uncomfortable situations—but Cohen was able to paddle these stormy waters. At the end of the war, he went AWOL for two weeks, asserting that his duty to the military was for the war period only. As punishment, he was again demoted to the rank of private.[126]

After the war, Cohen returned to Canada, where he settled in Edmonton. He introduced himself as a sergeant and made a celebratory announcement of his return to the local mayor. After he was formally discharged from the army, the Tong Meng Hui asked him to serve as spokesman for their organization and to assist them in publicity activities. Cohen became the English secretary of the organization. Canadian newspapers from that period document his powerful influence, noting that he was even able to sway the Chinese community's vote in the local elections. He acted as a vote contractor, and the local candidates negotiated with him. As his esteem grew with the Chinese, his status in Edmonton improved as well. He was elected a member of the Great War Veterans' Association and tried to use his status to promote the rights of the Chinese community in Canada. He also was in regular contact with senior officials of the Republic of China. When Chen Shu-ren, secretary general of the Guomindang in Canada, arrived in Edmonton, Cohen was the one to give him a tour of the area.

125 Levy, *Two-Gun Cohen*, 86–94.
126 Ibid., 104.

In 1922, Cohen began a new adventure. He sailed to China to negotiate a railroad deal for Sun Yat-sen. His first stop was in Shanghai, city of sin for Europeans in China. Under non-Chinese rule in the foreign concessions, the Europeans could do as they pleased. Shanghai was a perfect fit for Cohen's personality and aspirations.[127] While there, he arranged a meeting with Sun through American journalist George Sokolsky, who worked for the Chinese leader. The meeting was a success although, as he later attested, Cohen couldn't take his eyes off the leader's wife, Soong Ching-ling. Cohen was appointed to the position he had targeted—bodyguard on Sun Yat-sen's personal staff. His coarse Cantonese dialect was not an obstacle, as many in the Chinese leadership spoke fluent English.

Sun granted Cohen the title *fu guan*, aide-de-camp. Soon he was awarded two Chinese names: Kuo Han, which sounded similar to his English name, and Ma Kun, which stayed with him for the rest of his life. Sun and Cohen shared several traits that led to a feeling of brotherhood between them: they were both foreigners in their homes, exceptional individuals who had reinvented their pasts. Entranced by Sun's dreams of national redemption, Cohen was moved to act based on ideology and avoid the dishonest behavior of many of his fellow foreigners in Shanghai.

From 1922 to 1925, Cohen lived in Sun's household. In February 1923, Sun took a delegation to Guangzhou (Canton), where they met with members of the Communist Party to attempt to forge an alliance. Cohen was assigned to the highest echelon of the leader's personal bodyguards and helped train Sun's other guards. He learned to box and ordered the others to use their fists before pulling out their pistols. When Sun was appointed generalissimo of the military government in March 1923, Cohen stuck close beside his leader. In one battle Cohen saved Sun from a kidnapping attempt. In this well-known incident, Cohen was hit in the left arm by a machine-gun bullet, and Sun bandaged him. Cohen then trained himself to shoot with his left hand, in case next time he were to be wounded in the right. Subsequently he always carried two guns, one in each hand, earning him the nickname "Two-Gun Cohen."[128]

Cohen earned a decent salary but regularly squandered his earnings on gambling, women, and other earthly pleasures. He also told exaggerated stories that were largely fabricated. He crowned himself "general."

127 Ibid., 118.
128 Ibid., 125.

In March 1925 Cohen visited Canada, where he was received to great acclaim. But while there, Cohen received word that Sun Yat-sen had died of liver cancer, and the rug was pulled out from under his feet.[129] During that time, chaos reigned in southern China. Communists and Nationalists turned against each other. Some in the West even considered Cohen to be China's true leader.[130] Meanwhile, he was earning enormous sums through trade in weapons. In this venture he enjoyed the protection of Guomindang leaders such as Sun's brother-in-law, the banker T.V. Soong; Sun Yat-sen's son Sun Fo; and southern war heroes such as Li Chi-shen and Ch'en Chi-t'ang. However, Cohen did not have the support of Chiang Kai-shek, who had taken control of the Party. Cohen was promoted to brigadier general and then to major general.[131]

In 1935, Cohen went to England to visit his family, as his father was ill. His father died during the visit, and Cohen did everything possible to help his family, supporting them emotionally and financially. When the Sino–Japanese war broke out in 1937, Cohen lent his support to Soong Ching-ling, the late Sun Yat-sen's wife. He assisted her with her charity projects, and she rewarded him for his efforts. At this point he made his home in Hong Kong, where he assisted Jewish refugees who had come to China, mainly Shanghai. When the Japanese occupied the British colony in 1941, he remained in Hong Kong. The Japanese put him in Stanley Internment Camp, where they interrogated and tortured him, but he continued to feel that his fate was tied to China and remained loyal to that country. Acquaintances from the internment camp period related that he endeared himself to others and did his best to help them. In 1943, he was finally released as part of a rare prisoner exchange agreement. Cohen returned to Canada, where he married a Jewish woman, but he continued his travels and salacious lifestyle, and the marriage ended in 1956.

In his later years Cohen looked back fondly on old times and wove myths about his life in China. His name became connected with the building of the new China. As a Jew, he supported the Zionist project. Some say that when the Nationalist China representatives to the UN planned to vote against the partition plan that would enable establishment of the Jewish state, he convinced them to change their stance and abstain from voting in the General Assembly. This abstention helped achieve the majority that

---

129 Ibid., 139.
130 Ibid., 153.
131 Ibid., 187.

was necessary for the UN to approve the plan. At the initial stages of the Cultural Revolution, Cohen visited Israel and according to various witnesses, he expressed amazement at the success of the Zionist project. He attended a performance of a Yiddish play, *De Megille* by Itzik Manger. But his visit had no repercussions for Israel–China relations.

In his final years Moshe moved to Selford, a suburb of Manchester. He visited China regularly. As his name was connected to the nation's founding fathers, he was permitted to move freely between both the People's Republic and Nationalist China (Taiwan), a privilege reserved for a small number of unique individuals. Rumor has it that he even tried to bring about an agreement between the opposing camps. He also worked as a consultant for companies operating in China. His last visit to the PRC was in 1966, on the eve of the Cultural Revolution, as a guest of Premier Zhou Enlai. Cohen died on September 7, 1970 and was buried in the Jewish cemetery in Blakely, Manchester. His gravestone was engraved with epitaphs in English, Hebrew, and Chinese.[132]

Researchers of Cohen's life have never been completely able to decipher his character, and the gap between reality and myth, fact and fantasy will probably never be completely closed. Emily Han described this gap in the introduction to her 1988 book on Cohen. She relates how she met Cohen while writing another book on the Soong sisters. Cohen was sent by Mrs. Sun Yat-sen to express her indignation that Han had described her as a "Communist" in the book and to request politely that she change it. She wrote: "Did I ever see him carrying two guns? I don't think so. Usually he wasn't even wearing a uniform. But we called him 'Two-Gun' anyway, just in case those fearful guns really were present underneath the roomy coat he wore."[133]

Jacob Rosenfeld

Dr. Jacob Rosenfeld was another Jew who deserves mention here, as his imprint on the history of the new China was even more powerful than that of Moshe Cohen. Rosenfeld was born on January 11, 1903. He died before he reached fifty and was buried in the Kiryat Shaul cemetery in Tel Aviv. Rosenfeld was ostensibly an ordinary Jew, but beneath the marble

---

132 King, "Two-Gun Cohen," online document; Katzir, "Moshe Cohen, the Chinese General."
133 Portman and Kipfer, *Shadow over China*, 1–2.

tombstone that marks his grave lies an extraordinary story, and researchers of Jewish history are unaware of the depths of its mysteries. Rosenfeld's life story is even more exotic and unusual than the biographies of Moshe Cohen above and Shaul Eisenberg, whom we will describe below.

Rosenfeld was born in Lemberg, then part of the Austro-Hungarian Empire (today Lviv in the Ukraine). In 1928, at age twenty-five, he completed the study of medicine at the University of Vienna, where he specialized in urology and gynecology. Rosenfeld sympathized with social democracy.[134] He paid a high price for that privilege when he was arrested on suspicion of involvement in "subversive" activities. Shortly after the Anschluss in 1938, when Nazi Germany invaded Austria, Rosenfeld was arrested by the Gestapo and sent to Dachau and Buchenwald death camps. Historians do not know whether he was acquainted with Marxist literature before he was arrested, but he was undoubtedly exposed to it while in these camps together with Marxist prisoners.[135] The Chinese would eventually emphasize this anti-fascist aspect of the Rosenfeld myth. His fellow prisoners documented Rosenfeld's bravery and willingness to provide medical assistance to those in need, even risking significant danger to his own life. These exploits also appear in other documents collected on Rosenfeld many years later.[136]

After about one year in the camps, the authorities made a surprising decision that his offenses were relatively light, and he was granted a conditional release. The Gestapo gave him fourteen days to leave Austria. Undocumented reports note that he received assistance from Dr. Ho Feng-Shan, Consul General of China in Vienna. Ho, often termed "Chinese Schindler," helped many Jews whom he observed suffering from persecution in that city. From 1938 to 1940, according to his daughter, Ho issued hundreds, possibly thousands of Shanghai emigration visas (later called "visas for life") to Jews, thereby saving many lives. For this humane act, so rare in those grim times, Ho was granted the title "Righteous among the Nations" many decades later by the State of Israel.[137]

---

134 Kaminski, *General Luo Genannt Langnase*, 28. Kaminski also wrote *Ich kannte sie alle* (Vienna, 2002) which contain Rosenfeld's war diary.

135 Ibid., 48.

136 Ibid.

137 "Dr. Feng Shan Ho & Jewish Refugees—From Vienna to Shanghai," Shanghai Jewish Refugee Museum Website (retrieved August 26, 2011): http://www.shanghaijews.org.cn/english/article/?aid=64. Kaminski argues that "just a few visas [Ho issued] could be traced. He adds that after all "visas were not necessary for going to Shanghai...and that

In June 1939, Rosenfeld left Vienna, and after a long sea voyage he reached Shanghai. He opened a private clinic in the international concession. Although he could have earned a respectable income from his profession, he chose an unexpected direction—he joined the communist revolutionaries who were struggling to create deep socio-economic change in China and to overthrow the Japanese occupation. Rosenfeld may have been driven to this uncharacteristic step by the horrifying scenes of war and human suffering he observed in Shanghai. According to Friedrich Schiff, an Austrian Jewish painter living in Shanghai who knew Rosenfeld well, Rosenfeld could not bear the vast social gap he observed in the surrounding society. The foreigners enjoyed luxurious homes equipped with modern central heating, air conditioning, and swimming pools, while Chinese families lacked basic necessities and dirt-poor "coolies" roamed the city streets in the suffocating summer humidity and extreme winter cold. Rosenfeld felt he could not remain silent in the face of the mortal hunger, poverty, and degradation that he observed. He felt that he had to take a daring step, to make an outspoken and uncompromising political statement. He resolved to help the miserable and the downtrodden.

In early 1940, in the crowded Chinese city, Rosenfeld met a German communist who went by the alias Heinz Shippe (his real name was Gregory Grzyb). Since the 1920s, Shippe had been in close contact with members of the Chinese Communist Party. At Shippe's home in Shanghai, Rosenfeld met Dr. Shen Qishen, "health minister" of the New Fourth Army (one of the two commands of the National Revolutionary Army, then still in united Chinese control under Chiang Kai-shek). Shen spoke German, and the two developed a strong friendship. They enjoyed in-depth conversations on ideological issues, philosophical discussions on the nature of humanity, the Chinese Revolution, and the theory of Karl August Wittfogel.[138] Wittfogel was a well-known intellectual and German communist. In his book *Oriental Despotism*, he outlined an original theory on the historical development of vast empires like China and India. He described the agrarian production methods of these societies and analyzed their uniqueness. Wittfogel concluded that the character of these societies was determined by their need for labor-intensive irrigation works and a bureaucratic management structure. In his view, these countries developed "hydraulic cultures"

a few refugees used Ho's visas to flee to other places than Shanghai. Letter to the author, April 6, 2018.

138 Kaminski, *General Luo Genannt Langnase*, 49.

based on enormous water infrastructures. Wittfogel expanded this thesis into fascinating conclusions. In addition to discussing Wittfogel's theory, Rosenfeld and Shen had long talks on medicine, and we may assume that Shen visited Rosenfeld's clinic.

Rosenfeld's younger brother Joschi was also living in Shanghai at that time. The brothers tried their hand at international trade in Chinese silk, but their venture failed. Jacob was increasingly carried away by radical ideological romanticism. His views intensified along with Japanese attacks on China, and with the occupiers' increasingly cruel behavior in Shanghai and its environs. On one hand, Chiang Kai-shek's failure to remedy the catastrophic situation, and on the other his harsh operations against the Communists, whom many Chinese considered to be anti-Japanese patriots, darkened his halo as a leader. Rosenfeld fumed against Chiang Kai-shek's political party. The writing was on the wall: Rosenfeld felt he had no choice but to join Dr. Shen in integrating ideological activity and medicine in his life, and he threw in his lot with the Communists. The Austrian-Jewish physician abandoned Shanghai, and in March 1941 joined the Communists in the battle against the Japanese occupier, serving as military physician in the combat regiments.

Rosenfeld reached the ancient city of Yancheng in Jiangsu province on the northern banks of the Yangtze River. The city's name means "City of Salt," and it reminded Rosenfeld of Salzburg, the Austrian City of Salt. The Fourth Army set up its temporary headquarters in in an ancient temple in Yancheng. There Rosenfeld met army commanders Liu Shaoqi and Chen Yi, who eventually became heroes of the Chinese Revolution. By this point, he had become part of the backbone of the Chinese Communist movement. He spent long hours operating on the wounded, working non-stop and with an unusual dedication that impressed observers. He treated ordinary citizens, simple villagers, and dirt-poor commoners. As a gynecologist he cared for Chinese women, including those who asked to abort unwanted pregnancies during the stark wartime circumstances. When farmers demanded to know why their women weren't fertile enough, he was quick to retort with an ancient Chinese proverb: "The old man can't carry the burden and so he throws it down beside the gate."[139] Rosenfeld practiced his craft, including surgery, in inhospitable conditions, sometimes beside the very fields where the Chinese soldiers were engaged in desperate battle against the Japanese.

---

139 老头扛布袋,进门儿就倒 lǎotóu káng bùdài, jìnmén er jiù dào

On July 22, 1941, Yancheng fell to enemy forces. The Japanese attacked with small motorized boats, taking advantage of the river, which was swollen after powerful rains. Rosenfeld escaped to Kunming along with his medical unit, and after that the forces wandered the countryside. The constant movement proved exhausting for the medical team. Rosenfeld was given a horse for his own personal use, but he found riding difficult, so he usually walked and used the horse to carry the unit's equipment.

Eventually Rosenfeld was transferred to service in the Shanghai branch of the Eighth Route Army, and finally to the People's Liberation Army (PLA) in Manchuria (Dongbei), where he became an assistant to the Minister of Health in the temporary military government of the revolution. During his service he moved around to various locations in north and northeast China. He became medical commander and health minister in the army of General Wan Yi in Dongbei.[140] The general was very impressed by Rosenfeld's dedication and supported his advance in rank throughout his service, until the Jewish physician reached the most senior rank ever achieved by a foreigner in the Chinese revolutionary army.

After ten years of battle, while holding a rank equivalent to general, Rosenfeld became one of the heroes of the Chinese Revolution, like the legendary Canadian physician Norman Bethune. In 1945 the Japanese Empire collapsed, but the Chinese Communist revolutionary struggle was not over—a harsh and cruel civil war broke out in China. The Communist forces had separated from the Nationalist government forces under Chiang Kai-shek and the Guomindang and began their final attempt to take over the regime's strongholds and establish a new republic—the People's Republic.

Rosenfeld thought of himself as a true Chinese. Disappointed with his native Austria, which had capitulated to Nazism and betrayed him and his ilk, he made China his new homeland. He dedicated his life to the battle against the Japanese and Guomindang nationalism under Chiang Kai-shek. During the war, Rosenfeld applied to become a member of the Chinese Communist Party, as he wholeheartedly admired its unique values and purpose and adopted them as his own. He sharply criticized the practice of Leninist socialism as expressed in the Soviet Union. From his viewpoint, the Chinese Revolutionary Army was a marvel of humane treatment even toward its Japanese prisoners, and its soldiers acted according to pure democratic values.

---

140 Kaminski, *General Luo Genannt Langnase*, 141.

Almost nothing has been written about Rosenfeld's unique experiences during military service in China or about his unusual life. The only work that sheds some light on his story is a study by Gerd Kaminski.[141] His book documents the unprecedented sacrifice of a foreigner on behalf of a people whose language he did not know, while endangering his own life. He practiced military and civilian medicine under conditions that were unbearable, even compared to known battle situations elsewhere. The Chinese Communists who benefitted from his professional services showered him with love and warmth. In times when food was almost nonexistent, they gave him their crumbs of bread, bits of chicken, and rare tidbits. But within this sea of love, the man was lonely. Only one or two others around him spoke German. His Chinese was no more than basic, and the little that he did speak was acquired over many years and with great difficulty. He was often overcome with powerful feelings of longing for his family, especially for his sister Stefanie, whom he hoped to bring to China so that she could assist him. At one point his grateful hosts tried to arrange a marriage for him with an appropriate woman. In the Chinese worldview, a "good" wife meant a woman who would bear him a son, which they considered to be humanity's ideal achievement. But Rosenfeld rejected the matchmakers' proposals, insisting that he had no property or means to support a wife. Aside from that, if he had his choice among Chinese women, he asserted that he would prefer a luckless one with smallpox scars over another who might be charming and attractive.

Rosenfeld became close to Liu Shaoqi, the political commissar of the New Fourth Army who eventually served as chairman of the People's Republic of China. After the war and until he left China, Rosenfeld assisted in the construction of a major hospital in the region under the Fourth Army's control and worked to promote medicine in the new China.

In October 1949, Rosenfeld went to Europe, reaching Vienna in November. He intended to find his family in Austria, stay there for a while, and then return to China. He hoped to serve in a medical position, as befitted the status he had acquired during his demanding military service. He also toyed with the idea of serving in a respectable position in the Austrian representation in Beijing.

In Vienna, Rosenfeld discovered that his mother had died from illness on the way to Theresienstadt. He was happy to discover that his siblings

---

141 Ibid.

Jerome and Stefanie were still alive; however, he became severely depressed and his health began to decline to dangerous levels. He discovered that he had a serious heart condition, and he had to focus on caring for himself. He tried to write a memoir but was unable to find a publisher willing to take the financial risk of printing the book. In the crazy days of post-war Europe, interest in China was low. When the Korean War broke out and pitted China against most of the UN member states, European empathy waned toward Chinese history and culture. To Rosenfeld's further frustration, two books by Austrian doctors who had served in China were published. There was no reason to publish a third work on the same topic.

Rosenfeld considered returning to China, his only source of hope, but his dreams were never realized. He was caught in the web of Chinese bureaucracy. His colleague from the New Fourth Army, who had become China's ambassador in East Berlin, apparently did not forward his letter requesting to join the army again, perhaps because he did not want to take the responsibility. Despite the Jewish physician's unprecedented contributions to the success of the revolution, the new China presumably was not welcoming to foreigners, much less those who were interested in becoming citizens and settling there. Then, as now, ethnic homogeneity was a foundational principle in China. Despite Rosenfeld's poor health, he continued his efforts to obtain a permit for entry and stay in the country he loved. He received numerous rejections from the Chinese embassy in East Germany—they simply didn't want him! He was even willing to join the military again, this time to assist as a combat physician in the war in Korea against Western imperialism, then represented by the UN.

Rosenfeld was betrayed by the representatives of the very country he had called home for over a decade. Even his friends, including Dr. Shen, were unable to assist him. We may assume that they were afraid to take a stand against the authorities, including the secret service, which was undoubtedly involved in the rejection of Rosenfeld's application.

Homeless and estranged from his native Austria (even if it had been communist, it would have been under Soviet influence, which was unacceptable to Rosenfeld), the Jewish doctor was alone, without family, and desperate. His requests for asylum in the United States also went unanswered. Who in post-war America would welcome an enthusiastic supporter of the Chinese regime, a man who had lent a helping hand to the Communists? McCarthyist America was busy denouncing its own citizens who were even suspected of sympathizing with the "Reds"; there was no room for Europeans whose communist connections were proven beyond any shade of doubt.

The default option was Israel, and in late July 1951, Rosenfeld arrived in Tel Aviv, where he was welcomed by his brother Joschi and sister-in-law. His other brother Norbert was on his way to Canada. At first, life in Israel seemed promising, and Rosenfeld searched for work as a doctor for a health service or small town. Finally he was offered a position at Assuta Hospital in Tel Aviv. While job-hunting, he continued his attempts to obtain an entry permit and visa to the United States, where he thought he might find a cure for his illness—but to no avail. In 1951 he traveled to Switzerland, where he once more tried his luck with the Chinese. He contacted the Chinese consulate in Bern, but yet again luck frowned at him. He underwent a series of cardiac tests, and the doctors' conclusion was decisive: he needed a heart operation, but it was too dangerous. There was still no answer from the Chinese. From Switzerland he continued to Bologna, Firenze, and Zurich before returning to Israel. This time, it was his last stop. In March 1952 he suffered a heart attack and collapsed. He was hospitalized in Assuta, the hospital where he worked. He died on April 22 and was buried in the Kiryat Shaul cemetery.

To this day, the Chinese revere General "Long Nose" (Luo Shengte), as he was called during his military service. While during the Cultural Revolution, when his former friends Liu Shaoqi and Chen Yi lost favor, he was forgotten, after Mao's death and the inception of the liberal Open Door economic policy, the Chinese remembered him and he was labelled a national hero. They honored him by giving his name to a hospital in the city of Junan in Shandong Province. In 1992 they erected a statue of him at the entrance to the hospital. He was also commemorated in revolutionary songs and in the central museum adjoining the Mao Zedong Mausoleum in Beijing.

In 2003, on the centennial anniversary of Rosenfeld's death, a special exhibit in his honor was organized in Beijing at the National History Museum at Tiananmen Square by the Austrian-Chinese Friendship Association, the Chinese Friendship Association, and the Shandong Friendship Association. The exhibit included his diary, which tells the story of his life. To commemorate this friend of the Revolution, the Beijing post office issued a special series of three stamps. Earlier on, in 1999, Beit Hatfutsot at Tel Aviv University organized an exhibition in his honor. It was opened by Dr. Gerd Kaminski and the ambassadors of China and Austria. In October 2006, an exhibit on his life opened at the Jewish Museum of Vienna. In 2008, another exhibit opened in Washington, D.C., and the opening was apparently attended by his niece, Ann Margaret Rosenfeld-Frija.

After the Chinese embassy in Israel was opened, Chinese visitors to Tel Aviv paid their respects at Rosenfeld's grave. The secretary of the Israel-China Friendship Association, Dov Mirkin, related that the Israelis had no idea that Rosenfeld was buried right under their noses in Tel Aviv. The news got out only when a request was received from Han Xu, former Chinese ambassador in Washington, to visit the grave during his trip to Israel. The grave had been neglected, but the Austrian-Chinese Friendship Association and the Association of Former Jewish Residents in China initiated efforts to clean it and ensure that it received the care appropriate for a "hero of the Chinese nation," as he was described by members of the delegation.[142] Finally, faithful visitors paid their respects to this special man who died childless, and they remember his contributions to this day. There was more than a little irony in the Austrian government's declaration that Rosenfeld symbolized true friendship between China and Austria. His brother Adolph asserted that Jacob had often told him that he could never consider working as a physician in Austria, as he feared he might have to treat a person with Jewish blood on his hands.[143] Yet after his death, the man who had fled Austria, who adamantly denied any connection to his homeland due to its Nazi past and its post-war character, and who refused to return there to live, became a symbol of allegiance between Austria and China.

---

142 Immerglick, "The Chinese People's Hero Buried in Tel Aviv."
143 Kaminski, *General Luo Genannt Langnase*, 180.

Chapter Three

1948 to 1956—Behind the Scenes

Over the years, while the pendulum of formal relations between Israel and China was swaying from one extreme to another, a parallel, informal drama was acted out behind the scenes. Various organizations and political parties tried their hand at strengthening ties between Chinese and Israeli society, mainly through visits by Israelis to China. These Israeli visitors belonged to leftist socialist parties and to the Israel Communist Party (ICP, known in Israel by its Hebrew acronym, "Maki"). Often they adopted an attitude of reflexive, almost blind enthusiasm toward China. Their viewpoint was usually one of admiration for the success of the Revolution and glorification of the achievements of the new People's Republic. But some also preserved a hefty measure of sobriety and identified unwelcome phenomena that had spread throughout China. Undoubtedly the records and memoirs of these visitors open for the researcher an additional, valuable window into the historical narrative.

This appreciation and even admiration for the People's Republic of China was not limited to the Israeli Communist movement, but also characterized kibbutz members in Israel in the 1950s. Documents in the Yad Tabenkin Archives shed light on the informal connection created between Israeli and Chinese citizens and the Israelis' deep interest in events in China. These documents allow us a view beyond the formal dimension and offer evidence of the esteemed place that China occupied in the hearts, minds, and imaginations of defined groups in Israel.

In the first chapter of this book, we examined the formal aspect of Israel–China relations, from the founding of the state in 1948 until the 1956 Suez Crisis. The present chapter focuses on relations between Israeli civil organizations and Chinese society in various contexts. In this case

China adopted a "people-to-people policy"—a unique strategy that it used on occasion to overcome the boycotts that many governments waged against it.

Members of Leftist Israeli Parties Visit China

During the 1950s, members of the left side of the Israeli political map attended meetings and conferences in China. The Israelis demonstrated optimism and even admiration for the new China; however, they also expressed disappointment that Beijing recognized and communicated with Arab countries yet overlooked Israel. What role did the leftist parties in Israel play in relation to Israel's policy toward China? What was the nature of the relationship between the communist parties in the two countries? Did they influence the establishment of formal ties in 1992?

As early as 1949, members of the Israeli Communist Party (ICP) praised the rise to power of the Chinese Communist Party (CCP), as embodied in the declaration of the People's Republic of China under Mao. The ICP maintained close ties with the CCP until 1960. Later, an ideological chasm separated the two parties based on ICP's uncompromising support of Russian communism; the "orthodox" form"; and its refusal to accept the unique, independent dogma of the Chinese Communist Party.

In October 1949, ICP invited members of CCP to send a delegation to its eleventh congress, the first congress since the establishment of the State of Israel. Mao congratulated ICP on the congress and expressed his regret that it was too early to send a delegation from his party. Although Chinese representatives did not attend this Israeli congress, its atmosphere was imbued with the spirit of the Chinese success story. In his speech at the congress, Shmuel Mikunis, who represented ICP in the Knesset for many years (1948–73), praised the Chinese Revolution as a victory over the imperialist conspiracy in East Asia. Meir Vilner, another member of the party, emphasized the deep connection between the revolution in China and the Soviet example, asserting that China had achieved Soviet standards under Stalin's tutelage. He quoted Mao himself, who proclaimed that the Communist victory in China would never have been achieved without the Soviet Union's support.[144]

---

144 Shai, "Israeli Communist Party and PRC," 87.

To the Israeli Communists, China was an example and a model. They placed great hope in the Chinese Revolution, which they saw as the forerunner of other revolutions in Asia. They considered that the Chinese Communists had created a new archetype not just for undeveloped societies but also for developed states like Israel. The Israelis understood the quiet co-existence between national minorities in China and the Han people, the largest ethnic group in China, as an example of a peaceful means of conflict resolution. The Israelis hoped that they could implement this model. Additional Chinese initiatives, such as reforms in agriculture and education, were also considered prototypes for the transformations that the young State of Israel should adopt. Israel faced tough social challenges due to the waves of immigrants landing on its shores, and economic and social problems loomed. It was thus no surprise that the Chinese plan for eliminating ignorance and for transferring entire industries to the workers, as well as adoption of the progressive Constitution of 1954, were reported in detail in the ICP newspaper *Kol Ha'Am* ("Voice of the People"), published in fifty thousand copies per issue.[145] These were encouraging reports, written from a naïve, uncritical viewpoint that bordered on idealization of events taking place in that distant land. Aside from the Soviet Union, no other communist regime in the world enjoyed such a detailed survey or such lavish praise as the Chinese government and party received from the ICP spokesmen and journal.

The first visit of ICP members to China took place in January 1950, when Ruth Lubitz participated in the Congress of Asian Women in Beijing. There she met with members of the Central Committee of the Communist Party and held informal talks with them. Naturally, she expressed her party's position on issues such as the Arab–Israeli conflict and social and economic conditions in Israel and China. On January 15, at the Congress plenum, Lubitz declared that Western imperialism was the source of the ongoing Arab–Israeli conflict. In accordance with the accepted socialist line of reasoning, she added that when socialism strengthened its position in Israel, relations with China would improve concurrently.

In her book Lubitz described the visit to China as a historic visit. In fact, this was the first delegation to visit China, and its participants observed the buds of the new era of the People's Republic under Communist Party leadership. During the festive celebration at the Congress, the Israeli

---

145 Ibid., 87.

delegation was honored with an impressive reception, which was attended by government officials and representatives of a wide range of public organizations, including women's and youth groups. Children carrying flags and flowers added a particularly festive and colorful character to the event. However, Lubitz expressed disappointment that Mao did not attend the opening ceremony (he was busy attending a celebration in honor of Stalin's seventieth birthday). Lubitz sketched the experience of this gathering at the Congress in optimistic tones, creating a classic communist propaganda piece. In her descriptions she presented smiling, confident images of women as they boundlessly embraced and cheered for each other. Her phrases were peppered with socialist terms and expressed her anticipation of the end of imperialism throughout the world.

Lubitz's descriptions illustrated the widespread enthusiasm then inspired by the new China among communist and socialist entities, with their fascinating and unique combination of old and new. The difficult scenes that Lubitz and her colleagues witnessed in China—poverty, miserable living conditions, and child labor, all against the background of the mass destruction caused by the civil war—were presented as remnants of the previous era of capitalist exploitation, tenant farming, slavery, and imperialism. Lubitz methodically defended the new China and tried to avoid criticizing its regime, which she thought had led China's citizens from slavery to freedom. She sunnily described nursery schools that were "prepared for educating the children in the new spirit" and noted that the children were being educated for joy and happiness. In her view the revolution in China was a necessity that contained the kernel of hope for the entire Chinese nation.[146]

Lubitz did not mention the issue of Israel–China relations, and it is doubtful that this topic arose in her discussions when in China. On the other hand, she wrote copiously about the Soviet Union's relations with China. According to her, Moscow was "China's greatest friend," and without its help China would never have recovered. The proof was that the USSR representative to the Women's Congress was received with tumultuous applause. Like her colleagues, Lubitz criticized Chiang Kai-shek and the "Chinese bourgeois" that had helped destroy the country. She related what she had heard about battles and confrontations between representatives of the Nationalist regime and their Communist enemies before the

---

146 Lubitz, *I Chose to Live the Struggle*, 320–329.

Revolution. In one case, she wrote, factory laborers and pro-Communist farmers had convinced their enemies to unite around the flag of rebellion using appropriate arguments, instead of resorting to violence. Lubitz obviously believed these rumors, as this model of an internal ideological struggle seemed fitting to her and could even serve as a model in other locations around the world to replace bloody battles.

Lubitz also praised agrarian reform in China and echoed her colleagues in stating that this path would improve the standard of living, the status of women, and the fields of education and health. [147]

In October of 1950, ICP representative Shmuel Mikunis traveled to Warsaw to meet with the Chinese ambassador to Poland. Additional meetings were held in Moscow, Eastern Europe, and Beijing between communist activists from Israel and Chinese officials of various levels.[148]

In 1954, Yair Zaban, a leading member of the Israeli left, resigned from the Mapam political party and joined the ICP. Zaban visited China that year, and he wrote about the experience of travelling on the Trans-Siberian Railway, which made a powerful impression on him. He noted that booming speakers played the official railway song "Moscow-Peking" in Russian at the Moscow station, and when the train reached the station at the Manchurian border, the same song was played in Chinese. In an article published twenty-five years later, he quoted the refrain, "The pact of brotherhood will last forever." But in fact, this "pact of brotherhood" did not last. In 1960 a deep chasm opened between China and the Soviet Union, symbolizing the end of innocence and the belief that these two socialist countries would remain eternally united.

While in Beijing, the young Zaban attended a performance of a classic Peking opera. His escort, a young English teacher from the state institute of foreign languages, asserted that China had created a unique combination of cultural values and traditional forms of creative expression, and new values for life and society. The performance that he witnessed was not far from reality. It was based on a chapter from the traditional Chinese drama *Outlaws of the Marsh*.[149] This story presented ordinary Robin Hood-style

---

147 Vagman, "Agricultural Reform in China: Notes from a Visit."

148 Shai, "Israeli Communist Party and PRC," 88.

149 Also known as *Water Margin* and *All Men are Brothers*. One of the four best-known Chinese novels of the Ming dynasty, attributed to Shi Nai'an (1296–1372), but possibly written later by another author. The novel contains Robin-Hood style stories about 108 outlaw heroes who live at the edges of the water.

heroes as outlaws and had previously been prohibited as it was considered subversive. But with the Communist regime's support, the story regained popularity. When the Chinese escort witnessed Zaban chain-smoking, he revealed to the Israeli guest that he had quit smoking after Mao had ordered everyone to stop this dangerous practice. Zaban was moved by the depth of admiration and gratefulness that the Chinese displayed toward their leader. The feelings they expressed seemed untainted by hypocrisy or pretense. According to Zaban, the world had never before witnessed such blind willingness to follow their leader.[150]

Aside from Zaban's visit, additional contact took place between the ICP and CCP in the 1950s. In 1954 young Israeli representatives visited Beijing for a meeting of the Federation of Democratic Youth.[151] An ICP delegation was invited to China by the Chinese Association of Workers' Union to mark the founding of the All-Asian Union Organization. According to *Kol Ha-Am*, the Israeli participants discussed the issue of Israel–China relations with their hosts.[152] But the meeting was not utilized for exchanging messages intended to advance or change the status quo. Members of the two parties adopted a tactic of compartmentalization of information, intended to separate the level of official bilateral relations from the level of collegial relations between the two political parties. Other cases support this characterization, which is typical of this specific issue.

1956 was a relatively fruitful year, rich in encounters for ICP members. In April, the Twentieth Congress of the Soviet Communist Party was held in Moscow, during which Shmuel Mikunis discussed Israel–Chinese relations with his colleagues from the Chinese Communist Party.[153] That same month Ruth Lubitz visited Beijing again, this time for the congress of the International Democratic Women's Federation commemorating the tenth anniversary of its founding. The congress was attended by 183 representatives from forty-eight countries.[154] In September, just before the Suez Crisis broke out, senior ICP officials David (Sasha) Khenin, Fuad Houri, and Meir Vilner met with their Chinese colleagues for the Eighth Congress of the Chinese Communist Party. In his address to the Congress, Vilner defended

---

150 Zaban, "Confucianizing Marx?"
151 Protocol of the meeting of the United Kibbutz Movement secretariat, June 13, 1954. Yad Tabenkin Archives, 2-4/11/3.
152 *Kol Ha-Am*, December 10, 1954.
153 Shai, "Israeli Communist Party and PRC," 89–90.
154 Yad Tabenkin Archives, 15-36/3/1.

the Egyptian stance on the Suez Crisis. In his opinion, steps taken by the Egyptians would eventually serve to weaken imperialism in the region. He praised the achievements of the Chinese government and the CCP's successful implementation of Marxism–Leninism while adapting the ideology to China's unique conditions. He thus implied that what the Chinese termed "Mao's Thought" served as a bridge between Marxist–Leninist theory and the specific conditions prevailing in China.[155] As for strengthening Israel–China relations, Vilner noted the efforts undertaken by ICP members toward this end. At the same time, he admitted that the time was not yet ripe to establish full diplomatic relations between the two countries. This lecture was delivered in the presence of Zhou Enlai and other senior CCP officials, and they applauded the Israeli when he finished speaking.[156] On September 25, Zhou and Vilner met for an extensive conversation during which they discussed relations between the two countries.[157] At this stage, ICP members unconditionally and automatically supported each position of the Chinese government and every process that it initiated. It is no surprise, therefore, that they also justified Beijing's hesitant stance toward the establishment of full diplomatic relations with Israel.

But the discussions that ICP members held with CCP colleagues did not bear any real fruit. To a large extent this was a repeat performance, in an informal setting, of the initial Israeli efforts toward contact with China—efforts that were ultimately unsuccessful.

Other Israeli Visits to China

ICP members were not the only Israelis who visited China. Representatives of other parties also spoke with the Chinese despite the absence of a formal framework for the relationship. Two women joined Ruth Lubitz at the International Women's Conference as representatives of the Organization of Democratic Women in Israel: Yocheved Bat-Rachel of the Labor Federation and Emma Talmi-Levine of the United Workers' Party (Mapam). This visit by the three Israeli women was particularly important considering that it took place one year after the Bandung conference, which as mentioned

---

155 Schurmann, *Ideology and Organization in Communist China.*

156 Interview with Meir Vilner, home of the Chinese ambassador, Savyon, September 28, 1995.

157 Shai, "Israeli Communist Party and PRC," 89–90.

was a foundational but not positive event in the history of Israel–China relations.

In her book *In the Path I Walked*, Bat-Rachel describes her experience during the visit.[158] She details the various political issues that arose in the discussions and recalls the attitude of the conference participants toward Israel, mainly regarding matters that had arisen at Bandung. The conference participants identified with the spirit of the Afro-Asian conference, voicing condemnations of Israel alongside encouragement and support for the position of the Arab states, and this was expressed in the report that was published. The Chinese representative to the congress was the minister of health, whom Bat-Rachel describes as "an intelligent woman . . . who occupies a high position in public and political life." The Chinese minister attempted to suggest a compromise for the text on the universal desire for peace. In this proposal, objections were expressed to the "Baghdad Pact" (Middle East Treaty Organization) and support for the Bandung principles. This pushed the balance of support over to the Arab side. At the same time, the Chinese delegation did not call to adopt all the Bandung decisions and did not include some decisions in the congress report, such as the demand to return refugees from 1948 to territory of the State of Israel. Undoubtedly, from the point of view of China and the Afro-Asian states, the Bandung conference was a central signpost on the road to formulating their foreign policies. Bat-Rachel gained the impression that the Chinese were wooing the representatives of Arab countries and showed almost no interest in the Israeli delegation. The attitude toward Israel was as to a foreign growth that had no place among the Asian nations or the Third World.[159]

Representatives of the Israeli delegation visited the Natural History Museum in Beijing, and Bat-Rachel presented a gift to the museum manager—an album from the Ein Harod Institute of Arts. She tried to initiate contact between institutions, including an exchange of art works. But the Chinese museum manager gently rejected her proposal. As Bat-Rachel wrote: "I understood that he needed the approval of the government's Ministry of Culture in order to have any contact with foreigners."[160]

The May Day celebrations in China made a deep impression on Bat-Rachel and Talmi-Levine. Bat-Rachel wrote vivid descriptions of the sights and sounds and was impressed by the people's loyalty to Chairman

158 Bat-Rachel (Tarshish), *In the Path I Walked*.
159 Ibid., 270–275.
160 Bat-Rachel (Tarshish), "On Chinese Soil, 1956," Yad Tabenkin Archives, 15-36/3/1.

Mao.[161] The two continued on to Shanghai where notwithstanding the colorful and intriguing sights, they were witness to the poverty and shortages then prevalent in China. Bat-Rachel blamed colonialism. In a general meeting of the conference representatives, they met Soong Ching-ling, Sun Yat-sen's widow, and were impressed by her personality and knowledge. At this event Bat-Rachel again felt that the attention of the former first lady was focused on the Arab delegations. The Egyptians were singled out, and the head of their delegation was seated at the same table as the hostess and members of the Soviet delegation.[162]

In the summary of her visit that Bat-Rachel wrote for her party colleagues, she noted the partial success of the Israeli representatives in moderating the draft of the final decisions.[163] This was expressed in the fact that Israel was not mentioned separately in a critical tone. In addition, they initiated the establishment of a committee that intended to discuss Israeli compromise proposals. But the draft of Bat-Rachel's speech at the conference was rejected by the organizers because it emphasized the differences between the State of Israel and Arab states while highlighting Israel's positive points. In addition, Talmi-Levine disagreed with her colleagues.[164] The three Israeli women represented three different streams of political thought then present in their country. Thus tension reigned not only between the Israelis and the Chinese but also among the representatives themselves.

Bracha Habas, David Hacohen's second wife, who wrote under the penname Dvora Bat-Yisrael, was also interested in Israel–Asia relations in general and Israel–China relations in particular. Habas was an influential writer, journalist, and educator. In 1954 and 1955 she sent articles to the Israeli periodicals *Davar* and *Dvar Ha-Shavua* from distant Burma. She was forced to use a penname because government orders forbade the wife of a diplomat from expressing personal opinions on government matters, for fear of contradictions and discrepancies with official policy. Still, as the only woman who accompanied her spouse on the Israeli commercial delegation's visit to China, Habas undoubtedly made a significant contribution

---

161 Bat-Rachel (Tarshish), "Impressions from Peking on May 1st," Yad Tabenkin Archives, 15-36/3/1.

162 Ibid.

163 Yad Tabenkin Archives, 10-11/11/3.

164 Bat-Rachel (Tarshish), "Trip to the Congress of the International Democratic Women's Federation," Yad Tabenkin Archives, 15-36/3/1.

to the program.[165] She also participated as an observer and reporter at Beijing meetings between the Israeli representatives and representatives of the International Democratic Women's Federation, also attending meetings of representatives of the Writers' Association. In her reports, she paints an idealistic picture of Chinese society and the new regime in China. In her opinion, the Chinese nation was "master of its own life and fate." Habas viewed Chinese woman as "free" and as enjoying "equal rights in society." However, she also critiqued the uniform garb that Chinese women were required to wear during that period and the ethos of obligatory respect for Chairman Mao as indicators of enforced uniformity. She expressed doubt as to whether these were proper expressions of full freedom for women or even for the Chinese individual.[166]

Habas' unique position—both on her own and as a diplomat's wife—and her attitude toward China clearly outline the dilemma that the State of Israel faced in the 1950s. On one hand, representatives of leftist parties felt an obligation to endorse the official Israeli public relations stance. But on the other, they upheld their own independent viewpoints that did not fit the official party line. At any rate, these representatives had only a minor influence on the connection between Israel and China.

The Parliamentary Front in Israel

On the parliamentary front, ICP members were treated as almost total outcasts, both by the general public as well as by their colleagues in the Knesset. Still, they did recruit modest support for their position toward the new China. Members of Mapam and a minority in the Mapai governing party supported the Communist stance that protested the indecisiveness of Israel's government toward China and criticized American pressure, partially expressed in the Israeli position on the Korean War.[167] In their opinion American pressure was an expression of condemnable imperialism. ICP members initiated steps to prevent Israel from adopting UN decisions that named China as the aggressor in Korea, thus recommending the adoption of sanctions against China. But on this issue their efforts were in vain.[168]

---

165 Hacohen, *Burma Diary*, 271.
166 Bat-Israel, "With Leaders and Writers."
167 Shai, "Israeli Communist Party and PRC," 86.
168 Ibid.

On July 15, 1954, Mapam Knesset member Avraham Berman called for establishing diplomatic relations between Israel and China. He believed that such a process would improve Israel's international status and grant it economic prospects. However, his proposal was rejected by a majority in the Knesset. ICP and Mapam members who voted for the proposal remained in the minority. Two months later ICP again demanded that the Knesset order the government to establish relations with China, but again the motion failed.[169]

On January 13, 1955, ICP secretary Meir Vilner raised the issue of relations with China in the Knesset once more. He asserted that Israeli government policy was causing severe damage that was likely to leave Israel completely isolated on the Asian continent. In this region, he emphasized, China was considered the hero of the anti-colonialist struggle and a promoter of the independence of the region's nations. Vilner also observed that five years had passed since Israel had recognized China, and almost four months since Zhou Enlai had authorized negotiations on normalization between the two countries,[170] but still no positive results had ensued. He also criticized the position taken by the Israel delegation to the UN in 1954, which paralleled the position of the United States and voted against raising the Chinese issue at the UN. This step, according to Vilner, caused additional delay in the saga of China's attempts to gain and occupy the Chinese seat in the international organization. The ICP position was clear as the light of day: the Chinese regime on the Chinese continent was the only legitimate government of that country and the rightful holder of the UN seat, both in the General Assembly and the Security Council. The ICP considered every attempt to deny the Communist regime its legitimate rights to be an imperialist-inspired conspiracy. To Vilner, Washington's policy toward China was merely a repetition of Hitler's attitude toward the Soviet Union following the outbreak of the Second World War.

In his responses to Vilner's assertions, Foreign Minister Moshe Sharett expressed the Israeli government's hopes that the commercial delegation about to leave for China would lead to a breakthrough in relations between Jerusalem and Beijing. But once again the Knesset rejected the ICP's proposals.[171] Although Israeli government and Foreign Ministry policy in 1954

---

169 *Kol Ha-Am*, July 18, 1954.

170 Zhou Enlai's declaration of September 23, 1954 on the existence of contacts to establish diplomatic relations with Israel, mentioned in the previous chapter.

171 Shai, "Israeli Communist Party and PRC," 86–88.

and 1955 regarding China was not totally opposed to the ICP or Mapam position in the Knesset, in public expressions, especially Knesset discussions, the formal representatives erected a firm barrier against the ICP stance. They aspired to make achievements with regard to China while avoiding undesirable public repercussions that might aggravate Israel–US relations.

At the UN in 1954, members of the National Committee for Peace in Israel, headed by Mapam members (including Meir Ya'ari and Israel Bar-Yehuda) and ICP members (such as Tawfik Toubi) protested Israel's vote on China, which was unusual. On September 24 the committee sent a letter to Moshe Sharett and the Israeli delegation at the UN General Assembly calling for definitive support of People's Republic of China's bid for UN membership.[172] They protested what they called an "unnatural and illegal" situation that prevented a major country like China from representation in the international organization. How was it possible, they asked, that Nationalist China (Taiwan) could represent all the Chinese people on the global stage?

In general, in all the issues that concerned China in the internal sphere as well as the external arena, ICP adopted the international Communist line wholeheartedly. It called for non-intervention in China's internal affairs and considered Taiwan and Tibet to be internal issues. Regarding Taiwan, ICP argued that the agreements of the Cairo Conference of 1943, as well as the Teheran and Potsdam agreements, defined the island as an inseparable part of China. As for Tibet, ICP considered that sending Chinese military forces there in 1950 was not an act of occupation but rather legitimate enforcement of order over a rebellious region by the ruling government. All in all, ICP blamed international imperialism in the style of Great Britain, Japan, and others for carving up China into zones of influence. It considered Tibet to be a victim of this policy, and Beijing was obligated to return this region to the state and establish internal order there as necessary. To the ICP there was no harm in Beijing's attempt to bring the Revolution's message to the far-flung districts, including Tibet, where "parasitic religious priests" were exploiting the people.[173]

The ICP trumpeted China's policy in Asia and *Kol Ha'Am* heaped its praises on the agreements that China signed with India and North Korea,

---

172 Yad Tabenkin Archives, 15-31/26/3.
173 Shai, "Israeli Communist Party and PRC," 88.

especially clauses that addressed the food supply. The ICP noted with satisfaction that the new China was enjoying increasing recognition from international organizations.

As noted above, the Korean War put an end to Israel's non-identification policy, resulting in many years of postponing a China–Israel agreement on the establishment of diplomatic relations. When China actively and openly entered the military conflict in the Korean Peninsula, the leftist opposition in Israel considered that "the American war machine" was merely an instrument designed to exploit the Korean crisis and topple the revolutionary regime in China, thus reversing the social and economic achievements it had brought about. The declarations of President Truman and American generals strengthened the feeling that the anti-revolutionary process in Korea was planned in consultation with leaders of the Republic of China in Taiwan. In essence, the ICP viewed China's involvement in the Korean War as a step parallel to the sending of international anti-fascist forces to Spain during its civil war.[174]

After the war, ICP and other leftist parties attempted to turn back the wheel to a balanced policy between the blocs. Years later Knesset member Meir Vilner stressed in an interview that he had aimed to keep the China issue from disappearing from the Israeli agenda—to "keep it alive."[175] In this regard, the ICP was successful.

After 1956, when all hopes of contact between the two states dissolved, the ICP's activity focused on strengthening ties between itself and the Chinese Communist Party. However, the ICP was unable to achieve this goal. Although relations between the two communist parties were not completely cut off, continuing during the freeze in Israel–China relations, in the end the Great Leap Forward put a stop to these contacts. Like most of the communist parties around the world, the ICP viewed this unprecedented act, which included the Mao personality cult, as a distortion of and deviation from communism. Undoubtedly, it proved to be a painful awakening.

---

174 Ibid., 88–89.
175 Ibid., 87.

Chapter Four

1955 to 1978—No Contact

This chapter will reinforce Yigal Alon's statement in the late 1970s that "the Asian continent is very problematic from an Israeli point of view." I rely here on public documents as well as new primary sources and evidence.[176] Throughout the relatively long period surveyed here, communication between the two countries was practically nonexistent. Finally, in 1978 a breakthrough was achieved that renewed dialogue between the Israeli establishment and its Chinese counterpart.

The period discussed here begins on April 24, 1955, when the Bandung Conference concluded by noting the need to recognize "the rights of the Palestinian people" without mentioning the State of Israel. After this date, relations between Beijing and Jerusalem began to deteriorate and reached their lowest point with China voicing expressions of hostility toward Israel. At the same time, China entered a period of rapprochement with Arab states, particularly Egypt. Under Gamal Abdel Nasser, Egypt formally recognized the People's Republic of China in May 1956, on the eve of the Sinai Campaign (Suez Crisis). During this war the Chinese defined Egypt's battle against France and Great Britain over the Suez Canal as a struggle against imperialist powers, with Israel as their submissive servant.

Several factors contributed to China's intensifying criticism of Israel: the split between China and the Soviet Union in 1960; the continuation of the Cold War in the international arena; and the tightening of relations between Israel and the United States, mainly during the presidency of Lyndon Johnson. For its part, Israel backpedaled its attempts to woo the new China. At that point it was no longer possible to ignore the clear messages sent to Jerusalem by Israel's representatives in the United States, led by Abba Eban. These messages clarified unequivocally that Israel could not

---

176 Interview of Yigal Alon by Reudor Manor, Kibbutz Ginossar, August 26, 1979, on behalf of the Hebrew University Davis Center for International Relations.

make independent diplomatic overtures as if it were a non-identified state, particularly with regard to China.[177]

The Sino–Soviet split that deepened during the 1960s and 1970s intensified Beijing's desire to strengthen its influence in the Afro-Asian sphere in general, and particularly in the Arab world. China placed a high priority on pushing the Soviet Union into a distant corner in the international arena and creating a third bloc that the People's Republic would lead. During these decades, China attempted to strengthen its influence in Asia, Africa, and Latin American countries and continued its harsh criticism of the Israeli government. China did not accept Israel's position that its reprisal operations against its Arab neighbors (carried out in response to frequent attacks against its territory) were intended to prevent illegal infiltration of Palestinians into Israel. In addition, China viewed the establishment of the Palestinian Liberation Organization (PLO) in 1964 as an opportunity to advance its own objectives, and not surprisingly, it became the first non-Arab state to recognize the PLO. During that time China also tried to initiate another Afro-Asian congress to which the Soviet Union would not be invited. Again, as Zhou Enlai emphasized, China was willing to see Palestine as an integral part of the Arab world—an initiative that served to advance China's own interests.

An important signpost in the relationship between China and the Palestinian Liberation Organization was PLO chairman Ahmad al-Shukeiri's visit to China on March 22, 1965. The Israelis realized that this was a momentous occasion, and in response to the visit, Israel's delegation to the UN changed its usual voting pattern. As mentioned above, during that period the delegation usually voted in favor of granting the Chinese seat to the People's Republic, but in 1965 it voted to grant the seat to Taiwan. Delegation members had intended to cast their usual vote, but this time, Mordechai Arbel, a young, determined diplomat who had recently joined the delegation, insisted that the time had come to clarify to the Chinese that their enthusiastic support of the PLO could not continue without a suitable Israeli response. Mordechai Arbel sent his arguments to then Foreign Minister Golda Meir, who supported his approach and announced that this time, Israel would vote for Taiwan. That year the UN vote was decided in favor of Taiwan by a narrow margin. Years afterward, Arbel related in an interview, "The Taiwanese representative stood up, embraced me, and said,

---

177 Shai, "Strange Bedfellows," 149–150.

'You saved us.'[178] We can only guess at the Chinese reaction to the Israeli vote—what is certain is that from a diplomatic standpoint, the two nations continued to move further apart.

Another example that reveals how the Chinese were moving closer to the Palestinians is found in a statement made by Lin Biao, a key leader of the Chinese Communist Party, to the Lebanese newspaper *Al-Nahar*. Formal articles in the Chinese media that were dictated from above repeatedly emphasized that China would help the Palestinians to reconquer their entire homeland. This statement implied that Beijing refused to accept the very existence of the State of Israel and was essentially calling to wipe Israel off the map. The Chinese viewed the PLO and other Palestinian organizations as part of the international liberation movement that was fighting to remove the burden of colonialism and imperialism. The Chinese defined the Palestinian struggle as legitimate and just, similar to the struggle of the Third World nations following the Second World War. Therefore, from 1966 to 1969, China granted extensive assistance to Palestinian organizations, mainly the PLO and Fatah. It established military training bases for them in China (for example, at the Nanjing military academy) and supplied light weapons and medical equipment. Still, this material assistance was limited in part due to logistical problems in transporting supplies to their destination. In fact, China was dependent on the authorizations of Arab states through which the aid had to pass, and these states were under the powerful influence of the Soviet Union. This posed a political problem for China, which at the time was on a headlong collision course with Moscow.

Heads of Palestinian organizations were granted formal receptions in China at various events, such as support rallies for the Palestinian cause and the twentieth anniversary celebration of the People's Republic of China's founding. A PLO representation office was opened in Beijing in 1965. Undoubtedly, China's interest in supporting the Palestinians was not purely ideological as these organizations were mostly nationalist and did not sympathize with the type of communism that China represented. Rather, Beijing also intended to demonstrate that it supported a Third World anti-imperialist revolutionary movement. Paradoxically, the Chinese granted only limited assistance to the Popular Front for the Liberation of Palestine (PFLP), a Marxist organization headed by George

---

178 Telephone interview with Mordechai Arbel, Tel Aviv, June 2013; votes of the Israeli delegation to the UN, Foreign Ministry documents. See also SIGNAL, "The Geography of Sino–Israeli Relations," Tjong-Alvares (online document).

Habash, and the Popular Democratic Front under Naef Hawatmeh. China criticized these two marginal organizations for their Russian Communist slant. Beijing also condemned the Popular Front's tactic of hijacking aircraft, as done at Zarka airport in Jordan in 1970, calling this an "impulsive act."[179]

When the Six Day War broke out in June 1967, mass demonstrations of support for the Arab states were held in Beijing. China still pursued their policy of non-recognition of Israel's right to occupy any part of its territory, even areas inside the pre-1967 borders. Apparently, without getting into the thick of the issue, China expressed praise for "the heroic acts of the Palestinians in the occupied territories—in Tel Aviv, Haifa, Eilat, and Jerusalem." During the Cultural Revolution, such declarations stemmed from lack of knowledge of the reality in the Middle East and not necessarily from an educated, careful decision to completely reject the State of Israel's existence.

China applauded the 1970s crisis between Egypt and the Soviet Union, which reached its climax with the deportation of Soviet advisors from Cairo. The Chinese regime viewed the Arab governments as a revolutionary force that was acting against what they called "American imperialism" and "Soviet hegemony." During the same period, the regime in China tended to bind these two terms together. The attack against Soviet hegemony derived from a complex methodological and ideological problem: from a pure Marxist point of view, a socialist state could not be called "imperialist." This would be an internal contradiction as, theoretically, imperialism derived from the capitalist system. A socialist state that behaved similarly to capitalist-imperialist states was therefore called "hegemonic." This term became more common as the battle against the Soviet Union intensified.

Israel's stance remained as in the past. It was prepared to establish full relations with China and to accept its legitimate right to rule even in the regions under dispute, such as Tibet and Taiwan. The Israeli delegations to the UN usually continued to vote in favor of Beijing's right to serve as China's exclusive representative. But China did not return the favor—it continued to pursue its anti-Israel policy. The Yom Kippur War, which began when the Arabs launched a surprise attack on Israel in 1973, did nothing to change Beijing's policy. China favored the Arab states, which were involved in a dispute over rejection of the ceasefire that had been agreed upon by the

---

179 Ibid.

two major world powers. After the war China supported the oil embargo that several Arab states initiated against the United States and Great Britain in an attempt to convince these powers to roll back their support of Israel. China also favored inviting the PLO to become an observer at the UN and supported Resolution 3379 of the General Assembly, which determined that "Zionism is a form of racism and racial discrimination."[180]

Eventually, three events were to catalyze significant change in the relations between the two countries: the China–Vietnam War of 1979, adoption of the Open Door Policy after Mao's death, and the collapse of the Soviet bloc in 1989. After that point the two countries began confidential military and technological cooperation, with Israeli businessman Shaul Eisenberg acting as go-between. We will explore this story further in the next chapter.

The Israel Communist Party and the Chinese Communist Party: The Great Leap Backward

While relations were at a standstill, one remaining thread connected China and Israel: contact between the oppositionist ICP and the ruling Chinese Communist Party. What was the nature of the relationship between the two political parties? To what extent did they influence the establishment of formal ties between the two states in early 1992? What was the stance of the Israeli Communists toward the Chinese Communist Party and its practical and ideological fluctuations, the Great Leap Forward (1958–61), and the Cultural Revolution (1966–76)?

In 1949, ICP members praised the CCP for seizing power and for declaring the establishment of the People's Republic under Mao's leadership. As mentioned in Chapter Three, the ICP maintained close ties with the CCP until 1960. But after that their relationship suffered an ideological split due to the ICP's uncompromising support for the Soviet Union's orthodox form of communism and its unwillingness to accept the unique, revolutionary, and highly independent policy of the CCP. The ICP viewed the Great Leap Forward as pretentious, unfounded ideologically, and a distortion of pure communism. It also rejected the Cultural Revolution, which resulted from the Mao personality cult.

---

180 In 1991, when UN Resolution 3379 was repealed by the General Assembly (Resolution 4686), China was absent from the vote.

As mentioned, 1956 was a relatively productive year, rich in international meetings of ICP members such as the Twentieth Congress of the Soviet Communist Party. This historical congress marked the beginning of the process of de-Stalinization. During the meeting, Shmuel Mikunis discussed Israel–China relations with his colleagues in the CCP.[181] Here we recall Ruth Lubitz's second visit to China[182] and the conversations held by senior ICP officials David (Sasha) Khenin, Fuad Houri, and Meir Vilner with their Chinese colleagues in Beijing at the Eighth Congress of the CCP (during Vilner's first visit to China).[183]

At the time, Khenin was serving as ICP secretary for the Tel Aviv district. In a personal interview, he described the "ideological" visits to China made before the Suez Crisis[184] and recalled the delegation of Israeli youth that participated in the council of the World Federation of Democratic Youth in 1954. Delegation members included Yair Zaban and George Toubi (Tawfik's brother). From 1956 to 1960, additional visits were made by individuals such as Tawfik Toubi, Samih al-Qasim, and Zvi Bernstein (husband of Esther Vilenska). In 1959 Bernstein made an official visit to China for the tenth anniversary celebration of the Communist Revolution. All the visitors traveled to China through Moscow, and as Yair Zaban noted, this enabled ICP members to meet with senior officials of the Soviet Communist Party. Khenin considered it unimportant that the two senior leaders of his party, Moshe Sneh and Samuel Mikunis, did not visit China. His explanation for this was that the two were concerned with other, more urgent affairs. In 1957 Mikunis met Mao in Moscow at a gathering of communist leaders. Mikunis reported that Mao demonstrated knowledge of the history of Jews in China, but beyond that no progress on the issue of relations between the two states was made during their meeting. Khenin attempted to convince Mao to intervene with Nikita Khrushchev on behalf of Russian Jewry, but it is doubtful that this initiative bore any fruit.[185]

David Khenin visited China again in 1960, this time as a member of the ICP secretariat and central leadership. His visit was planned for an entire month, but he unexpectedly shortened it to two weeks. According

---

181 Shai, "Israeli Communist Party and PRC," 89–90.

182 Yad Tabenkin Archives, 15-36/3/1.

183 Interview with Meir Vilner, home of the Chinese ambassador in Savyon, September 28, 1995.

184 Interview with David (Sasha) Khenin, July 17, 1995.

185 Ibid.

to him, he saw no reason to continue his travels throughout China. Like his colleague Vilner, he was deeply disappointed with the Chinese leadership during that period, particularly from the steps taken as part of the Great Leap Forward. Khenin related that the concept of making one big jump to a utopian regime was wrong, and even worse, it was completely non-socialist. According to Marxist theory, making progress at the correct pace toward the ideal socialist society was very important. For this reason, Vilner and Khenin viewed the "Great Leap Forward" as a serious move backward. Eventually, these two harshly criticized the Cultural Revolution and rejected it outright. In addition, during their visits they could not ignore the barbs of criticism that official China flung at Israel.

Just before Khenin's trip to China, Mikunis returned from the congress of communist parties in Romania, where he openly and outspokenly attacked Mao's position. During that period, the ICP clearly had adopted the Soviet approach. The ICP objected to China's steps, viewing them as an ideological distortion of the communist legacy that should be rejected. Not long afterward, relations between the two parties cooled for an extended period.

In 1965 a split divided the ICP. The rebels, those who would eventually inherit the ICP label, tried to present their opponents, known as the New Communist List, as pro-Chinese. But this charge was ridiculous, and *Pravda* newspaper even corrected it in a later report.[186] Yair Zaban, a member of the camp that opposed the views of Khenin, Vilner, and Toubi, eventually admitted that the attempt to connect the split to the debate over the pro-Soviet and pro-Chinese stance was "completely blown out of proportion" by the ICP. In fact, this was a tactic designed by the ICP to taint the New Communist List (NCL). The goal of the two political streams that came out of the mother Israel Communist Party was to earn Moscow's approval.[187]

In fact, neither of the two Israeli communist parties supported the Chinese party line. In the mid-1960s, most Israelis considered a connection with China to be extremely problematic ideologically, even within communist circles. Years later during the Cultural Revolution, both the ICP and the NCL refused to support the ideological line followed by China. The Israeli

---

186 *Pravda* ("Truth" in Russian) was a well-known Soviet newspaper that expressed the views of the Communist Party in the USSR. Interview with David (Sasha) Khenin, July 17, 1995.

187 Interview with Yair Zaban, Tel Aviv University, July 7, 2011.

parties even objected outright to the Mao personality cult and to China's many other ideological departures from orthodox communism.

ICP policy toward its sister party in China did not remain one-sided. From that point on, the Chinese refused to host Israeli representatives even if they were representatives of the communist parties. In 1962, at the conference of the World Federation of Democratic Youth in Warsaw, Zaban reported that the Chinese representative abstained from a political debate that broke out between the Arab delegations and the united ICP delegation refusing to participate.

From the 1950s through the 1970s, the ICP newspaper *Kol Ha-Am* served as an unusual cultural platform for the works of Chinese writers and poets. This journal was undoubtedly one of the few channels through which these rare works could be read and studied in Israel. In addition, ICP contacted the Chinese Academy of Sciences and organized meetings in Israel, China, and Eastern Europe of communist youth and athletes from Israel and China.[188] Still, the semi-formal visits and discussions held during these meetings did not lead to any concrete results. Thus we may say that the connection between the communist parties in both countries did not serve as a bridge or alternate path to overcome the disconnect between Jerusalem and Beijing. The decade of the Cultural Revolution (1966–76) and the two years after Mao's death, through 1978, did not lead to the anticipated contact between the two states. In that period, no dialogue developed between China and broad areas of the world outside the Soviet bloc.

According to Khenin, Israel had no interest in a relationship with China. Like his colleague Vilner, Khenin was unable to identify any noteworthy influence that their activity had on the ties between the two states. The success of the Israeli Communists, as Vilner defined it, was very modest, and at best permitted them to raise the issue of China in the Knesset on occasion.[189] Beginning in 1955, the ICP significantly reduced its formal parliamentary activity on the issue of China and focused only on maintaining ties with the Chinese Communist Party.

View from Afar: "Going Behind the Wall"

Examination of documents from the Israel Foreign Ministry reveals that the Israelis were closely following events in China. Emmanuel Gelber, the

---

188 Shai, "Israeli Communist Party and PRC," 90.
189 Ibid., 87.

Israeli consul in Hong Kong from 1973 to 1975, served as one channel for sending information to the Jerusalem office. The attempt to develop energy sources in China was an important topic, as these had remained "a mystery to the West for many years." Israel also maintained close watch on China's relationship with Russia and the influence of the Sino–Russian relations crisis on the situation in China. Gelber compiled and submitted reports packed with details, always adding the caveat that much of the data was based on estimates and not on proven numbers.

On the energy issue, the popular assumption in October 1974, for example, was that "China was on its way to becoming an oil power." In this context, Gelber examined gasoline imports to China from Middle Eastern countries. He also studied negotiations on the import of technology and equipment from the United States, Singapore, Japan, Norway, and Denmark. Gelber demonstrated competence in the Chinese way of doing business. He considered that even if deals were signed, the Chinese would not agree to integrate foreign companies as partners in the development of energy sources. He anticipated that the Chinese would permit Israel to purchase knowledge only, while preserving Chinese exclusivity in supervision and management of the oil fields. He also sent back to Israel summaries of lectures and memos written by his acquaintances, including historians, diplomats, Sinophiles, and anyone who he thought could supply information that would help decipher the Chinese riddle, then and in the future. He himself also wrote comprehensive reports on various individuals. As for Mao's leadership, as early as October 1974 Gelber noted that preparations should be made for his departure from the arena, even anticipating developments that would take place in the post-Mao era.[190]

Gelber continued to follow the discussions in China, such as the debate over the possible choices for Mao's successor (two years before his death) and the speculation that surrounded this issue—names that were mentioned included Zhou Enlai and Madame Mao. The consul noted that this problem and other issues within the Party had yet to be resolved. The Party reached a certain *modus vivendi*, which was not meant to be determined conclusively until after Mao's death. In November 1974, after Foreign Minister Ji Penfei was replaced, Gelber sent a report on the new minister, Qiao Guanhua, to the Asia and Oceania Department of the Israel Foreign Ministry. In his report he emphasized Qiao's relatively moderate positions

---

190 From the collected correspondence of Emmanuel Gelber, personal copy: "Sources of Energy in the PRC," Israel Foreign Ministry, October 16, 1974.

toward the West, expressing hope for some change.[191] The previous January, he had reported personnel changes in the Chinese military. This, he said, was announced "in the typical Chinese manner—with an incidental mention of meetings between military leaders and the public. This is how the government publicized these changes in the leadership of the Chinese military, the broadest ever since the ousting of commanders after the failure of the Lin Biao uprising in 1971." He analyzed the replacements and ascribed them to the central leadership's attempt to remove discreetly the local commanders whom it considered to have acquired too much power.[192]

Gelber demonstrated deep understanding of the processes that were taking place throughout China. He related thoroughly to Beijing's relations with Taiwan and Hong Kong[193] as well as to cultural issues (as evidenced in a commentary he wrote on anti-Confucius propaganda in 1973).[194] He even wrote about China's policy toward Israel and the Jews. Immediately following the Yom Kippur War, which was covered widely in the Chinese media, he sent a detailed report to Jerusalem on its consequences for the relationship between the two states.

In general Gelber concluded that Israel was not a significant factor for China, and only slight attention was paid to it. As there were almost no Jewish communities in China, and China had no historic debt to the Jewish people or to the State of Israel, relations with Israel in the 1970s were insignificant. The entire Middle East, despite its oil reserves, did not occupy a prominent position in China's global strategy of that period. Beijing's main motivations in the Middle East were the desire to be the leader of the Third World and to garner the support of the Muslims in Southeast Asia. The rift with the Soviet Union had continued for over fifteen years and was also part of China's global strategy. China was surprised by the Arab states' dependence on Russia, as revealed in the war in the Middle East. This fact clarified to China that it still had a long way to go to achieve the position of leader of the Third World.[195]

Gelber thought that China's interest in the continued existence of the State of Israel derived, ironically, from the fact that Israel was an important

---

191 Gelber, "Replacement of the Foreign Minister in China."
192 Gelber, "Replacement of Personnel in the Chinese Military."
193 Gelber, "China and Hong Kong."
194 Gelber, "Anti-Confucius Campaign."
195 Goodstadt, "The Middle East Backlash," *Far Eastern Economic Review*, vol. 82 (November 12, 1973). Gelber relied on Goodstadt's article on this issue.

obstacle to Soviet domination of the Middle East. Still, he argued that Israel could not expect a drastic change in Beijing's negative attitude toward Jerusalem, as China intended to make full use of its connections with the Arab states.[196] China's formal position blamed Israel for starting the war, asserting that its motivation was largely a desire to conquer additional territories. The Chinese placed heavy emphasis on the success of the Arab armies and terror organizations in the early stages the war. They noted that the Soviet Union had "aided the Israeli war effort" by permitting Russian Jews to emigrate to Israel, thus granting a much-needed infusion of human resources to the Jewish state. After the ceasefire, the Chinese media dropped its interest in the Middle East.[197]

At Gelber's request, information was also gathered by American Jews supportive of Israel who visited China. They took notes on popular opinions about Israel, Jews, and the Zionist project. These unofficial impressions clarified that the Chinese viewed Zionism as a branch of imperialism, which is how it was described by the Chinese media. These opinions were mainly "stereotypical and dictated." The media repeated the theory of Israel as an aggressive occupation state "in the same category as racist Portugal and South Africa." Undoubtedly, in that period only a limited number of Chinese had any knowledge of the history of the Jewish people and their suffering. Gelber's overall attitude was that Israel should continue to try, even in unconventional ways, to influence China and strengthen ties with it. For example, he proposed "reaching out to the Chinese" through Americans who had friendly ties with China and who were also friends of Israel, or through ordinary citizens of China who might be impartial. Throughout his career, Gelber hoped that someday Israel would succeed in "going behind the wall, if only to avoid discouraging Jewish friends who visit there from trying to act in our interest."[198]

The discussion over Asia's importance to Israel also arose in an interview with Yigal Alon,[199] who emphasized that this continent had been "perhaps the least important in Israeli foreign policy throughout the entire existence of the State of Israel, for well-known reasons." He criticized this attitude and also the decision to end the activity of the Israeli embassies in

---

196 Gelber, "China and the War in the Middle East," November 27, 1973.
197 Ibid., "The Yom Kippur War in the Media of the PRC," Israel Foreign Ministry, November 26, 1973.
198 Ibid., "Israel's Image in Communist China," Israel Foreign Ministry, October 3, 1974.
199 Interview by Reudor Manor with Yigal Alon, Kibbutz Ginossar, August 26, 1979.

South Vietnam, Laos, and Cambodia. On the other side, Alon noted the foot-dragging and hesitation of Japan, South Korea, and the Philippines regarding ties with Israel. Although he did not mention China directly, Alon recalled the major oil fields discovered there and expressed hope that if China became Japan's major supplier of oil, China would no longer fear the Arab states' reaction should it establish open diplomatic and commercial relations with Israel. He thought that if the road to Asia were opened, this would make up for the diplomatic losses that Israel incurred in other Communist countries that broke ties with it because of the 1973 war. For example, he recalled the "special relationship" between Israel and Taiwan. Taiwan hoped that Israel would stand by its side in its struggle against the People's Republic of China in the international arena, despite Israel's 1950 recognition of the government in Beijing.

In 1974, after Alon was appointed as foreign minister, he delivered a speech in the Knesset in which he mentioned China for the first time in public, stating that Israel was interested in establishing joint relations. He expected China to change its stance toward Israel. In a lecture at the Shiloah Institute at Tel Aviv University that year, Alon went further and said that renewing ties with the Soviet Union could be destructive to the State of Israel in relation to future ties with China. In 1975, he raised the issue of China about seven times at numerous opportunities and hinted that both states harbored a basic desire to improve relations covertly. Still, Alon's assumed that ties with Moscow were preferable to ties with Beijing. The questions that arose were as follows: Can the enemy of my enemy be my friend? Would China and Israel begin a rapprochement, considering that both were in conflict with the Soviet Union? Because China had no anti-Semitic, Christian tradition as in Europe, Alon was encouraged to think there might be a significant opportunity in the long-term to promote Israel–China relations.

Alon recalled his meetings with David Hacohen and emphasized that he had agreed with Hacohen with regard to Israel–China ties. We may assume that on the issue of the "missed opportunity" with China (surveyed in Chapter One), he would agree with Hacohen's position as well. To advance ties with China, Alon enlisted the assistance of individuals that he recruited, including Henry Kissinger, Senator Hubert Humphrey, and other senior American officials who were in close contact with Chinese representations in the United States. Romanian head of state Nicolae Ceaușescu and George Macovescu, Romania's foreign minister, had excellent ties with China on ideological grounds, and Alon asked them to help as well. He reported that he also contacted the widow of Edgar Snow, journalist and China expert, who was pro-Israeli; an American businessman who promised to arrange a meeting for him in China; and representatives of the socialist left in Great Britain, who also promised to help. He mentioned Shimon Peres' attempt to use his contacts with German politician Franz Josef Strauss to put out feelers to the Chinese on the Israel issue during Strauss' visit there. According to Alon, Kissinger asked him to be patient, as a breakthrough in China–Israel relations could not take place solely on the basis of the establishment of diplomatic relations between Washington and Beijing. Rather, Israel had to wait for full normalization of relations between the United States and China.

Ostensibly positive signs appeared here and there. For example, in a speech at the Chinese military academy, the Chinese defense minister praised Israel as a militarily strong country. Finally in the late 1970s, informal, confidential contact began between Israel and China with the intervention and assistance of Jewish businessman Shaul Eisenberg. Eventually Eisenberg initiated contact between Israel's military industry and the Chinese military establishment. This development took place against the backdrop of the China–Vietnam war and the failures of the Chinese military during its preliminary stages.

The period surveyed here was thus characterized by an almost total lack of contact between China and Israel. Any contact that did take place was coincidental and led to no breakthroughs in relations between the two states. The communist parties in both countries were also unsuccessful in acting as occasional bridges between them. The dialogue between representatives of the two parties, despite occurring in a wide variety of forums at numerous opportunities, produced no positive results—apparently, ideological affinity was not enough. Ironically, contact between the United States and China, opposing ideological regimes from both sides of the political map in the international arena, was initiated during the period of President Richard Nixon, a manifestly right-wing leader. It was Nixon who became the one to pave the road to China while admirers of China and its ideology on the liberal American left were left behind.

Chapter Five

Clandestine Contact—Shaul Eisenberg in China

Shaul Nehemiah Eisenberg was a mysterious and powerful individual. This became readily evident at the large meetings and receptions that he attended and in the way that interviewees spoke of him after his death. Even those who knew him only superficially or who had heard of him second- or third-hand became his admirers.

Eisenberg was born in Munich in 1921, the fifth of six children of Sophie and David Eisenberg.[200] His mother was from Krakow and his father from Warsaw, but both had immigrated to Germany in their youth, so the language they spoke at home was German. Three of Shaul's siblings were also born in Munich. One of the brothers, Raphael, was ordained as a rabbi. Shaul was also given a religious education and was exposed to a traditional atmosphere at home.

After Kristallnacht in late 1938, when Shaul was seventeen, the family was deported to the no-man's land on the Poland–Germany border.[201] He fled to Switzerland where he worked for ten days pushing an apple cart. On the eleventh day he was detained, as he lacked the proper formal documentation. He would later relate that he made the first deal in his life in this quiet, mountainous country. First he located other individuals who needed documents. Then he went to the consul of Paraguay, who issued papers for the clients. The two split the payment of one hundred francs per customer.[202] Eventually, Shaul used the money he had saved to help his parents emigrate to Shanghai. As for himself, after his Swiss residence papers expired, he crossed the border on foot into France. Then he went to

---

200 "The Business Empire of a Global Mystery Man," *Business Week* (November 16, 1981).
201 Levin, "The Man Who Buys and Sells Everything."
202 Ibid.

Luxembourg and from there to Belgium and Holland.[203] Throughout his life he would criticize the leaders of the Jewish community in Switzerland for their failure to offer any shelter and assistance to him or to other refugees. While in Antwerp he worked in a vegetable store, where he earned sixty Belgian francs per week, a paltry sum that forced him to steal food for survival.[204]

In Holland, Eisenberg was caught by the border police, as once again he lacked the proper documents. The authorities took him in for investigation and sent him to a refugee camp, where he was detained for six weeks. Then, in May 1940, he was given permission to sail outside the country. He boarded a British cargo ship and, after a stay in Singapore, he finally reached the cosmopolitan city of Shanghai, where his parents and one of his siblings were living.[205] His ticket was paid for by a non-Jewish family he had met who happened to own the shipping company.[206] While at sea Eisenberg began to do as he had on land—make business deals. This time he worked with a British national who operated the ship store. Eisenberg sold whiskey and cigarettes to the ship's Chinese passengers, and the two shared the profit.[207] In distant Shanghai he quickly realized that finding a job was not at all simple. He refused to depend on the Jewish community's charity organizations. He thus went to Manchuria (Manchukuo), the puppet state that the Japanese had created and controlled, and from there he sailed to the Land of the Rising Sun—Japan.

Global Business

Eisenberg made his way to Tokyo, where there was a Jewish community. There he met the Yamada family and went to live in their home. He began his career in the business world by buying scrap metal (such as tanks and armored personnel carriers) and selling it to the Japanese government. Japan was then involved in military operations in China and preparing for attacks on Southeast Asia, and it needed large quantities of steel.[208]

---

203 Ibid.
204 Ben-Porat, "I Nicked Vegetables So I'd Have Something to Eat," first article in the series "Conversations with Eisenberg."
205 "The Man in the Middle," *Ha'Aretz* supplement, November 20, 1981.
206 Ben-Porat, "I Nicked Vegetables So I'd Have Something to Eat."
207 Lipkin, "He Began with Fifty Dollars and Ended with Over a Billion."
208 Levin, "The Man Who Bought and Sold Everything."

One year later, Japan entered the Second World War, and Eisenberg married Lea Nobuko-Freudelsperger, daughter of a Japanese-Austrian family. Her father, Herman Freudelsperger, was a graduate of the Vienna Academy of Art. He fell in love with Japan, settled there, and painted portraits of members of the Japanese aristocracy and banking families. He established a network of contacts in commercial and financial circles and it was apparently through these contacts that Shaul developed his own personal contacts. As a foreign citizen of one of Japan's allies, he was able to carry out unique transactions, and his business began to prosper. For example, he purchased iron ore from Australia and the Philippines and sold it to local manufacturers who were trying to rebuild their factories. He expanded his purchases of iron ore to the United States, India, and Chile and became the main steel supplier for the giant Japanese manufacturer Yawata. Eventually he occupied such a prominent position in Japan's steel industry that after the war, the Japanese included him in the first industry delegation to the United States.[209]

The Japanese respected Eisenberg as a foreigner who had chosen to live in their country. As his wife was half-Japanese, the natives felt they could trust him in business as an agent and go-between. In the difficult post-war period following Japan's surrender and the dismantling of the giant Japanese corporations, one way he could assist them was to register property temporarily under his name. When the limitations were lifted, he assured his clients, he would return the property to its owner. After the restrictions finally ended and the Japanese could again reconstruct their giant corporations, Eisenberg returned ownership honestly and without hesitation. In exchange he gained the goodwill and trust of his business partners. This was an important asset that bore fruit in the future.[210] In the 1950s, he constructed the Jewish Community Center in Japan, which became a meeting point that united the local Jewish community.

After the establishment of diplomatic relations between Israel and Japan in 1952, Eisenberg donated a building for the use of the Israeli ambassador.[211] In addition, he served as an agent for creating the first commercial ties between the two countries. He was instrumental in making the connection for constructing a bulk carrier between Zim, Israel's shipping

---

209 "The Man in the Middle," *Ha'Aretz* supplement, November 20, 1981.
210 Interview with Gabriel Gidor, 2004.
211 Eitan, "Eisenberg: Money Breeds Money."

company, and a Japanese shipyard. When the Israeli national soccer team visited Tokyo in the mid-1950s, Eisenberg hosted them at his expense, providing them with housing, transportation, and support staff.

Business in Korea

After the Korean War ended in 1953, Eisenberg began to do business in South Korea. Although the country was half-destroyed, he believed that it held enormous potential for the future. He found its citizens more open than the Japanese and quicker to learn business methods. His goal was to open Korea to the wider world by acting as a business agent. Eisenberg became the key for companies like Siemens and General Electric that wanted to enter the Korean market. He served as the agent for establishing power plants, steel factories, railroads, and ports in South Korea.[212] He also worked on Israel's behalf: he petitioned Great Britain, Austria, and West Germany[213] to obtain the initial credit needed to pay a South Korean shipyard for the construction of three Israeli ships.[214]

One of Eisenberg's strategies for increasing profits in Korea and other developing markets was to add special clauses to the contracts he brokered, specifying conditions for the purchase of spare parts for the products supplied. In these clauses, the client committed to purchasing spare parts exclusively from the supplier for extensive periods of up to forty years— even though everyone realized that the original parts would only last for a few years. Eisenberg amassed enormous profits in this manner. Gabriel Gidor, then chief executive of Israel Aircraft Industries (IAI), explained that in the power plant sales contracts signed through Eisenberg in Korea, Eisenberg was sometimes willing to compromise on the amount of his commission when he stood to earn many times more on the spare parts. Thus Eisenberg's profits largely depended on long-term planning and his willingness to wait, as eventually he would realize the profitable clause in the contracts.[215]

In the early 1970s, while Eisenberg was enjoying weighty influence in South Korean governmental circles, South Korean President General Park Chung Hee decided to manufacture an atom bomb. In 1972 Korea began

212 Interview with Gabriel Gidor, 2004.
213 "The Man in the Middle," *Ha'Aretz* supplement, November 20, 1981.
214 Eitan, "Eisenberg: Money Breeds Money."
215 Eitan, "Eisenberg: Money Breeds Money."

secret discussions with France to purchase a plutonium reprocessing plant. Despite Washington's objection to the deal, Korea and France signed a contract in early 1975. In an interview with the *Washington Post*, the South Korean president clarified that if the Americans dared to place obstacles in its path, South Korea would develop nuclear weapons on its own.

Next the Canadians became involved, as they were an important supplier of nuclear components. They realized that often, client countries like India that declared their purposes to be civilian were in fact using Canadian nuclear products for military use. Thus Canada decided that when selling their nuclear components, they would demand assurances that the final product would be used for civilian purposes. Further, Canada decided that Canadian companies would have to obtain advance permission from their government before beginning the process of enriching high-level uranium, reprocessing, or reusing nuclear materials. In 1976 Canada signed joint agreements on this issue with Argentina and South Korea.

Eisenberg entered the picture when he attempted to broker the sale of a reactor manufactured by the Canadian company Candu to Korea. When it was learned that Korea attempted to purchase a plutonium reprocessing plant from France, which could be interpreted as an intention to use the reactor to produce a nuclear weapon, Canada informed Seoul that under these circumstances, it could not agree to the processing of nuclear materials. This amounted to cancellation of the deal. Following American pressure, Korea seemed to abandon its activities in this direction, as Taiwan had previously. However, rumors persisted about the continuation of the Korean initiative. The Canadian state comptroller's report of 1976 revealed that in addition to losses of some one hundred million dollars, the company Atomic Energy of Canada Ltd. (AECL) had committed financial miscalculations related to deals made with Korea and Argentina. These included enormous payments using unauthorized bills.

According to unauthorized reports, eighteen million dollars was transferred to Eisenberg in the Korean deal through unexplained channels. The Canadian parliament began a formal investigation on suspicion of bribery and corruption. However, it was stymied by lack of cooperation from senior directors of AECL, who refused to produce financial records and answer questions. Canadian Prime Minister Pierre Trudeau defended the basic decision to supply nuclear technology to countries such as Korea and Argentina. He stated that Canada had a moral imperative to share its knowledge in this field with Third World nations, and that Canada must accept their clients' commitments to use that knowledge only for their declared intentions. Canada's minister of energy, Donald McDonald, followed suit in defending the decision.

However, in December 1976, in an effort to avoid criticism at home and abroad, Canada adopted even tougher demands on this sensitive issue based on the nuclear non-proliferation treaty. From then on, Canada would cooperate in the nuclear field only with countries that had signed the non-proliferation agreement. Korea had signed this agreement and accepted the Canadian requirements, which paralleled the supervision and control requirements set by the International Atomic Energy Association (IAEA). Thus the road was paved for the sale of Canadian nuclear products to Seoul.

In the meantime the Canadians conducted a thorough investigation on the issue, including the suspicion of bribery in the Korean deal. Although Eisenberg's company was cleared, its mention in this affair proved damaging to its image. Competitors both inside and outside Korea took every opportunity to harm Eisenberg's company, and it lost deals to others. Thus on the one hand Eisenberg had earned the highest Korean medal, but on the other hand he was hurt and felt that his basic rights had been undermined.[216]

Following this affair, Eisenberg's dealings in Korea were significantly reduced, and he began to focus on business in the Philippines, Latin America, and then China.

On the Road to Israel

From the mid-1950s onward, Eisenberg's business activities reached global proportions. They included exports of military equipment (mainly boats, airplanes, and ammunition to various countries), of Israeli electronic components, and extensive connections with Israeli companies Tadiran and Elta. In addition, he was involved in the attempt at "making the desert bloom" in Egypt in cooperation with Tahal, the Israeli water planning company. He also bought and sold cement factories, flour mills, seed oil factories, a factory for processing sunflower seeds in North Dakota, and factories for producing alcohol from sugar in the Philippines and Hawaii. Eisenberg also dealt in oil, invested in films, financed a project for developing solar energy, and purchased 11 percent of the stocks in the American

---

216 Ibid.

textile giant United Merchants. In the early 1990s he was even involved in setting up an experimental farm in Uzbekistan to improve cotton crops and save water.

In the 1960s Eisenberg founded United Development Company in Panama. He also brokered numerous deals for selling merchandise and constructing infrastructure and factories. These included mines in Chile and India; coffee processing factories in Thailand and Taiwan; a canned goods factory in Vietnam; a paper factory in Iran; water purification systems in the Virgin Islands; steel factories, telephone networks, railroads, cement factories, textile factories, and chemical factories in South Korea; an agricultural-industrial concern of over sixteen million acres in Brazil; irrigation systems in Peru; and an iron factory in India in a joint business deal with Romania and West Germany. He also acted as an agent on behalf of a conglomerate of companies from five countries, led by France and Belgium, in a competition for construction of a high-speed train in South Korea.

Eisenberg also continued to broker international deals in many fields, including telephone networks, railroads, textile and chemical factories, irrigation systems, paper manufacturing, canned goods, and solar energy. In addition to activity in Asian countries (India, Thailand, Taiwan, and the Philippines), his companies also began to work in the Americas. His business knew no boundaries. He stretched his arms out to Brazil and the Caribbean islands at the same time as he broadened his dealings in Central Asia. In Uzbekistan, for example, his companies expanded in agricultural fields (experimental farming, improving cotton yields, and economical irrigation).

In the 1960s Eisenberg worked to move his business headquarters to Israel, where he planned to make his home. During that period, Sir Isaac Wolfson and Sir Charles Clore asked Israeli Minister of Finance Pinchas Sapir for a tax exemption that would permit them to manage their international businesses from Israel. They explained that passing such a regulation would help Israel become a center for broad international activity. They also mentioned Eisenberg's companies in this context. Eventually, the Knesset did pass a law that permitted international business operations in the proposed tax-free framework. In the end Wolfson and Clore did not move their businesses to Israel, but Eisenberg took advantage of the opportunity at hand to expand his activity there. The law became known as "the

Eisenberg law," and Eisenberg began to navigate the complex web of his global businesses from his new headquarters in Tel Aviv.

In 1968 Eisenberg founded the Israel Corporation in partnership with the Israeli government and under the direction of Pinchas Sapir. While putting down stakes in Israel, he continued some of the business activities that he had begun earlier, such as purchasing the Israeli investment company Piryon, which had originally owned a single bakery. In addition, he founded Nesua Real Estate Company, which purchased plots for development, including Villa Melchett Villa on the Sea of Galilee. The company bought forty acres of fields from Beit Berel and an impressive plot on which he built the family home. Other Eisenberg projects worth mention from that period are the construction of Asia House and Africa House in Israel; founding a company for exporting Israeli factories such as Elite and Etz Hazayit; cooperation with Elite to build an instant coffee factory in Romania; export of textile products from Israeli companies Ata and Lodzia; founding a palm oil factory in Eilat together with Etz Hazayit for export of factory equipment; similar factories in East Asia and South America; founding Atesco, a company for refurbishing jet airplanes; and purchase of the First International Bank of Israel. In addition, Eisenberg invested in Israeli companies such as Ata, Lodzia, Delta, and Rapac Electronics, as well as shipping companies, supply and cooling, and citrus groves. He purchased companies such as the Israel shipping bank and bought stocks in the Paz fuel company.[217] In parallel he expanded his dealings in products of Israel Military Industries, as well as Israeli industrial manufacturers of advanced electronics, cement, water, flour mills, and a variety of other products.

In the mid-1970s, after the long, draining war between the United States and Vietnam, Eisenberg began activities to help rehabilitate Vietnam. In this he took advantage of his close ties with the Vietnamese minister of international trade.

---

217 Six companies were registered in Eisenberg's name, four of these in Israel: Eisenberg Export Company, Eisenberg Company for Export of Industrial Factories, Bar-Gad, Asia House. The two that were registered outside Israel were Atesco (Aircraft Trading and Services) and Universal Seed and Oil Products. He also purchased two-thirds of Intergamma Company, the Israeli representative of Kodak; the Israeli agent of Olympus cameras, Amisar company, and a public investment company. Eisenberg also gave ten million dollars toward the construction of a hospital in Jaffa in his mother's name, but construction was halted after the frame was built.

One Billion Chinese Await

After Mao died, Hua Guofeng was pushed aside and Deng Xiaoping's status rose. The momentum of the Cultural Revolution gradually slowed, opening a window of opportunity for Shaul Eisenberg into the enormous Chinese market. Eisenberg's previous successes were based on the rehabilitation of economies, rather than on activity in already developed countries like the ones in Western Europe. Post-Mao China was a natural destination for Eisenberg. He was willing to invest time and energy there, even at the price of cutting back or even halting minor activities elsewhere that might interrupt his entry into the desirable market that awaited him. After four decades, the international entrepreneur returned to work in the very location where he had started his business career—Asia.

Through the good services of the Chinese ambassador in Vienna, Eisenberg made an important breakthrough for his business in China. Yet he insisted that the Chinese government send him a formal invitation and that his connection with Israel be openly known. In 1978 he arrived in Beijing at the invitation of the chairman of a ministry-level organization—the Chinese Council of International Trade. He met with the deputy prime minister and ministers of industry and economy. Against the rising tension between China and Vietnam that developed into a major war, he had to decide between commencing activity in China and continuation of his broad operations in Vietnam. He decided in favor of China. From then on, Eisenberg became a pioneer for Israeli business in the Chinese market. The Eisenberg Group of companies sold Israeli agricultural technology, communications products, and a wide variety of industrial products. The Group also brokered the sale of Israeli potash to Chinese government organizations. The sale was accomplished despite an initial hitch, as the Chinese were used to red potash from China and had to be convinced to purchase the Israeli version, which was white. Finally, Eisenberg succeeded in convincing Sinochem to become the first Chinese company to purchase white potash from the Dead Sea Works.

In the late 1970s Eisenberg moved the headquarters for his China operation from Hong Kong to Beijing, where he rented a small office and slept in one of its rooms. He developed close ties with Jiang Zemin, who was then deputy ministry of electronic industries and responsible for military purchasing (he later became mayor of Shanghai). Eisenberg then began sales of Israeli military equipment to the Chinese. Their existing stock was outdated, and Eisenberg paved the way for sales of improved, modern military components and ammunition to the Chinese—such as tank parts and enhanced artillery originally manufactured in the Soviet Union.

Eisenberg served as the broker for many other deals and deepened his involvement in China. Some of the deals began without his involvement but were frozen until he entered the picture—one example was the glass factory constructed in Shanghai. In one case, he served as agent between the Chinese and British parties who had reached a standstill in their negotiations for this factory.[218] In 1979 the Chinese had contacted the British company Pilkington Brothers and requested a license to manufacture glass under their exclusive British patent. After some delay and even disengagement between the sides, Eisenberg began to act. He brokered and pushed, and the deal went through as a joint initiative of the Eisenberg Group, the People's Bank of China, and the Chinese government. Eisenberg was the main catalyst behind the deal. He invested the commission that he earned in a new, related business in Shanghai: a dock for unloading raw materials for manufacturing the glass, and on the opposite side another dock for loading the finished product.[219]

Eisenberg's business in China continued to grow. At the height of activity, Eisenberg's investment company United Development had over twenty offices in China. The company signed hundreds of import and export contracts and built 250 factories for manufacturing, communications, energy, and agriculture, among other purposes.

Other activities in China included bringing various factories to the Middle Kingdom. Eisenberg also established a corporation of large coal purchasers from various countries to fund mines, railroads, and a port in China. Other companies that benefitted from Eisenberg's brokering skills included Elin, an Austrian company that developed a facility for economical production of electricity from water; a French company that built water treatment factories; another Austrian company that built a factory for synthetic fibers; an Italian company that sold to the Chinese know-how for manufacturing sewing machines and bought raw materials from them; and ECI, a public American company owned by the Israeli Clal concern, which sold to China a machine that doubled the output of communication lines.

---

218 "The Man in the Middle," *Ha'Aretz* supplement, November 20, 1981.
219 Levitsky, "Shaul, King of China."

Eisenberg's Influence on China–Israel Relations

The unprecedented infrastructure that Eisenberg created in China, together with his connections in the highest echelons, paved the way for Israel's military industries to enter China in the late 1970s. During the initial battles of the Sino–Vietnamese war, the Chinese army suffered harsh blows that damaged its morale. Beijing, as Jonathan Goldstein pointed out, "sought overseas sources for advanced weaponry. Israel was a state-of-the art arms manufacturer and a logical supplier of precisely the type of combat-tested weaponry China needed."[220] Eisenberg's diverse services in the military realm were now required. And indeed, he arranged for the Chinese to upgrade China's outdated military equipment by purchasing Israeli products.

At that time, Israel and China did not have official relations. In late February 1979 members of the first delegation sponsored by the Israeli Ministry of Defense arrived in China. The delegation numbered some thirty individuals, who had to travel under false identities. The group was led by Gabriel Gidor, CEO of Israel Aircraft Industries, and also included David Kimchi, director of the Mossad's foreign relations department. Gidor reported that to organize this trip, Eisenberg made at least five solo trips to China between May 1978 and February 1979.[221]

The delegation's visit was preceded by a meeting between Eisenberg and then Minister of Defense Ezer Weizman, in which Eisenberg declared that he could open the door to China for the Israeli defense establishment. He was even willing to offer the use of his private jet to do so. Also in preparation for the delegation's visit, Prime Minister Menachem Begin met in May of 1978 with a limited number of senior Israel Aircraft Industries officials at the company's offices in Lod. IAI representatives included CEO Gabriel Gidor and Chairman of the Board Yisrael Sakharov. At the meeting Begin expressed his desire for the company to penetrate the Chinese market.[222] Thus Eisenberg's proposal came at the right time and fell on willing ears. In parallel, Egyptian president Anwar Sadat visited Israel, leading to a vast improvement of Israel's position in the international arena.

---

220 Goldstein, Jonathan. "A Quadrilateral Relationship: Israel, China, Taiwan and the United States since 1992," *American Journal of Chinese Studies,* October 2005 and Barzilai, "Weizmann Initiated Eisenberg's Involvement in the Arms Deal with China Twenty Years Ago."

221 Interview with Gabriel Gidor, 2004.

222 Barzilai, "Here's How to Break Down a Wall."

Establishing security ties with China could transform this rising power into a client of the Israeli defense industries. Contact with China could also replace Israel's connection with Iran, which waned and disappeared following the dramatic change that took place in Tehran. Further, in that period the Americans were very suspicious of China. They feared its rising power and refused to transfer any technologies that might become a long-term strategic threat. In the situation that developed, Israel became one of the first Western countries that was willing and able to help China, to upgrade its weapons systems, and provide service in its time of need.[223]

Eisenberg had already begun working with IAI in the early 1970s. In fact, he had become the IAI's weapons dealer in Asia. But when Israel made the breakthrough for the sale of military supplies to China, Israeli government leaders raised the issue of his involvement in this contact. Was it appropriate that here as well, he would serve as the major go-between? Was there room to accept his demands for exclusivity and payment of enormous commissions of 7, 10, and even 20 percent of the sales?

Prime Minister Begin and Foreign Minister Moshe Dayan first tried to involve other powerful and wealthy individuals in the nascent deals, such as Nissim Gaon, Azriel Einav, and Yekutiel Federman. But Defense Minister Weizman insisted that Eisenberg was the one and only person for the job, and that he was the one who had the best chances for success. "Who else could create such important ties for Israel?" he asked. In the end Weizman won the debate, and Eisenberg was given the job of brokering Israel's entry into China on military matters.[224]

Following cancellation of China's aid contract with the Soviets, separation from its "ideological mother," and continued isolation from the West, China found itself at a military disadvantage for equipment and technology. It wanted to purchase know-how and technology that would improve its position. The military conflict with Vietnam in the south and tension with the Soviets in the north intensified the feeling of urgency in China on this issue. In addition, following the Yom Kippur War, Israel possessed valuable knowledge for China regarding advanced Soviet weapons and defense systems.

These general conditions created a sense in Israel that it had much to offer to the Chinese in the form of upgrading Soviet technology, new

---

223 Interview with Amos Yudan, July 21, 2004. See also Shichor, "Israel's Military," 68–91.
224 The code name for the secret initiative was "Olympia." See, Barzilai, "Here's How to Break Down a Wall."

know-how in fire control and night vision, and the hybrid vehicle field. The technological abilities and the creative gifts of Israeli inventors led to the expansion of Israel's own skills as well as the potential for exporting the products of this talent—first and foremost, in the field of defense. Still, Israel lacked the required scope of manufacturing necessary to compete with the major, experienced powers. At any rate, the breakthrough was made. The Israeli military industry succeeded in its mission, and the Chinese were even willing to compensate the Israelis well for their services.[225]

Members of the military delegation took Eisenberg up on his offer and flew to China in his private jet. Gidor related that they were prohibited from revealing their Israeli identity. Back in Israel only a few individuals knew about the trip. The cover story was that the plane was flying to the Philippines. Along the way, it deviated from the usual route and turned toward China. Once in Beijing, the Israelis gave the Chinese a wealth of information on military and technological matters. The Chinese were anxious to dispel their ignorance on the mechanics and ability of Soviet weaponry, and the Israelis were only too happy to assist.

Eisenberg played an active role in the visit. He participated in some of the discussions with the Chinese colleagues and aided from the "war room" set up in a Beijing hotel. He also maintained contact with Israel while delegation members were isolated in the Chinese government's official guest house. Without Eisenberg, Gidor related, nothing ever would have happened. Eisenberg suffered many setbacks, including being forced to accept some of his payment from the Chinese in kind—low-quality Chinese goods for which he had no need. Still he persevered, and his patience paid off when he achieved his goal of profit through generous commissions. He made connections and accumulated a long list of individuals who owed him favors. He exercised his skills at analyzing situations and opportunities, identifying factories that did not have enough work, and ordering merchandise from them at low prices.[226]

In 1979 and in the 1980s, relations continued between the Israeli military establishment and parallel Chinese organizations. Agreements were signed in the fields of knowledge and weapons. As usual, Eisenberg served as go-between while raking in vast profits—at least half a billion dollars, according to some reports. Although contact between the two countries

---

225 Interview with Gabriel Gidor, 2004.
226 Ibid.

was carried out under a strict veil of secrecy, reports occasionally surfaced in the foreign media, but these raised more questions than they answered. For example, in 1984 the British military weekly *Jane's* reported that China and Israel had conducted arms deals valued at $3.5 billion.

Israeli businessman Amos Yudan also described deals between Israel and China and Eisenberg's key role. Yudan went to China in the 1980s to carry out business activity (some of which was military) on behalf of Tadiran company, which was then owned by Koor. Due to the prohibition against formal business dealings between China and Israel, the sales were made through a third party. Yudan confirmed that another reason for this was suspicion regarding Eisenberg. In 1988 Yudan received a proposal from Sergio Itzhak Minerbi, deputy director of the Israeli Foreign Ministry and head of the economic affairs department, to establish a secret company for establishing ties between the two states. Reuven Merhav, who was then serving as Israeli Consul General in Hong Kong, related that he was approached by some "confused" Chinese who asserted that Eisenberg was managing Israel's business. The Chinese believed that everything related to Israel had to go through Eisenberg. They were thus surprised when Israeli military representatives would suddenly appear out of the woodwork, announce that they were responsible for advancing Israel's interests in China, and propose various deals.

Due to this state of affairs, the Israelis decided to set up an office in Hong Kong. On the outside this office would appear completely Chinese, but in fact it would be managed and controlled by the Israeli government. Business would be conducted through this office instead of the consulate. The proposal was authorized by the cabinet: Yitzhak Shamir, who was well-acquainted with the Mossad and had friendly ties with it; Shimon Peres, who was sharing the post of prime minister with Shamir by rotation; and Ariel Sharon, then Minister of Industry, Commerce, and Employment. Under Yudan's direction, Copeco Company was founded. Yudan observed that the company operated successfully and wove ties with senior Chinese officials, including Jiang Zemin himself. However, the company did not operate in the military sector, which was still under Eisenberg's exclusive control. Copeco brokered deals between Israeli and Chinese companies, brought Israeli technology to China (greenhouses, drip irrigation technology), and sent delegations between the countries. Sometimes these were Israeli government delegations that went to China disguised as business missions.

In the early 1990s senior Chinese officials met with Yudan and asserted that "the old man," meaning Eisenberg, was a very good person, but that his commissions were too steep. They proposed avoiding his services and doing business directly. The field they were interested in was aerial refueling of aircraft. Accordingly, Yudan contacted Moshe Keret, then CEO of Israel Aircraft Industries. But a few hours later he received a phone call from Reuven Merhav, who attacked him furiously: "Are you crazy? Don't you know that belongs to Eisenberg? How dare you?" The attempt to sidestep Eisenberg almost cost Yudan his job. As it turns out, Eisenberg had a well-oiled network of contacts who kept him informed, both inside IAI and at the other Israeli entities that were involved in China. Evidently, Eisenberg occupied an unprecedented position and wielded incomparable influence within the highest echelons of Israeli government, as well as having unique contacts in China. Years after his death, many in the Israeli defense industry felt indebted to him for his initiative, not only in creating ties in China but also in the development of Israel's military industries. This chapter in the history of Israel–China relations is inextricably connected to Eisenberg, as Israel benefited enormously from the meetings he held, his hosting of high-level Chinese delegations in Israel, and other contributions. Just months before his death, Eisenberg hosted the vice premier of China on his visit to Israel, during which he met with Prime Minister Benjamin Netanyahu. Representatives of the Mossad foreign relations department joined Eisenberg's delegations, and his contacts proved vital for Israel's relationship with China well before formal ties were established between the two countries.

Before his death in March 1997, his conglomerate United Development Inc. had amassed unprecedented power and influence throughout China. It traded with China and operated inside the country in a wide range of innovative fields including the transfer of agricultural technology, communications and industrial products, and sales of Israeli white potash.

In 2003, an Israeli writer published the following poem, under the pseudonym Dalia Falach:[227]

---

227 Dalia Falach, Am Oved, Tel Aviv, 2003.

Eisenberg 1979

Mao died, while on the other side,
The Shah lost his power; his throne shook.
It was time to sell,
And Eisenberg said he could do it.
On February 22, 1979, he flew his plane to China,
He took with him:
- The general-director of the Ministry of Defense;
- The head of defense exports support in the Ministry of Defense;
- The director of the security department in the Ministry of Defense;
- The head of the foreign relations branch of the Mossad;
- The CEO of Elta and the CEO of Elisra;
- The CEO of Tadiran and the CEO of Raphael;
- The deputy director of Israel Military Industries for production coordination;
and others.
They flew together, in secret,
Wearing no ID tags on their clothes.
What a touching sight
To see them crowded together in the plane.
They stayed there for three weeks (this is the "cool" part, right?)
They lectured to the Chinese about all that they had and all that they knew,
And then the Chinese bought.
The media that covers such deals
Estimated the amount of sales at 3.5 billion dollars up to 1984.
China paid in goods: silk.
If I understood correctly, Eisenberg sold the silk, all of it,
At market price (in the West),
Then took his percentage:
15%, as agreed with the Israeli cabinet
(Begin, Weizman and Dayan).
He added another 2% to cover unexpected expenses.

After Eisenberg's Death

In 1997, at age seventy-six, Shaul Eisenberg died of a stroke. Thousands attended the funeral at the cemetery in Savyon, Israel—business people, politicians, and diplomats; the Chinese ambassador; and members of the senior Chinese diplomatic staff.[228]

Until his dying day, Eisenberg continued to manage his businesses in his energetic and focused manner. He continued to press forward with activities in China (after he purchased the controlling share of Israel Chemicals in the mid-1990s, he expanded the company's economic projects in China).[229] Still, some argue that in the years leading up to his death, China and the Chinese business world no longer needed a man like him. China had developed increasing access to the West and the international economy. In the new interconnected world of fast and sophisticated communication techniques, and with the incredibly rapid pace of China's opening to this world, the role of middleman became outdated and superfluous. Eisenberg was apparently unable to adapt his businesses to China's new global reality.[230] Still, even in the mid-1990s he earned respectable profits from commissions on China's military acquisitions from Israel.[231]

After his death, the Eisenberg Group followed its founder's lead and continued attempts to develop business activity with China. For example, in mid-1998 the Group and the Dead Sea Works reached an agreement with the Chinese government to construct a factory for potash production under the joint ownership of these three entities.[232] In addition, the group served as a broker for selling the Phalcon airborne early warning radar system to the Chinese.[233] This deal created a diplomatic incident due to the problematic triangle connecting China with Israel and the United States. However, when the dominant figure of Eisenberg left the ring, the close ties that connected his company to China were loosened and never returned to their previous level during his lifetime. His son and heir, Erwin, appears to be a cautious leader who does not rush to initiate multiple new projects around the world but rather focuses on preserving existing dealings and concentrates most of his activity in Israel.[234]

---

228 Golan, "Thousands Attend Eisenberg's Funeral."
229 Peretz, "The Heir is Already Apparent."
230 Galili, "The Next Generation's Turn."
231 Oren, "The Sparkling Burglar," (Hebrew: "*Haporetz Hanotzetz*").
232 Steinberg, "Agreement between the Eisenberg Group and the Chinese Government."
233 Ben, "The New Phalcon Rules."
234 Rosen, "When I Whistle, My Employees Come Running." On the Phalcon affair, see Chapter Seven.

Chapter Six

How to Lose Money in China—The Stories of Four Israeli Companies

The Chinese market was wide open for a period following the Opium War in the latter half of the nineteenth century and especially in the first half of the twentieth century, until the People's Republic of China was founded in 1949. China had no functional sovereign authority, and it promised a healthy income to Western merchants. A series of agreements imposed on China by foreign powers left its products exposed, without any protective mechanism. In practical terms, China was the victim of informal imperialism. As opposed to the areas settled by the major empires as formal colonies, China did not benefit from the few advantages those colonies enjoyed. It had no imperial mother-figure that took care of its residents in sectors traditionally managed by government, such as transportation, education, justice, or defense from outside enemies. Its riches and its enormous market were left completely vulnerable to the power holders. From the viewpoint of any private or government company that desired China as a platform for commercial activity, the sky was the limit.

But that dream of El Dorado, the mythological city of gold, was not always realized. Numerous European companies failed in their attempts to do business in China, despite the mammoth advantages that foreigners initially enjoyed—such as the protection of their governments and the extraterritorial regions that granted legal shelter. The cultural gaps, the differences in consumer patterns, and the difficulty of operating in such a foreign cultural environment created commercial barriers and stinging failures. The meeting point between the Chinese and Westerners was characterized by this paradoxical situation. On one hand Westerners had lofty expectations of enormous profits, but on the other they sometimes met with bitter disappointments and heavy losses. This pattern has continued from the nineteenth century to this day—but the Westerners never seem to learn these lessons. Although the loser retreats in shame, the inexperienced colleague that has never experienced the uniqueness of China still harbors illusions about the country, the dreams of treasure hunters—as if the Chinese market with all its riches has been waiting just for him to arrive. One investor fails, another pops up in his place, and the cycle continues.

In the 1930s, as Sherman Cochran showed in his study,[235] the Swedish Match company chalked up heavy losses in China, despite seemingly careful and wise preparation. An in-depth analysis of this company's history reveals that despite the training they received, on many levels its managers did not internalize the uniqueness of China and its culture and were unable to work with the foreign mentality. Further, the representative of the Chinese side deceived the Swedes and led them astray. In the interface between the two cultures, the hand of the Chinese merchant was almost always on top despite his country's perceived inferiority in the global arena.

The foreigners' lack of skill in promoting their initiatives in China's unique conditions (the language barrier is only one example) meant that they and their businesses were almost always on the losing side. This phenomenon was called "imperialism imprisoned"—a situation in which the seemingly weak prevailed over the strong, proving that the words of Proverbs, "By wise counsel will you wage your war" (24:6), applied equally to economic battles.[236]

After China adopted its Open Door Policy in the late 1970s, the dam broke and China became a fertile field for foreign investment. It now offers a comfortable environment for the activity of foreign companies searching for cooperative ventures beyond their native borders. Special economic zones and preferred treatment for joint ventures and foreign direct investment (FDI) are conducive to the business activity there. Alongside this, China has initiated reforms in commerce, pushed for innovative development of

---

235 Cochran, *Big Business in China*.

236 For more on the topic of attempts to exploit China versus the opposite, see Shai, *The Fate of British and French Firms—Imperialism Imprisoned*.

industries, created of millions of jobs, acquired technology, and achieved an appreciable improvement in its standard of living and economic capabilities. These elements have acted and are still acting as valuable leverage for expanding the dimensions of China's international commerce. However, China continues to receive much lower amounts of direct foreign investment than other countries. Many foreign investments are short-term and in limited sectors.

One of the difficulties that foreign companies still face is the government model, which largely avoids transparency in the business system and demonstrates a lack of continuity in laws and regulations. The cultural differences between China and other trade partners often lead to misunderstandings. China has yet to implement free market principles completely, or to the extent that Westerners might expect. The economy is planned from above, policed, and centralized. The issue of copyright also has an impact on multinational commerce. The Chinese philosophical view on this topic is different from the accepted view in the West: copyright infringements and illegal copies are a common phenomenon and are not expressly prohibited. The issue of 关系 (guānxi), the special relationships sometimes needed to promote a deal, can be an obstacle as well as a useful tool for leveraging business.

In recent years, diplomatic research on China's foreign relations has become a topic that overlaps with business history, as it offers another prism through which we may analyze additional layers of relationship. Deng Xiaoping's well-known saying from the 1980s that foreign products must serve China expressed the essence of Chinese thinking on relations with foreign countries. As for joint initiatives, the implication of the leader's statement called for viewing cooperation as a vehicle for improving Chinese technology, ideally without supplying the required capital from the Chinese side. In this manner the Chinese would provide the land for constructing the factory as well as infrastructure, labor, and raw materials. But the foreign investor would have to supply the technology, most of the equipment, the management strategy, and the active capital—as necessary as oxygen—for the initiative. The foreign investor was also expected to give the funds for advertising the product. Of course, we can explain this approach as deriving from the Chinese people's deep historical sense that they had been exploited for decades by foreign imperialists and enjoyed only paltry rewards in exchange for the resources and labor that they provided.

Israeli Businesspeople Try Their Luck in China

Shaul Eisenberg's extensive experience in China paved the way for other Israeli businesspeople, both directly and indirectly—but where Eisenberg met with enormous success, many others experienced only failure.

In the 1980s, before the establishment of formal diplomatic relations between Israel and China, Israel established an agency in Hong Kong to encourage Israeli exports to China. This agency had a local representative in Beijing. During that period, the amount of indirect trade between the two countries was very modest—around fifty million dollars per year (aside from sales of defense and military products). After normalization of relations in 1992, and mainly starting in 1999, direct trade between the two countries developed at exponential rates. China became the most important Asian target for Israeli exports. Trade thrived, the number of Israeli companies that operated in China grew, and joint ventures also proliferated. Exports from Israel to China reached over three billion dollars in 2017, not including diamonds, while imports from China totaled around eight billion dollars. The question of the relationship of imports to Israel from China and exports from Israel to China remains a significant issue today. Israel has not been able to increase its exports to China in comparison to imports from that country.

In 2004 the Ministry of Commerce, Industry, and Labor defined China as a target country for advancing Israeli exports. As part of this program, entrepreneurs were given government grants in the fields of information technology, agriculture, water quality, and environmental protection. Bureaus of commerce were opened in Beijing and Shanghai. The breakthrough in relations between the two countries was characterized by new initiatives, such as establishing representative offices for companies, signing agreements, holding conferences and congresses on trade and economy, and sending reciprocal visits of delegations. The governments performed (and still perform today) periodic checks of the trade barriers between the two countries, and joint economic studies are a regular part of the relationship. For example, in 2010 Prime Minister Benjamin Netanyahu asked the Ministry of Industry and Commerce to establish an inter-office committee to examine ways to increase Israeli exports to China. The working assumption was that the Chinese economy would continue to grow, and Israel should take advantage of the window of opportunity that presented itself.

Three branches of industry made a significant contribution to the increase in Israeli exports: engines and electrical equipment (medium high-technology industries); fertilizers (medium low-technology); and control and measuring equipment. Israel had a clear advantage in the high-technology products in addition to its relative advantage in innovation, entrepreneurship, and human capital.

Sano and Osem were among the first companies that tried their luck in China in the 1990s. Many Israeli companies gazed longingly at the growing market that had just opened up to Israeli initiatives in many areas. First to delve in were companies from the fields of agriculture and water, in which Chinese regulation was more moderate. Then came companies in various other fields, including Netafim (drip irrigation solutions), Amiad (water filtration for irrigation), Hazorea (exporting fish and water plants) and Haifa Chemicals.

Soon after, China passed laws and regulations in the field of communications, and Israeli companies operating in this area also began to enter China (such as ECI Telecom, Tadiran, Electra, and Gilat Satellite Communications). The next wave began in the late 1990s and mainly included hi-tech and electronics companies, as well as other companies that had not participated in the first wave, such as Checkpoint (cyber security), Comverse (telecommunications software), Alvarion (autonomous Wi-Fi networks), and VCON (communication). They were soon joined by real estate, insurance, and venture capital companies.

The Case of Sano

Bruno Landesberg, controlling owner and former chairman of Sano-Bruno Enterprises Ltd., a major Israeli cleaning products company, was first drawn to the Chinese market after a Chinese delegation that visited Israel in the 1980s expressed interest in his products. Delegation members proposed that they establish a similar factory in China. Landesberg was excited by the idea and began to act. Along the way he was enchanted by the Chinese culture and people. He set himself the goal of putting down stakes in China. First he consulted with Shaul Eisenberg, and the two began to work together in the early 1990s.[237]

---

237 Interview with Bruno and Alex Landesberg, July 10, 2011.

Sano top managers met with members of a Chinese commercial delegation in Cyprus, and Landesberg and his son Alex presented samples of the company's products. The Israeli delegation included the company's chief chemist, another chemist, a supplier of raw materials, a representative of the advertising company attached to Sano, and a translator. In preparation for the meetings, Sano created an image film about the factory and a detailed presentation including a proposal for the planned project. The Israeli delegation was welcomed warmly by the Chinese. Landesberg ascribed the positive atmosphere to his knowledge of the Russian language and culture, with which the older Chinese were also acquainted. In this unexpected manner, the language barrier almost disappeared. Quality food and beverages accompanied by Russian music also had their effect.

At the next stage, discussions were held in Shenyang, Manchuria (Dongbei) the planned location for the factory. According to Landesberg, in those days Shenyang looked like an enormous slum. On this visit as well the Sano representatives were given a warm welcome, "like emperors," as Landesberg reported. The delegation was received by a convoy of "twelve Mercedes." But the negotiations on the plan for the factory, how to construct it, and its manner of operation were long and tedious. Every single issue was discussed for long hours, and even when it seemed that an agreement had been reached, often the Chinese reopened the discussion on one question or another, as if they had not already debated it fully—a veritable war of attrition. Furthermore, during their visit the Israeli delegation members were kept in complete isolation and prohibited from having any contact with the surrounding environment. During the day the Israelis were distracted with rich meals and alcohol, while the business discussions were held at night. The Chinese aspired to obtain a majority in the joint board of directors that the two sides would establish. Finally, the Chinese got what they wanted—fifty-five percent control in the factory. In this situation the Sano representatives were forced to accept the conditions that the Chinese set. The Israelis' influence was almost completely neutralized, and they were prevented from having any say on the appointment of laborers, clerks, or local management in the factory.

Finally, after Sisyphean discussions, the agreement was signed and Sano established a factory in Shenyang as a joint venture with a Chinese company selected by the Chinese side. Sano was responsible for constructing the factory and supplying all the needed technological equipment. The land was allocated by the Chinese government. As was the accepted procedure, Sano was not permitted to purchase the required land but could only lease it. Under the agreement, the Chinese were responsible for the marketing aspect.

Sano prepared the plans for constructing the factory and left it up to the Chinese partners to implement them. But there was a huge gap between the original plans and the implementation. Landesberg asserted that a conspicuous example of this was the issue of allocation of areas inside the factories. Generous areas, which the Israelis considered extravagant, were set aside for the management offices. The offices were furnished in grand style and equipped with adjacent bathrooms (even for Landesberg, who had no idea that this was in the plan). The laboratory and production areas, by contrast, were smaller than required. In addition, the final cost of construction was higher than the original amount planned. Sano had to bear the discrepancies on its own, and this caused a serious disagreement between the two sides.

Another problem arose with regard to hiring the professional staff for the factory. Sano invested significant sums in training Chinese professionals, flying a dozen of them to Israel, putting them up in hotels, and providing professional training—all at Sano's expense. But after the experts returned to China, the Chinese fired all of them except for one and replaced them with their own cronies. Even the factory manager was appointed on a political basis, in complete opposition to Landesberg's preference for an experienced manager with a full command of English. The Chinese demanded that all communication with them be conducted only through a translator of their choice. In this way they hoped to keep an eye on the data that was sent to their Israeli partners. Partnering with a Chinese company that had government ties had seemed at first to be a supporting advantage, but in the final analysis Sano realized that it was an obstacle. The Chinese were first and foremost interested in political and governmental connections instead of talents and achievements. The decision-making process was also cumbersome and difficult.

Sano made the decisions about which products to manufacture. But because the Israeli staff was prohibited from any contact with Chinese clients by holding the necessary objective market surveys, the Sano staff was unable to obtain appropriate market information. The Chinese had their own ideas. They followed the surveyors closely and often skewed the data obtained. They channeled matters according to the views dictated to them by their superiors. In hindsight Landesberg decided that the choice of product (refill bags for liquid cleaning products) was wrong, and Sano would have done better to supply products that were less sophisticated and more urgently needed, such as bug sprays.

Under the contract Sano had to use local companies for marketing and advertising, although these fields were still in their nascent stages in China. Although the company assigned to Sano had government connections, it did not have the necessary experience, and it failed in advertising the products. For example, Landesberg related, Sano suggested the propagandizing method, which was cheap and appropriate for conditions in the field. But the Chinese insisted on TV advertising despite its much higher price and inaccessibility to the low-income target market. In many areas the product was also unavailable in stores. It was placed on shelves immediately preceding visits of the Israeli staff and removed immediately following. The Chinese side refused to hold market surveys and prohibited Sano staff from any contact with the Chinese population. Landesberg reported that his company tried to learn about methods of penetrating the Chinese market privately through companies in Hong Kong. But the price of this consultation was high. Throughout the process Landesberg had the feeling that the Chinese were constantly trying to milk funds from the foreign companies that attempted to do business with their country.

From the first moment of contact with the Chinese until the termination of the joint venture, Sano's activity in China lasted for about five years. After the partnership was dissolved, Sano was forced to leave behind the factory that it had funded and equipped—and the vast knowledge invested in it—without enjoying any profits whatsoever. The factory was opened in 1995 with some forty employees, but production halted after just a few months. The first investment totaled about three million dollars. But Landesberg added that this was only the original amount, "before we became the cash cow . . . . The Chinese were always coming up with new excuses for additional expenses."

According to the contract, Sano was prohibited from pursuing any legal action related to the initiative. The sides had established that in case of a disagreement, they would go to a mediator, and the Israelis were assured that the Chinese respected this technique deeply. The Landesberg family's legal advisor suggested that should mediation be necessary, it should be conducted in Switzerland. But the Chinese insisted that as a trust-building step, mediation would be conducted in China. When disagreement arose, the Chinese did not honor the agreement, and mediation never happened.

For their part, the Sano staff were suspicious of a compromise process that would take place in China, as they felt it would naturally be skewed toward the opposing side. They thus decided to abandon the idea.

In addition to a cleaning products factory, Sano also founded an advertising company that operated in China, also as a joint venture with a Chinese company. Sano invested hundreds of thousands of dollars in establishing and developing the company. A building was purchased and renovated to serve as an office building, and its value rose over time. The company began to function, but the data that Sano management received from China were few and far between. While Sano paid generously for attorneys and accountants, it never received the requested information. The feeling within Sano was that the Chinese inflated the expenses so as to collect unjustified funds. Despite this, the company did turn a profit. But when Sano asked for its portion, the Chinese announced that Sano was not eligible for it, as it had significant debts. Again the Israelis were left with the sense that they were being exploited by their foreign counterparts, although the Beijing government acted in such a way that permitted the existence of the foreign companies and made no moves to nationalize them. Thus it was careful not to slaughter the goose that laid the golden egg; it made sure to squeeze profit from the foreign companies by roundabout means.[238] For example, foreign companies had to provide housing for all Chinese employees.

When Sano realized that it could not trust the Chinese attorneys or accountant to solve its problems, it contacted the Israeli partner who was responsible for advertising and asked him for assistance. This initiative bore no fruit. The Chinese simply suggested that the Chinese mother company would purchase the company with its commercial name, offices, and employees for the paltry price of twenty thousand dollars. Thus any grievances on the part of the Israelis would disappear. Although the office building alone was worth several hundred thousand dollars, Sano management decided to give up and accept the offer. As had happened with the cleaning products factory, Sano again preferred to absorb losses rather than wage a long, expensive, exhausting legal battle against the Chinese. Eventually, Sano learned that the advertising company was still in existence and was enjoying admirable success. Today it is traded on the stock market

---

238 See, for example: Shai, *Imperialism Imprisoned.*

in China and is apparently located in the Shenyang region. Furthermore, the company still uses the original name—Sano.

In hindsight, Landesberg decided that it was preferable not to pursue joint commercial ventures with China—better to enter the Chinese market alone and on an independent basis. That way, the Chinese would not hold the position of status as hosts who could make all the decisions for themselves whenever conflict arose with their partners.

Despite these negative experiences, Bruno Landesberg did not regret his adventure in China. Looking back, he viewed it as a learning experience, a romantic dream that in a more fitting time and place might have come true. He noted, "When we walked through the streets of Shenyang to the factory and saw the Chinese flag hanging on one side of the entrance and the Israeli flag on the other side, we didn't care about the money or the profits." His son Alex shared a more realistic, bitter side of the experience. In his opinion, the Chinese deceived Sano and even lied brazenly regarding the costs involved. He estimated Sano's losses at between two and three million dollars. These losses might have been even greater if Sano had not rushed to abandon the venture at the right time. He asserted that possibly, he and his father were naïve. Their worldview was that when doing business together, partners must behave fairly. "We are a fair company, and we expect the other side to act fairly as well, whether Chinese, Indian, or Israeli." At first, the Chinese made an excellent impression with their warm attitude. But as the relationship progressed, Sano realized that the Chinese were willing to cause the capitalist company sizeable losses under the assumption that the Israelis had untapped reserves of capital and that it was their duty to exhaust the foreign funds.

Not Worth Peanuts—The Case of Osem

The name Shaul Eisenberg again arises in the case of Osem, as Eisenberg served as mediator between the Israeli company and the Chinese company that Osem had contacted. Eisenberg was supposed to be one of the investors in constructing a new joint factory on Chinese soil. According to the original plans, the company constructing this factory was to be divided equally among three entities: Osem, Eisenberg, and the Beijing Agricultural Industrial Company (BAIC). The Chinese company owned farms and agricultural terrains on which profitable buildings had been built, such as hotels and factories. In the mid-1990s, representatives of the Chinese company visited Osem factories in Israel to study its line of products. They showed particular interest in Bamba, the puffed peanut-flavored snack. The Chinese proposed constructing a Bamba factory in China and even took back samples of the snack to their country, intending to begin the venture.[239]

Meanwhile, Eisenberg decided he was not interested in investing funds in the joint factory in China, and he pulled out of the partnership. Still, he did not take any payment for the mediation and consulting services he provided to Osem and its CEO Gad Propper regarding the entry into China.

Osem and the Chinese company reached an agreement. According to Propper, they decided that Osem would retain ownership of 51 percent of the company, which gave them the controlling interest they desired so intensely. They also agreed that Osem (Israel) would be responsible for importing the technology and know-how for establishing and managing the factory in China. Based on their knowledge of the local market and the know-how they already possessed, the Chinese were supposed to focus on providing the land and building for the factory as well as carrying out marketing and sales.

Propper described the experience of signing the agreement and the preliminary business dealings as positive, despite the very different way of thinking in Chinese business and business ethics. At that stage and as the negotiations proceeded, Propper had no suspicions that the other side intended to cheat him or cause him losses.

The Osem factory in China was developed and constructed over a period of one year on the foundations of a former ice cream factory that had gone bankrupt (a joint venture with a Western company). Osem spared no expenses for labor and equipment and supplied up-to-date technology for the factory. It even adapted its methods for the needs of production in the new location. Lior Ben-Tzur, an employee of Beijing Eisen Lubao Oil, a manufacturer of edible oils, was appointed as the CEO of the new company.

The factory in Beijing was dedicated at a festive ceremony attended by Ora Namir, Israel's ambassador to China. Production began, and at first the work progressed smoothly. The Bamba snack product was sold to wholesalers, who distributed it throughout Beijing. Distribution to other districts was planned appropriately, but after a while the wholesalers complained that the stores were not paying them for the product. Demand was lower

---

239 Interview with Gad Propper, August 14, 2011.

than expected, so the retailers refrained from ordering new merchandise and delayed payments.

Propper blamed the low sales on his Chinese colleagues' faulty performance in advertising and marketing the product. The Chinese conducted market surveys and posted advertisements on buses, and the product was sold in the large supermarket chains. But after the initial disappointment at failing to meet the anticipated volume of sales, and due to the accumulated debt, the Chinese partner company refused to inject additional funds into the project beyond its first investment. It transferred only the preliminary payments for the advertising, marketing, and formal permits required. Thus an uneasy situation was created. Additional obstacles appeared when the company tried to take loans from Chinese banks. Still, Osem agreed to continue their investment. In light of the asymmetry that developed, the Chinese agreed to reduce their share of profits in the company from 49 percent to around 40 percent.

At this point Propper contacted Nestle, which then owned eleven factories in the Beijing region (this was before the eventual unification between Osem and Nestle). Nestle offered modest assistance, providing consultants for the initiative but not financial means. Nestle was then facing high expenses in China. For example, Nestle established a milk products factory, which then required it by contract to purchase milk in regular quantities from thousands of dairies. Nestle's manager responsible for marketing and sales on the Chinese market told Propper that he used to wake up in the middle of the night covered in cold sweat—he suffered from a recurring nightmare that he was drowning in rivers of milk. The questions that disturbed him: how could he handle the company's sales obligations and what would he do with the overabundance of milk?

As a last resort, Propper contacted the Osem board of directors in Israel and requested an additional injection of funds. This step was not easy but was expected to produce long-term profits. But because Propper had no firm guarantees that the investment would bear fruit, he received authorization for one-tenth of the sum he had requested—only about half a million dollars. With this the fate of the Osem factory in China was sealed. The factory was moved to Papua New Guinea, where it enjoyed success. Meanwhile, the factory building on Chinese soil remained in Chinese hands.

Propper believed that the Chinese managers were as disappointed as he was by the rapid collapse of the joint venture. On a personal level he felt enriched by the experience. He had met people who were intelligent and friendly and who were filled with admiration for both Jews and Israelis. He said that his partners always demonstrated willingness to help. Still, he said, they were unskilled at thinking outside of the box, and their managerial style was inflexible and bureaucratic. Possibly, he thought, the Chinese colleagues profited at Osem's expense. As with the Sano initiative, the Chinese insisted on selecting the local workers that the partnership company would employ, with almost no possibility of using non-Chinese experts who could make valuable contributions. The Israeli companies were also required to provide lodging for the employees and to pay for full social benefits. In addition, they were forced to purchase the means of production from Chinese sources at uncompetitive prices.

Propper adopted a philosophical approach to the Chinese experience, both in his attitude toward the distress caused to him and his staff and regarding the losses he incurred. After all, he considered, when it came to knowledge and technology, it was hard to place an exact price tag on the effort that he had invested but that had not borne fruit. He estimated the total loss at several hundred thousand dollars, maybe half a million. The Chinese had also invested in purchasing the technology, he noted. The disappointment of failure distressed him more than the financial loss. Unlike Alex Landesberg, Propper did not feel that the Chinese had tried to cheat him or to get rich at his expense. Rather, he thought that the Chinese side had not made enough of an effort to save the joint venture. In his words, the Chinese "walk straight ahead, like horses wearing blinders—they can't look right or left." From the sobering perspective of experience, he related that he would never again get involved in such a venture, even if the situation in China were to change. In his opinion the Chinese mentality remained the same, and further, many companies were still under government control.

Lessons Learned

Amos Yudan, one of the first Israelis to develop business relations with China, had a definitive opinion on the fates of Sano and Osem there.[240] In the case of Sano, he believed that the main error was in the company's structure. Bruno Landesberg did not maintain the necessary control over the initiative, especially in the field of marketing inside China. Without

---

240 Interview with Amos Yudan, July 21, 2004.

such control, failure was only a matter of time. In addition, the Chinese side did not function as required and was unwilling to invest the necessary resources. Thus, although the products were excellent, sales failed.

Osem made a similar mistake: marketing was left to the Chinese side, which did not meet its obligations. The products stood on the grocery store shelves, but the local consumers heard nothing about them. The Chinese assumed that investment in advertising was too expensive, and they completely neglected the marketing aspect. Because Osem itself didn't undertake that task, the fate of the initiative was sealed.

According to Yudan, who as previously noted was well-acquainted with the Chinese arena and the Israeli businesspeople who had sunk into the Chinese quagmire, success would come only to those who thought long-term and who were willing to invest repeatedly in new products or technologies in China. A permanent presence in China was also obligatory and remains so today. Because the activity of a foreign company in China involves high costs, some have thought there was no point in investing in services or a broad range of contacts in this far-off country. In cases where the scope of business activity was not large enough to justify the required investment, the potential investor should have been aware of the limitations in advance. Investment in market research that addresses the unique conditions in China remains vital. Many Israeli companies are looking for a quick fix—they hope to sell without incurring heavy expenses. By contrast, the Chinese are interested in long-term investments looking many years ahead.

Yudan's perspective points to a common trait of many Israelis who deal in trade and business contacts with China: the unwillingness or inability to rely on experts on China (Sinologists). While companies willingly pay exorbitant amounts to attorneys, brokers, and translators, their managers are usually overconfident in their abilities and experience and do not consider the possibility of paying Sinologists or consultants who are acquainted with the Chinese mentality. Yet China is a culture and way of thinking that is very different and difficult to comprehend. Some businessmen who have been burned are willing to admit that they made this mistake. According to Bruno Landesberg, in those days the only relevant China expertise belonged to Shaul Eisenberg. Although Eisenberg was not a Sinologist in the academic sense, he was highly knowledgeable. Due to the close connections between them, Landesberg received advice on the feasibility of his investment, what to be cautious about, and other issues.

Unfortunately, Eisenberg's advice proved insufficient—constant follow-up was required.

Propper also spoke of Eisenberg when asked about the need for consulting with China experts. "When I received one hundred percent of the recommendations from Eisenberg, I felt no need to investigate further," he admitted. "If I had hired a Sinologist, he might have explained to me that even after obtaining good data from market surveys, there was still no promise that the business would succeed. Then the red light would have been lit for me at an earlier stage." Had he then possessed the knowledge that he has today, said Propper, he would have asked the Chinese to come to the table with recognized financial reserves for investment in case the initiative needed emergency rescue. He would even have demanded more control over decisions, including in the marketing field.

In the twenty-first century, now that China's value and economic power has earned global recognition, the field of consulting on this unique country has developed widely. Still, in the current age, with readily accessible information on many topics and applications that can translate sentences from one language to another in microseconds, many individuals instantly give themselves the title of China expert. Yet even in a society like China that is undergoing such rapid change and development, the history of the country plays a vital role in the game of economic and diplomatic relations. The foreigner's exploitation of China in the past two hundred years has left its mark on the Chinese in many variations. Naturally, we must add to this the many layers of China's history, its unique philosophy, and the religions and beliefs that it has developed over thousands of years.

From their viewpoint the Chinese have every justification (and perhaps even a national duty) to exploit whenever possible the resources of foreigners, Westerners, and particularly "capitalists," with all the accompanying resonance of this term. Certainly the Chinese have no reason to consider foreigners or their interests during negotiation and signature of agreements with them.

A Guide to Losing Money in China: The Next Generation

In the first eighteen years of the twenty-first century, Israeli companies have still found themselves groping in the dark with regard to promoting their businesses in China. In the second-generation ventures, we identify aspects that appeared in their predecessors, as well as aspects that differentiate them from the first-generation efforts. What is the magic formula for business success in China? Does such a recipe in fact exist?[241] It seems that we have not yet found the path to guaranteed success in the Chinese market. Even today success is hardly guaranteed, and many Israeli companies bleed heavily in China. We will now turn our attention to two of these second-generation efforts—DavidShield and Kardan.

DavidShield

In many ways, DavidShield International Medical Insurance is representative of the attempt of second-generation companies operating in China. Alon Ketzef, DavidShield's CEO, believes that in order to successfully penetrate this key market, Israeli and other foreign companies must internalize the existence of three models for doing business in China: import of products from China, export of products to China (or models of "doing business *with* China"), and doing business *within* China. Foreign companies have wrestled with this concept for many decades. The professional literature also contains lengthy discussions on business with China and within China. In the semi-colonialist period and until the rise of the Communist regime in 1949, foreign activity in China was characterized by political, strategic, and military advantages—what was often called "gunboat diplomacy." After the end of the Opium War, foreigners could threaten China's leaders that unsatisfactory treatment would provoke military or semi-military responses. These threats were effective. But of course, after the Communist regime took control of the People's Republic, this method was no longer appropriate. Further, in the 1950s a transformation took place in this arena.[242] In many ways the foreign companies came under the control of the new regime. The model of business within China became an entirely different game, although many were still not aware of the transformation.[243]

In 2008 Ketzef met a senior Chinese-Australian businessman in New York through a major American insurance company. The businessman asserted that he had the ability to implement a program on behalf of China's National Development and Reform Commission (NDRC), in

---

241 Israeli businesspeople and academic experts on China discussed this issue at a series of conferences held at the Faculty of Business Management at Tel Aviv University in June and July 2013.
242 See Shai, *The Fate of British and French Firms in China.*
243 Interview with Alon Ketzef, David Shield offices, Netanya, Israel, August 3, 2014.

which DavidShield would be invited to play a leading role in insurance activity in China. In the framework of the five-year plan, or the "green book," the Chinese government body would open up a new field: travel insurance abroad. According to the businessman, the initiative would provide health insurance coverage for the masses of Chinese citizens that were expected to begin traveling outside the borders of their country for business, tourism, or with various delegations. From the Chinese viewpoint, travel insurance was vital in case of emergency or crisis to prevent damage to Chinese pride and China's image abroad. Without proper insurance, sick or injured Chinese travelers were likely to be stranded in the world's capitals, leaving behind unpaid bills with doctors, clinics, or hospitals in the West. Any Chinese citizen who traveled outside China, especially on official delegations, would be required to purchase appropriate travel insurance. This essential task was delegated to the People's Insurance Company of China (PICC), the largest government company in China for all types of insurance except for life insurance. Lacking professional knowledge in the area as well as the necessary links with physicians, clinics, hospitals, and global health systems, the Chinese needed a relationship with an international company that had expertise in this field.

Before the meeting in New York, PICC had met with the Chinese-Australian businessman, who was also a physician and owned a medical assistance company in Beijing, to engage his services as a go-between and appropriate partner in the West. This man was considered the right fit for the job, as he had participated in writing the NDRC five-year plan and had been responsible for identifying the required contacts. After the meeting in New York, Ketzef traveled to Beijing for more meetings on the subject. He saw it as a unique opportunity: "Elijah the Prophet was knocking on my door, and I had to open it for him," he said, describing his lucky feeling.

On experiencing the wealth and power of China, Ketzef felt that he had arrived in the land of unlimited opportunity. He was treated to unbelievably rich meals, drinks, ceremonies, and honors. He and his colleagues were the honored guests at every event. Ministers, ambassadors, Communist Party representatives, district heads, chamber of commerce officials, and other high-level individuals all wanted to be his close friends. Ministers from Israel who supported the future initiative with excitement also met with him in China.

Not surprisingly, one year later the first business deal of its kind was signed. DavidShield would supply medical services to PICC for its clients—Chinese working abroad, from diplomats to construction workers. To implement the deal, DavidShield worked with Global Doctor, an Australian company that was connected to the Chinese-Australian businessman. DavidShield had previous experience with Global Doctor, which had been the service supplier for DavidShield's insurance customers in China. The Chinese government issued a tender for selling insurance policies to its citizens in foreign countries, and DavidShield and Global Doctor cooperated in submitting a proposal. The tender was meant for Chinese insurance companies with foreign partners, and this was how the cooperation began with the Beijing branch of PICC. The agreement with this branch was defined as a trial for three years, but DavidShield hoped that successful activity would lead to expansion of the agreement and inclusion of additional units of the Chinese corporation in the future.[244] The two companies, Israeli and Chinese, had equal shares in the new company established in China. Global Doctor was supposed to invest twenty million dollars in creating the initial service network and in advertising the service in China.

According to attorney Gideon Weinstock of Weinstock–Zecler Law Offices, who promoted the project, the deal was the perfect example of an integration of Israeli know-how and experience with the enormous potential of China. Alon Ketzef, CEO of DavidShield Israel, was also chairman of Global Doctor. He related that as part of the preparations, the new company intended to establish a subsidiary in Russia that would supply services in Arab countries where Chinese companies operated.[245]

A lavish launch ceremony for the joint project was held in 2009, with the Chinese media in attendance. Ketzef was investing all his energy in the deal and flying to China once every two weeks. He was given a seat of honor in the front row of the hall, and he felt pride and satisfaction.

As part of the deal, the parties agreed that the Chinese government representative would become a partner holding 50 percent of the new company, while DavidShield would hold the remaining 50 percent. The defined purpose of the company was to supply an international infrastructure for providing services to Chinese citizens traveling outside of China. The services would be provided through a foreign travel insurance policy, according to the usual package. PICC would be responsible for distribution,

---

244 Stein and Pe'er, "Phoenix Expands: Proposes to Purchase 50% of David Shield Agency."
245 Beit-Aryeh, "David Shield Enters China."

marketing, and sales of the services. The presentations and explanations that DavidShield's representatives received regarding the expected distribution and, of course, the resultant earnings seemed like a dream come true.[246]

Ketzef considered that the company's connections with the Chinese government were the main attraction of the deal with PICC. In the final analysis, PICC was the financial entity responsible toward the customer, the body that took upon itself the insurance risk. He also said that the partnership with PICC was designed to enable the project to reach an enormous market of government company employees and Chinese government entities who needed insurance outside of China.[247] DavidShield was given a floor in the PICC management building in Beijing.

But the moment the deal was signed, the treats ended and the problems began. First, the Israeli representatives were required by law to establish a registered company in China and to obtain a license for operation. Ketzef reported that the bureaucratic process at this stage involved many complications. The company was duly registered as a Wholly Foreign Owned Enterprise (WOFE). But despite fulfilling the requirements, the Israelis learned that China's insurance supervisor had instructed the PICC to sign a guarantee for the requested license as a condition for issuing the final license. The Chinese were willing to do so but demanded that the individual who would hold the company stamp be Chinese and not a foreigner. Ketzef had no other choice but to accept the condition. This meant that despite the formal equality between the two sides, the balance of power was tipped in favor of the Chinese—in fact, the Chinese government. The deeper significance was that in the case of disagreement in the future, the Israelis would not be able to sue the Chinese side.

Still, at this stage the Israelis remained optimistic and trusted their "Jewish smarts" to help them face future challenges. DavidShield intended to maintain the confidentiality of its international infrastructure and purchasing contracts over which it had exclusive control. The Chinese company was only supposed to purchase insurance services from DavidShield. Ketzef hoped that even if the Chinese side had a certain advantage in the practical balance of power in the new company, the Israelis would preserve the decisive advantage in the venture thanks to their ownership of the know-how

---

246 Interview with Alon Ketzef, August 3, 2014.
247 Stein and Pe'er, "Phoenix Expands: Proposes to Purchase 50% of David Shield Agency."

and the network of services acquired from various suppliers: physicians, hospitals, and medical technology companies around the world. Still, DavidShield found itself tangled in a web of disagreements and misunderstandings, some related to the work of the translators that were serving the Chinese side. Sometimes material was incorrectly translated—whether accidentally or on purpose.

In late 2009 the Israelis received monetary returns from the Chinese company for the project's activity. But they were surprised to find out that the Chinese did not hand over all the proceeds. The Israeli computer system listed a known number of insured customers who had paid their premiums—but payment was received for only 90 percent of them. Why didn't the Chinese pay DavidShield the entire amount? The Israeli company investigated and discovered that the Chinese partners had siphoned off money from the premium payments. DavidShield's attempts to file complaints against the perpetrators were met with herculean efforts to suppress the incident and transformed DavidShield and its managers into "problematic partners."

Ketzef was unwilling to fight on foreign turf. He realized that under those conditions, he would never gain the upper hand. He packed his bags and left China. To Ketzef the "China affair" of 2011 and 2012 was a veritable Third Lebanon War—the Israelis went out to battle accompanied by loud fanfare expecting to conquer and win, but they conceded defeat and were forced to beat a humiliating retreat. The monetary loss was the least important part of the affair.

Other interviewees documented that they had seen foreign businessmen who had suffered severely. Some were interrogated by government authorities and withdrew leaving their property and dreams behind. This brings us to ask, are activities in China worthwhile? Is it possible to work with such a foreign mentality and under a completely different regime? By extension, does Israel have a chance of doing business in the other "BRIC" countries—Brazil, Russia, and India?

We can learn many lessons from Israelis who have tried unsuccessfully to do business *in* China, as opposed to those who have done business *with* China. Getting a license is one thing, but holding it depends on the government's policies—the regime gives, and the regime takes away. In China, many assert, businesspeople must keep three different sets of books.

Even if the Western partner holds all the shares in the company, this has no practical meaning for the balance of power. As long as the business is operating on Chinese territory, it is for all practical means in the hands of the Chinese, as if it were legally owned by them. Another problem is related to authorization for sending profits over to the West, to company headquarters outside China. Even if it seems that the money was indeed sent outside of China in payment for business activity inside China, usually these are no more than financial shenanigans. In the world of finance, it is easy to convince an accountant that your property or shares are worth a certain amount and to translate this amount into value on paper. But in actuality, no real cash is generated. As an example, Ketzef believes that not one dollar of the tangible profits produced from deals inside China ever reached Tel Aviv. This is because as soon as the Chinese notice that a foreign company partnered in a joint venture with China has accumulated enough cash in a Chinese bank, they will find ways to prevent the transfer of these funds abroad. The tactic that the Chinese use is to offer the foreigner an incredibly attractive option that can be implemented only in China—in real estate or the seductive field of technology, for example. The impression in the books is that profit has been generated, but this profit is only a line in the accounting ledger.

In the departure lounge at Beijing Capital International Airport, Ketzef relates, on Thursday evenings while waiting for the flight back to Tel Aviv he would often come across Israeli businessmen who were shattered after a week of trying to do business in China. It became the stuff of bitter folklore, mainly a story of how the Chinese were succeeding in crushing the average entrepreneur. From the highest peak of the "Startup Nation," Israeli investors frequently fell into a deep pit, feeling frustrated and exploited.[248] The problem is that the Israelis refuse to learn from their predecessors. They're always certain that "it will never happen to me"—and so the illusion persists. Here is where the various "China advisors" come in, often making their living by leading their clients astray.

Ketzef and other foreign business people who operated in China suspected that if China did not change its ways from one extreme to the other, some potential entrepreneurs would stop dreaming about it. In July 2014 he was approached by a delegation from a well-known insurance company in China with a balance of half a billion dollars. They asked to meet with him—but he refused. His dreams were shattered, shelved in the back row. China was for the Chinese only, he concluded. In the past it was the

---

248 See Senor and Singer, *Start-up Nation: The Story of Israel's Economic Miracle.*

West that had robbed China—now it was China's turn to exploit the West's representatives.[249]

Kardan Israel Ltd.

The next second-generation company that we will analyze here is Kardan Israel Ltd. This company made a strategic decision to participate in new opportunities in two industrial sectors: construction and water treatment.

The company heads knew that a major issue bothering China was where to invest the billions of extra dollars available. In the early twenty-first century China was enjoying accelerated growth thanks to the broad reforms carried out in previous decades, and one of the main results was a massive process of urbanization.

McKinsey Company estimated that by 2025, China's cities would add 350 million inhabitants. Two hundred cities would contain over one million inhabitants, and fifteen major cities would claim over twenty-five million inhabitants each. To house this growth, China would need to construct some five million new buildings. In Chinese cities, the skeletons of multi-story buildings began to sprout like mushrooms after a rain shower.

Kardan entered China in 2005, with Yosef Greenfeld and Avner Schnur at the helm. Erez Applerot, until recently CEO of GTC China, a Kardan subsidiary responsible for the group's real estate activity, said that the urbanization of China was comparable to the entire population of the United States moving to a new home.[250]

This enormous potential involved significant risk due to the character of the regime. China is not a democratic country. Its authoritarian government holds almost unlimited control over the country's resources, including real estate—the land belongs entirely to the government. The areas set aside for construction are leased to private entities but remain under state control. In addition, as we have seen, the business culture is different from Western ways and is mainly based on personal relationships (Guānxì 关系) and local reputations. Under these circumstances, the foreign company that enters China may be harmed by the smallest mistake.

Alon Shlank, who until recently headed Kardan's activity in China, asserts that the business of foreign companies in China divides into two

---

249 Interview with Alon Ketzef, August 3, 2014.
250 Avisar, "How Is Kardan Trying to Breach the Wall of China?"

types: "business with Asian entities and business conducted with other countries." In his opinion, for non-Asian countries entry into and activity in China are more difficult, as they often adopt a patronizing attitude. Sometimes they initially offer low prices for their products or services to penetrate the market, and then they raise the prices. The Chinese consider this inappropriate behavior.

Shlank is well-acquainted with China and has been a regular traveler on the Tel Aviv-Beijing line for over a decade. He noted that Kardan's status as an Israeli company gave it a relative advantage in its activity in China.[251] "Unlike other countries, where we tend to downplay our Israeli identity, in China we emphasize it. The Chinese love Israel and especially the Jews, mainly because of the common denominator of a long history, going back thousands of years."

As we have emphasized, despite China's massive potential, Israeli companies do not find it easy to operate there. Kardan succeeded in penetrating China slowly and carefully, and only after it accumulated experience in another developing market—Central and Eastern Europe. "We wanted to duplicate our success in Central and Eastern Europe in a new location," Greenfeld said of the company's decision to enter the Chinese market. "China is a place that to a certain extent matches the reality that existed in the central region of Eastern Europe in the early 1990s—a new market that was previously closed to private initiatives, with high demand in the real estate sector. Transformations such as what took place in those countries, which are meant to close gaps of decades against more developed nations, take place only once in centuries. From our point of view, China is the gate to entering Asia. It is leading the entire continent to accelerated economic development. According to research carried out by the OECD, in 2020 the middle class in the Asia-Pacific region will reach 1.7 billion people, and will represent 54 percent of the middle class in the world."[252]

In 2003 Kardan sent Shlank to China to examine the feasibility of activity there. For over a year he investigated the potential market, and finally the company decided that the best way to penetrate the Chinese market was by connecting to a local partner. Accordingly, Kardan connected with Lucky Hope Company, headed by Professor Wilson Yang, a Chinese academic

---

251 Interview with Alon Shlank, May 7, 2014. For detailed information on Kardan's activities mainly in China through March 2017, see Kardan N.V., Barnea Report dated March 23 (retrieved November 12, 2017), especially chapter C.

252 Ibid.

who had moved into the real estate market. In 2005 Kardan leased its first terrain in China. Within six years Kardan's activity in China had expanded significantly, and it employed six hundred individuals, 98 percent of them Chinese. The company owned a number of housing projects and shopping malls in several cities. In 2007 it began activity in the field of water purification in several Chinese districts.

Shlank identified a number of complications and obstacles in promoting business activity in China. He emphasized that the culture is different, and that in China it is vital to understand the other party. Successful local cooperation depends on continuously maintaining mutual interests. When examining a new business, foreign companies must gain awareness of the other party's considerations and try to understand them. This applies to both private and public entities. The long meals that the two sides share are an important part of the local business activity and help to achieve this goal of mutual understanding.

In 2016 Kardan's real estate initiatives covered a combined area of three million square meters in cities that were second- and third-tier with regard to size. In total, Kardan had invested some 350 million dollars of its own capital, and the total investment in the new businesses in China was expected to reach one billion dollars. The China investment produced yearly IRR (internal revenue return) of at least 15 percent per property.

Greenfeld explained that Kardan decided to invest in second- and third-tier cities because the level of risk in the very large first-tier cities such as Beijing and Shanghai was higher due to variable land prices and property values. A possible decline of 10 percent in property value might translate into large sums. In addition, the competition in these locations was against large companies or government companies, which had structural advantages over any private company, making competition with them undesirable. By contrast, markets where no company held a significant advantage were more attractive for investment. In cities with three to ten million inhabitants, the local government viewed Kardan's activity favorably and invited it to participate in additional initiatives.

One of Kardan's projects is an apartment building in Xi'an, a city with 8.5 million residents. By Chinese standards this is a medium-size project—but by Israeli norms, it is enormous. The project, called "Olympic Garden," is designed to house twenty-five thousand individuals in 9,363 housing units. During the Olympics every city in China was permitted to use this name for one of its housing projects, and the name helped Kardan to promote its project. Olympic Garden extends over 135 acres and was built with an investment of 350 million Euro. The project boasts a luxurious sales office similar to sales offices for luxury apartments in Israel. The company employs a team of marketing and sales people who start their mornings with an exercise regimen before beginning another day of selling apartments.

From the films documenting the sales events, we can observe the buyers' excitement, even hysteria. Customers stood in a lengthy line, and drawings were held for choosing apartments. Some said that the lofts were snapped up like hot rolls. One factor that contributed to the project's success was the emphasis placed on construction of educational institutions. "In this project, we provide a solution for education, with a Singapore-style kindergarten and school that are operated by a high-quality educational institution. This enabled us to attract a quality population," Applerot related in an interview with *Globes*, the Israeli business daily. The school has nine hundred pupils, and this number is expected to grow to two thousand. At first the school was built as a marketing tool (the population requested it), but later it became an independent, profitable project in its own right. Whatever the reason, apartment prices rose by about 10 percent.

With the confidence Kardan acquired from this business success, it then moved on to its real field of expertise: construction and operation of shopping malls. In 2010 Kardan opened the Galleria Mall in Chengdu, which covers a gross area of ninety-two thousand square meters. Some fifteen million residents live in metropolitan Chengdu, which is experiencing accelerated construction and is branded as a "healthy" city. It is a young city with an elevated level of consumerism. This is where Kardan decided to construct an impressive mall, and this is also where Applerot asserted one may experience a taste of the "new China," an Eden for innovative architecture.

Kardan did not stop with real estate. After searching and studying, the company entered activity in the water sector, mainly waste water treatment, where return is between 15 and 18 percent. Iris Arbel, manager of Kardan's water operation in China, noted that China uses one-fourth of the world's water, and that it suffers from a shortage of potable drinking water. China was unaware that this was a precious commodity that must be conserved, so water prices were low—too low. In developed countries, water is between 2 and 3 percent of income, while in China it was only 0.3 percent. More importantly, while the government was hesitant in the real estate sector and activity there was sometimes challenging, in the water treatment sector the path was relatively smooth. The government encouraged—and still encourages—new initiatives, particularly if they are backed by promised investments of foreign capital.

In the field of real estate Kardan develops its projects from zero. But in the water sector it purchases existing facilities, streamlines and improves them, and sometimes even initiates and constructs new factories. For example, the company purchased a facility for forty million dollars in a city near Beijing, and then upgraded it. Purification of water from the river adjoining the facility is performed in three stages. At the end of the purification process, two-thirds of the water is returned to the river from which it is pumped. The Israeli company then sells the remaining one-third of the water for use by industry in the region in cooperation with the government, which is encouraging the field.[253] This process is considered more profitable, and the company made an advance agreement with the government on the price.

It thus seems that until recently, Kardan's history in China exemplified success. Its secret included considerate management and paying attention to the cultural differences between China and the West. This was done not by remote control from Tel Aviv, but from within China (Shlank divided his time equally between the two countries, while Applerot lived in China). Only when the managers live in China can they accurately evaluate risks and opportunities, avoiding the trap of misleading sentiments and impressions. According to Shlank, a commander who is disconnected from the business front will never be given the full picture.

China has presented impressive growth figures, rapidly reducing the gap with the United States. Within a few years it is expected to replace the United States as the largest economy in the world. Still, we cannot ignore the fact that despite its enormous size, China is still dependent on the global economy and influenced by it, as it is mainly an export economy. The crises currently affecting the United States and Europe call into question China's ability to continue to grow at the same rate as in recent years. Yet it is possible that local Chinese consumption will slowly replace its dependence on the rest of the world, and China's huge reserves will help it overcome the global slowdown. Shlank believes that even if China is hurt by the decline in US consumption, it will have the independent means to compensate for

---

253 Interview with Alon Shlank, May 7, 2014.

this. Investments will come from home. For example, the subway project in Dalian in the north, planned to begin in 2018, was pushed forward by several years to contribute to growth. Still, this may have negative consequences, mainly accelerated inflation and a real estate bubble.

In other words, the question arises as to whether the window of opportunity that pushed Kardan ahead in China is limited, and to what extent positioning Kardan as a Chinese company may endanger it in the long term. In addition, we also ask if we can correctly evaluate Kardan China, which is a subsidiary dependent on the activity of the group in Eastern Europe, as a separate unit—and to what extent its status as part of this group endangers it.

Still, it is clear that Kardan in China did not repeat the mistakes made by the "first generation." It checked the needs of the Chinese more cautiously and carefully studied the regulations that applied in the country. For example, its status as a foreign company actually gave it a relative advantage, as local governments were measured by the foreign investments that they were able to bring to their fields. As noted, Kardan approached the second- and third-tier cities, locations where foreign investors (and even local ones, to some extent) were not standing in line to operate. Using its relative advantage (construction of commercial centers) and creating the correct, judicious combination of mall occupants and residential projects proved to be a breakthrough formula.

In contrast to the past, Kardan did not face any difficulties in sending profits outside China. If there had been any difficulty, it was expressed in the prohibition against bringing in loan money for real estate. We may assume the purpose of this prohibition was to prevent an unwanted bubble. There was no such limitation on equity capital. In the water sector there were no limitations, mainly due to priorities set by the government.

Kardan analyzed the local needs and preferences, and they thus internalized local policy and found the openings that enabled maximum exploitation of their business advantages. They were also able to define the product that the local clients would prefer; they understood what kind of apartment would appeal to the Chinese family, what kind of bathroom and shower they would prefer, and how to plan the bathroom—all while taking Feng Shui philosophy into consideration. The project managers also paid attention to issues such as obtaining the necessary permits and financing, relying heavily on local partners.

In the housing field Kardan faced no dilemma regarding the Chinese consumers' payment practices, since the method determined was that the purchaser would pay the entire price of the apartment in advance. Even if the purchaser took a mortgage on the apartment, this was the purchaser's responsibility, and managing the details of the deal was between the customer and the bank. The company received payment well before completion of construction, sometimes three or four months after signature of the contract.

In general, Kardan moved to working on large projects—development of commercial properties. In the final analysis, this is what gave added value to the shareholders. Kardan managers thought that their relative advantage might fade with time, but meanwhile they had stability and income. Managing projects after completion of construction was also important and offered a significant advantage. Proper management and maintaining the project appropriately increased its value. This attitude is not characteristic of the Chinese investor, who viewed the building as the main asset, while Kardan viewed the tenant as more important.

Sales of commercial properties were made not to tenants but to investors, as partial sale of the property caused deterioration and reduced its value. The concept of the "integrated project," in which an apartment building was constructed next to an office building, both of which were then offered for sale, improved the overall project and assisted in financing construction of the center, which usually remained under company ownership.

Kardan purchased Tahal, Water Planning for Israel Ltd., from the Israeli government. Tahal specialized in planning and implementing projects in the water sector. In China Kardan founded a new company that held discussions with local governments on constructing water and waste treatment plants. Usually, a company was given a concession for a period of twenty-five years, whether designated for the entire project or part of it. Company activity was backed by local government guarantees, and after the concession period, the company would return the license to the authorities. Usually, Shlank said, in most locations the company would find an organized facility with appropriate infrastructure. Sometimes, the company decided to improve the existing facility and operated it only after the necessary investment.

The company's advantage was mainly in unique fields such as multiple usages, which means purifying water and selling it for cooling turbines and other purposes. Water that had undergone professional treatment could be used for agriculture, industry, and watering gardens. In the fields of infrastructure and water (in light of the threat against the continued expansion of the Chinese economy due to environmental problems), there was a risk of social discontent at certain locations. An urgent need arose for a solution to a wide range of problems, and China decided to open the gates to business in these fields to foreign entities, who would bring with them experience as well as financial means. Thus the government accelerated the process of developing the infrastructure and water fields.

Yoram Gavison, business writer, observed that although Kardan's was a success story of an Israeli company in China, this did not necessarily mean financial success for the entire Kardan Group represented by mother company Kardan N.V. In July 2014, for example, Kardan N.V. management acted to secure the resources required for payment of its debts.[254] It was given a "B" rating by the S&P Maalot ratings company. At the same time, a negative rating forecast was made for the company's bonds due to delays in obtaining the required cash, past the September 2014 deadline. Suspicion arose of a failed quarter after a "Going Concern Notice"[255] due to a debt of 130 million Euro between the monetary resources available to Kardan and its monetary requirements (between June 2014 and the end of 2015). The problem was payment of the capital and the interest, which meant the company had to quickly sell property to meet the payments. The forecasts predicted that Kardan Land China, which represented 70 percent of the value of the entire company's assets, would be forced to contribute its relative portion by selling properties, even though the Chinese company was profitable. The economists assumed that KFS (Kardan Group's financial arm), which was active in the financial market in Eastern Europe, was the main reason for the losses. Accordingly, in March 2015, the media reported that Kardan N.V. had taken several steps, mainly sale of its operations in the industrial water sector in China, alongside additional moves such as selling partial ownership of Kardan Land China.[256]

---

254 Gavison, "Maalot: Kardan NV's Only Opportunity."
255 Note attached by a company accountant to its financial reports, if there is any suspicion that it might not continue as an active business.
256 Gavison, "Kardan Completed the Sale of 75% of the Chinese Water Company for 100 Million Euros," *The Marker*, March 3, 2015; see Michael Rochvarger, *Ha'Aretz*, January 6, 2016. Indeed, Kardan was undergoing serious dynamic changes. For an updated account on Kardan, see Kardan N.V., Barnea Report dated March 23 (retrieved November 12, 2017), especially section C.

Beginning in spring 2015, the company experienced several difficulties, while in China the residential market wavered. The future success of the joint venture was undermined. Although completed projects were sold at a profit, some were left unfinished and caused cash flow problems. Greenfeld was left 350 million NIS in debt. In recent years, the value of his shares in Kardan N.V. and Kardan Yazamut had plunged 95 percent, and one of the banks began bankruptcy proceedings against him.[257]

At a conference on the issue of foreign and Israeli firms operating in China, Ohad Cohen, head of foreign trade in the Ministry of the Economy and the man responsible for formulating export policy and promoting Israeli exports to China, asserted that over the past twenty years, Israeli exports had been diverted from Western markets to China.[258] Israel's export obstacles to China include limitations on exporting products to the Middle Kingdom and a lack of businesspeople who are knowledgeable about China and its ways. Still, Cohen noted a trend of improvement on both sides while recognizing the uniqueness of each economy. Cohen described steps that his office took to strengthen exports to China: aid in understanding regulation and Chinese bureaucracy, aid in funding representative offices in China, and giving topic-specific grants, among others.

Gal Furer, an attorney who worked in China for many years and attempted to promote business there, agreed that misunderstandings often resulted due to a lack of appropriate communication, language barriers, and cultural differences. Expanding on this, he listed the issues of regulation, corruption, and failure to honor contracts, as well as the legal aspect and the political agenda, which involve an inherent culture of bribery and protectionism that are difficult to circumvent. He also noted the problem of the Chinese go-between who is sometimes appointed a manager on behalf of the company. Sometimes a foreign company might hire a Chinese person, thinking that his craftiness would prove useful. But the foreign company fails to realize that this local hire was likely to act against the interests of his new employers.

In general the two sides seem to have suffered—and still suffer—from the sin of hubris, or false pride. Westerners tend to define themselves as "China experts" after a short learning period despite their paltry experience.

---

257 Sadeh, "Yosef Greenfeld's Battle for Survival," *The Marker*, April 24, 2015.
258 Conference on doing business in China, Faculty of Business Administration, Tel Aviv University, July 2013.

Arrogant "Orientalist" attitudes still prevail, leading to lack of willingness to accept the aid of individuals with many years of experience in China.

The Chinese are also arrogant following their economic success, currency reserves, and other achievements. Indeed, when European nations are desperately begging China to purchase their bonds or invest in infrastructure projects in their countries, China is well able to exploit the situation to its advantage.

At the conference mentioned above, attendees also discussed the question of whether Israeli companies had a future in China. Alon Teichtal, a senior vice president and director of the Asian region for Netafim, noted that professional consulting was lacking. He admitted that his company had learned from its mistakes—(the company's initiatives in Guangzhou and Shenyang had ended on a sour note). Thus while throughout the globe, Netafim dominates some 35 percent of the drip irrigation market in the agricultural sector, in China it holds less than 1 percent.

Boaz Horowitz, CEO of China Direct, and Iris Arbel, who worked for Kardan in China, noted that management according to a "female" model was appropriate for activity in China. In this model, managers avoid direct confrontations and embarrassing the Chinese, and try to learn and understand the other side's wants and aspirations. For his salespeople, Horowitz added, he didn't try to recruit the best manager in the field but rather outstanding women who were university students. In a brief time, they became senior managers and were remarkably successful.

In an interview[259] Arbel recalled an important entity: China's National Development and Reform Commission (NDRC). This commission has much influence, and if foreign companies approach it with ideas that its managers support enthusiastically, as in Kardan's case, the companies can achieve excellent results. Proposals made to the Chinese should fit Chinese policy at that moment in time. If a specific field of activity is not designated for backing, it will be difficult to achieve results. It is therefore important to obtain correct and current information in this area.

This chapter has analyzed the activity of four Israeli companies in China, with the goal of studying and comprehending their modes of operation and the consequent results. Possibly, there are one or two lessons to be learned from the case studies presented here. Many Israeli companies have tried their luck in China—some of them well-known. As some of the

---

259 Interview by Or Biron with Iris Arbel, Tel Aviv, July 18, 2013.

interviewees here noted, luck was often a factor in the functioning of the companies, whether in success or failure. Established Israeli companies that have acted and are still operating in China and that have faced regulatory and other obstacles include Super-Pharm, Ormat (operating in the field of energy, electricity, and power stations that use alternative energy, mainly geothermal), Gadot Biochemistry, Teva, and the Israel Corporation (under Idan Ofer, who absorbed losses of hundreds of millions of dollars from the company's investment in Qoros, the Chinese car manufacturer).[260] This list is only partial. From the case studies above, we may assume that a number of these companies lost money. Only some are willing to admit this openly, much less to give detailed information about the extent of the losses and the reasons surrounding them.

---

260 Hagai Amit, "Four Billion Shekels—2014 Was a Record Year for the Growing Businesses between China and Israel," *The Marker*, March 9, 2015.

Chapter Seven

1992 to 2018: Beijing and Jerusalem—The Last Battle?

On their visits to China, Israeli leaders have discovered an impressive modern state. While the international community expresses admiration for China's unprecedented construction and outstanding level of manufacturing and exports, China's leaders are not content to rest on their laurels. This foreign praise often contains a hint of arrogance, as representatives of the developed world point to the admirable progress of a state that was considered backward in recent history. Thus China is now focusing on transforming this image, aiming to translate the impressive achievements of the Open Door Policy, which began in the 1980s, into global influence—strategic, political, and diplomatic. The Olympic Games in 2008 and the Expo 2010 exhibition were mere steps on this ladder.

In recent years visits of Chinese leaders to South America and Africa have become part of this new approach, guaranteeing China political sway that will empower it to enter other parts of the world and accumulate more power in the global arena. Beyond honor and prestige, China craves influence that will enable it to immortalize its achievements in the world. Until the outbreak of the economic crisis in 2008, world powers battled over access to raw materials. However, this was only a prelude to the economic and diplomatic crises that visited the world in the following decade. In the context of crises on the world markets, such as in the summer of 2011, and the conflicting predictions that are voiced regarding China's future, questions arise regarding the shape of future competition between China and the United States. Issues on the contemporary agenda include control over raw materials and political hegemony in various areas of the world, particularly Asia and Africa. As for Israel, the contemporary situation inspires us to ask: what approach should Israel adopt with regard to China?

In general the United States is no longer flying high as in the past. In fact, it might even be sinking in its own economic morass. The swollen budget deficit has led to an increase in American debts both at home and abroad.[261] In contrast to the Chinese, the American government spends much more money on defense than it collects in taxes. At present, the United States is collapsing under the financial burden of loans taken at home and abroad. The government is not the only American entity that spends more than it collects: national savings and the real estate market are both registering downturns.

In the past, approximately forty-two cents of each dollar that the US government spent was not American money—instead, it came in the form of loans, which have reached the astronomical sum of 14.3 trillion dollars.

In theory, China and the other nations that hold some 50 percent of US Treasury bonds could flood the market and thus raise interest rates and inflate the US national debt. Such a scenario could turn into a vicious circle in which the interest rates continue to rise and the debt continues to inflate.

In complete contrast to the situation in the United States, in mid-September 2011 Italy asked China to purchase a portion of its bonds. Spain, Greece, Portugal, and Hungary followed suit for a total value of ten billion Euro. By doing so, China assisted the governments in stabilizing their economies as well as the global market economy. China began to pave a road that could transform it into the savior of the world economy, taking the place of the United States, which had previously played this role. Although in the past this scenario may have sounded like something out of a science fiction film, today it has become realistic.

In light of this situation, clearly the United States cannot dictate steps of any kind to China. Gently but firmly, Beijing deflects the attempts of the decision-makers in Washington to detect its global interests and block them. China continues to put down stakes in South America, Saudi Arabia, Iran, and many other countries, including the Middle East.[262] It is also consolidating its position in the China Sea while attempting active defense of the islands in the region. In the spring and early summer of 2015, tension rose surrounding the controversial islands in the South China Sea in reaction to the news that China had armed the artificial islands it created in the area. This tension continues to date.

---

261 Rivlin, "The Economic Melt-Down (1)."
262 Many articles address this topic. See, for example, Johnson, "Balancing China's Growing Influence."

Previously the United States had acts that Beijing considered provocative. In January 2010, the Barack Obama administration informed Congress that they planned to sell $6.4 billion worth of weapons to Taiwan. Three weeks later, on February 8, 2010, Obama held a historic meeting with the Dalai Lama during which he offered American support for preserving the status of the exiled Tibetan leader. These two acts provoked furious reactions from Beijing.

Even if the delicate equilibrium between the two powers has not been violated, we can no longer ignore the developments and dynamics in the global arena.

China's economic statistics are impressive. By 2007 China was exporting more than it imported. In that year its trade balance reached over $256 billion—much higher than that of the United States. This balance remained stable even after the global economic crisis of September 2008. In April 2009 China offered its Asian neighbors twenty-five billion dollars in credit, aiming to help them overcome the crisis. These generous offers had an overt political motivation—strengthening China's influence in the region. These offers of financial assistance made China the first to show public signs of recovery from the crisis. China was the third largest economy in the world, and it rapidly advanced to second place. In March 2009 the Central Bank of China announced that the economic steps the government had taken late the previous year had pulled their country out of the crisis. By 2012 China's economy was growing at unprecedented annual levels.

In 2016 China's exports totaled $2.06 trillion while its imports totaled $1.32 trillion, resulting in a trade balance of $0.74 trillion. In 2010 China's GDP was estimated at $5.87 trillion (thereby bypassing Japan, whose GDP was estimated at $5.47 trillion). With this, China became the second largest economy in the world after the United States. In 2016 China's GDP increased to $11.20 trillion, and by 2020 it is expected to become the largest economy based on GDP. Recently, China has even bypassed the United States to become Europe's largest trade partner.[263]

Since the beginning of economic reforms in China in the 1970s and 1980s, the poverty level has significantly declined. Income per person in

---

263 OEC, http://atlas.media.mit.edu/en/profile/country/chn (retrieved April 2, 2018), and "China Surpasses U.S. as EU's Top Trade Partner," *Xinhua*, October 16, 2011: http://news.xinhuanet.com/english2010/china/2011-10/16/c_131194386.htm

2016[264] was equivalent to \$15,500 in purchasing power parity (PPP).[265] In December 2016 China's foreign currency reserves stood at just over three trillion dollars. This was after China's foreign exchange reserves had fallen for a sixth straight month after authorities stepped in to support the yuan.[266] Its rate of savings (gross savings as a share of GDP) remains almost the highest in the world: some 50 percent of GDP, as opposed to the global average of around 30 percent.[267]

Furthermore, China makes wise use of "soft power" to improve its global image. As Indian researchers Parama Sinha Palit and Amitendu Palit indicated, the Chinese use this strategy regularly to advance their political goals.[268] "Soft power" acts like a gentle spearhead, enabling breakthroughs into markets and neutralizing criticism of the Chinese regime on human rights issues. The Chinese adopt this approach with consistency and determination, aiming to create a more moderate image of their country and deflect criticism of their policies on controversial issues. The expression "soft power" appears in China's ancient history as far back as the time of the philosopher Lao Tzu. In modern times, it has been mentioned and discussed by E. H. Carr and Joseph Nye. The Chinese ideal of the "good neighbor" (睦邻友好 mulin youhao), which means that one should behave in a generous and friendly manner toward partners and neighbors, is also based on this philosophical core. One example of the implementation of this philosophy is the nearly five hundred Confucius Institutes that the Chinese government sponsors around the world.[269] Thousands of foreign representatives from these institutes, including artists, intellectuals, and academics, visit China at the invitation of the Chinese government, and they enjoy an enthusiastic reception.

Yet although economic and cultural measures earn world recognition and seem to indicate the rising power of Beijing, we cannot ignore

---

264 Not including Hong Kong and Macau.

265 https://tradingeconomics.com/china/gdp-per-capita-ppp (retrieved November 28, 2017).

266 https://www.cnbc.com/2017/01/06/china-foreign-exchange-reserves-fall-in-december-to-lowest-since-february-2011.html (retrieved November 28, 2017) and Urbanek, "China's foreign exchange reserves."

267 https://www.cnbc.com/2015/10/25/china-savings-rate-versus-the-world-in-a-chart.html (retrieved November 28, 2017).

268 The concept of "soft power" was studied intensely in 2012 and 2013. For more on "soft power" in China's foreign and domestic policy, see Barr, *Who's Afraid of China?*

269 "China's Confucius Institutes to reach 500 global cities by 2020," *Xinhua*: http://news.xinhuanet.com/english/china/2013-03/11/c_132225228.htm, March 11, 2013.

the theory of an approaching collapse. This theory was common before the recent economic crisis and is bolstered by findings that call into question the optimistic forecasts regarding China's future.

Back in 2001, Gordon Chang wrote in *The Coming Collapse of China* that China might strengthen its economic hold on Asia and throughout the world.[270] He admitted that China had the potential necessary to achieve this goal and therefore it demanded international recognition as a global power equal to the United States and the European Union. Still, Chang also presented the possibility that China is merely a "paper dragon" on the edge of collapse (hinting at the phrase "paper tiger" that Mao used for the states that threatened China). Among the signs indicating reinforcement of this trend, Chang noted corruption within the Chinese government and the Communist Party; the "battalions of unemployed" in the streets throughout the state; unprofitable companies under government ownership (State-Owned Enterprises, SOE); loans given by Chinese banks that were not repaid; and China's budget deficit, which swelled in the years preceding publication of his book. According to Chang, even the fact that China joined the World Trade Organization was no harbinger of good tidings but rather "undermined China's foundations." In fact, he argued in a somewhat determinist manner, China's leaders had no way to prevent the "tragedy in the making" that was rapidly approaching.

In the seventeen years since publication of his book, Chang's pessimistic forecasts have not been realized. For example, China's joining the World Trade Organization led to no harm. Still, Chang's basic argument was voiced and even sometimes accepted in professional circles. The journal *Alternative Perspective* adopted a similar line of thought. In a detailed article, Madhukar Shukla made assertions similar to Chang's, casting doubt on China's promising future.[271] The journal emphasized these facts: over 50 percent of China's international trade was carried out through foreign direct investments, over 50 percent of this trade was intra-company trade (between branches of the same company), and China was sometimes the last link in the global supply chain. This last fact caused trade deficits against most East Asian economies, although China has still had hefty trade surpluses against the United States (and against other developed countries as well).

---

270 Chang, *The Coming Collapse of China*.
271 Madhukar, "A World Deceived by Numbers/Facts."

A high percentage of China's international trade is export of raw materials and half-finished products. In addition, a few years ago the Chinese government determined that the level of poverty is seventy-six dollars per year (compared to $365 per year, the usual level given in World Bank reports). Further, China has the widest income disparity in the world between village and urban populations.

Another chilling forecast regarding China's future was published in 2011 by Nouriel Roubini, who earned the nickname "dark prince of the financial markets" after he predicted the crisis of 2008. Roubini criticized the infrastructure initiatives in China, which he asserted were not at all necessary in a country of China's level of development. Roubini also predicted that China's policy of "overinvestment" was doomed to failure both at home and abroad. Therefore, its growth would experience a significant slowdown as soon as it could no longer expand investments in fixed properties (fixed investments), apparently beginning in 2013.[272]

Carl Walter and Fraser Howie expressed a similar opinion in their 2011 book, *Red Capitalism: The Fragile Financial Foundation of China's Extraordinary Rise.*[273] Their theory is based on data provided by Chinese financial institutions, mainly banks. They argue that China's economy is no different from other economies in the world, and that we cannot attribute China's smooth sailing through the global economic crisis to its closed financial system. The design of their system does not permit individuals or companies to adopt any position that opposes the government. Thus while the private sector in China that deals in exports was severely hurt in 2008 and 2009, meaning loss of jobs, income, and even closure of small businesses and larger companies, the Chinese banks did not experience this setback. According to the authors, the government-owned economy is "inside the system" while the private sector will always remain "outside the system." In addition, local debt is high in relation to GDP and is expected to increase further in the coming years.

Various data indicate that Chinese debt is likely to grow far beyond the international standard. In other words, China has accumulated a very

---

272 For more pessimistic forecasts on China, see:
Roubini, "China's Bad Growth Bet," *Project Syndicate*
http://www.projec. syndicate.org/commentary/roubini37/English
http://www.bloomberg.com/news/2011-06-28/shilling-why-china-is-heading-for-a-hard-landing-pt-3.html

273 See pp. ix, x.

large public debt and, like other countries in Asia, its budget also relies on the continuation of debt accumulation. In China the government controls the banks, and the government orders them to give loans to state-owned institutions. This mode of activity prevents transparency in the Chinese economy. In the case of Greece, for example, preliminary financial data met the requirements for entering the European Union, and it took more than a decade for the failures and problems to surface. If such a scenario happened in the Greek economy, which is an open economy, we may assume that in the controlled Chinese economy it will take even longer for the truth to be exposed. Therefore, economic crises might come knocking on China's door. Further, comprehensive reform in the Chinese banking system does not seem to be on the horizon. Even if such a reform were considered in the past, we may assume that the lessons of the economic crisis of 2008 pushed China even further away from this direction. The bankruptcy of companies such as Lehman Brothers in 2008 weakened the arguments of those who called for greater transparency in China and for openness and international activity in the Chinese economy.

Walter and Howie note that China explains the complexity of its economic system in a declaration that appears accurate: "Our economy is different from the Western model, and therefore the Chinese market also operates differently from the Western markets." They continue: "From the outside, the Chinese economy seems like a success story. Exponential growth began and has continued throughout the past decade. But this is only the external package . . . . There is no way to know whether the words 'stocks,' 'bonds,' 'capital,' or 'market' have the same meaning in the economy and political system in China."[274]

Other information supports these pessimistic assertions. Before the economic crisis of 2008, at least 150 million villagers migrated from the countryside to the cities, searching for jobs. Many of them were forced to take temporary jobs at low salaries and untenable conditions. In addition, China's population is aging at a rapid pace due to the one-child policy it has followed since the 1970s. Another threat to China's growth is the ecological and environmental issue: air pollution, water pollution, and continuous sinking of the groundwater level, particularly in the northern part of the country. The problem of soil erosion and continued economic development is leading to widespread loss of agricultural lands.

---

274 Ibid., 214.

However, when we compare the two types of forecasts, it seems that the optimistic forecasts have the upper hand. The reason for this is that China has been able to identify problematic global trends and stabilize them. The Olympic Games of 2008 and Expo 2010 aided China in promoting its position and image in the economic and political arenas as well as overcoming problems at home. Additionally, the Chinese government took drastic steps to stabilize and overcome the negative consequences of the economic crisis of 2008. Clearly, the relative weakness of civil society on one hand and the government's ability to neutralize a majority of public objection on the other enabled the regime to overcome all opposition successfully.

Furthermore, during the "Arab Spring" and the intense socio-economic protests in Israel in the summer of 2011, citizens in the West called on their governments to tighten their supervisory roles, increase budgets, abandon extreme free market models, and adopt economic policies that were more planned and centralized—in other words, to take a more active part in the national economy. Such changes were unnecessary in China, as it was already following these policies. This undoubtedly represents China's relative advantage. As a socialist state with unique characteristics, it can easily avoid a market economy that is too free. Other countries find it difficult to make this decision unilaterally.

The seeds of China's economic future were sown during Hu Jintao's term as president of China. In his speech at the Eighteenth Congress of the Communist Party in November 2012, Hu presented an ambitious plan, which included reorganization of the Chinese economy, doubling of the 2010 GNP by 2020, nurturing growth in the field of green energy, and encouraging local consumption.[275]

In March 2013 during the conclusion of the National People's Congress, China's new leaders Xi Jinping and Li Keqiang presented a plan with even more far-reaching steps—a list of broad reforms expected to be carried out in the state by 2020. These include easing the "one child policy," which levies sanctions against families that have more than one child; annulment of capital punishment for certain crimes; and closure of the labor camps, which are a constant target of harsh criticism by global human rights organizations. Alongside additional improvements in the fields of human rights and ecology, the publication also mentions economic reforms that will reduce

---

275 "Full Text of Hu Jintao's Report at 18th Party Congress," *Xinhua*, November 17, 2012: http://news.xinhuanet.com/english/special/18cpcnc/2012-11/17/c_131981259.htm

the government's involvement in the economy, encourage privatization, and remove limitations on business initiatives and activity, mainly in the real estate field.[276]

What is the relevance of these issues for our discussion of China–Israel relations?

Apparently, the answer is that Israel's attitude toward China must continue to evolve if it is to preserve its success and pace of growth in future decades. This is particularly true if the United States continues to undergo political, economic, and even military decline, as Emmanuel Wallerstein and other experts on history and political science have argued.[277] In addition, the American government during Barack Obama's second term as president adopted a slightly more critical stance toward Israel in the international arena, a deviation from the "special relationship" that had characterized relations between the two countries in the past. The question relating to the Trump administration remains open. It seems, however, that he is adopting what may be described as a "pro-Israel" policy.

At any rate, Israel may have to periodically reevaluate its longstanding policy on China and adopt a more assertive and innovative stance. Perhaps Israel should even encourage broader involvement for China in the Israeli–Palestinian problem, as well as in the tense situation between Israel on one side and Syria and Iran on the other.

Some argue that in the broader international sphere, Israel–China relations are not so important. China–US relations, the China–India–US triangle, and even China's status in the UN Security Council—all these are certainly much more important. But we argue that Israel–China relations do have significance, especially with regard to Israel's strategic and military role in the Middle East equation. China is interested in becoming a full partner in the peace process. We learn this, for example, from the Chinese government's appointment of a special envoy to the Middle East and from

---

276 "China Legislators Vote to End Labour Camps," *AFP* (retrieved December 24, 2013), http://news.yahoo.com/china-formalise-reforms-one-child-policy-labour-camps-033439167.html and Ben Blanchard and Kevin Yao, "China Unveils Boldest Reforms in Decades, Shows Xi in Command," *Reuters*, November 15, 2013, http://www.reuters.com/article/2013/11/15/us-china-reform-idUSBRE9AE0BL20131115 For the March 2018 National People's Congress, see http://www.npc.gov.cn/englishnpc/news/ (retrieved April 15, 2018).

277 Wallerstein, Immanuel, "The United States and Israel: The Approaching Separation," *Mita'am* 12 (December 2007): 89–99.

China's growing concern about the Israeli–Palestinian conflict. China also seems to expect Israel, especially within the Belt and Road Initiative, to become one of China's major suppliers of advanced technology, share its know-how and success in the realm of innovation, and perhaps even renew cooperation regarding security and military equipment.

China, Israel, and Hong Kong

With Hong Kong's accelerated economic development since the 1960s, Israeli companies (like others around the globe) have used this port city as a center for shipping and local trade. Hong Kong has benefitted from a well-developed economic and communications infrastructure as well as a free economic climate, and its connections with China have granted it a significant additional advantage. Hong Kong has served as the regional headquarters for the Israeli Zim Shipping Company in East Asia and as a central port for exports and imports to states in the region, including sporadic, indirect deals with China.[278]

In 1973 Israel opened a consulate general in Hong Kong, which sparked hopes for renewed relations with China. But two years down the road, the Israelis realized that their efforts to improve relations with China were doomed to failure. What was more, due to budget constraints, Consul Emmanuel Gelber was sent home from the British colony. The consulate offices continued to function, albeit at a more modest level, under the direction of a local Jewish businessman who was appointed honorary consul.

The 1984 Sino–British agreement on the future of Hong Kong and its return to China created a new window of opportunity for promoting cooperation between Jerusalem and Beijing. A paragraph in the agreement determined that "representations of the countries that do not have formal diplomatic relations with China may remain in Hong Kong or become semi-formal representations." Following this, Israel reopened the consulate general, and hopes rose that the city would become an important bridge to greater China, a meeting point for formal and informal contact with the Chinese. Indeed diplomats, businesspeople, academics, and tourists from Israel took full advantage of the new situation. Aside from contact with the

---

278 Merhav, "Dream of the Red Palaces," 567.

local Jewish and Israeli communities and routine promotion of contacts with Israel, the consulate general offered its services to Israeli companies.

Diplomat Reuven Merhav was sent to serve as the Israeli Consul General in Hong Kong, and one of his missions was to examine possibilities for creating ties with China. According to Merhav, Hong Kong could serve as a bridge for promoting ties between the two countries. As a first step, Merhav began by constructing a foundation for academic ties. In 1987 he visited Beijing, thus becoming the first Israeli diplomat to be granted the opportunity to bridge the gap between the two states. One year later Merhav was appointed as director general of the Foreign Ministry, and he continued his efforts in the China sphere.

After 1997, when Hong Kong became an integral part of China as a "Special Administrative Region" (SAR), Israel's relations with the former British colony continued normally. For many years Hong Kong was one of Israel's major trade partners in Asia. It was a gateway for Israeli merchandise entering China and for Chinese exports to Israel. However, the establishment of full diplomatic relations between Israel and China in 1992 largely limited Hong Kong's importance in the fabric of relations between the two states.

Patience Pays Off: Gradual Establishment of Diplomatic Relations

Reopening the consulate in Hong Kong played a foundational role in the creation of diplomatic channels between China and Israel. The academic ties that were made possible largely thanks to this office played a central role in paving the way toward diplomatic connections. Business relationships between the states began to form, as we learn from the story of Shaul Eisenberg (although his efforts began much earlier, in the late 1970s). This was made possible thanks to the rise of Deng Xiaoping and the policy of the Four Modernizations that he announced. Israel had much to offer in fields that interested China: agriculture, science and technology, industry, and national defense.

Israeli agricultural experts came to China as early as the late 1970s. But at this stage, China still upheld a defiantly negative stance toward Israel—it constantly rejected Israel's policies and maintained its position as a friend of the PLO and Arab states. A certain change in China's attitude was recognizable following Egyptian President Anwar Sadat's visit to Israel in 1977 and the inauguration of the Israeli–Egyptian peace talks. Although the

Chinese did not cease their propaganda attacks on Israel, they refrained from criticizing the nascent peace process, and their attitude to this development seemed positive.[279]

In the 1980s China's attitude toward the State of Israel gradually began to thaw. This process is illustrated by a study of statements made by various senior representatives. Alongside condemnations, China began to recognize Israel's legitimate status. During a 1982 visit to Cairo, Chinese Prime Minister Zhao Ziyang said that all Middle Eastern states—including Israel—should enjoy recognition of the right to exist and to independence. However, China conditioned this acceptance on Israeli withdrawal from the territories occupied in 1967 and granting the Palestinian people the right to self-determination and their own state.

During his visit to Egypt in 1985, the Chinese foreign minister declared that China would not establish official ties with Israel as long as Israel continued to uphold its policy toward the Palestinians. Still, in an unprecedented step, he added that China distinguished between the Israeli government and the Israeli people and that it did not rule out academic relations with Israeli experts as individuals, through international organizations as intermediaries. From that point academic exchanges began between the two states.

At first, Israeli scientists visited China, and these were followed by student exchanges. These visits played an important part in upgrading Israel's image in the eyes of the Chinese, who were impressed by the tiny state's scientific achievements and welcomed its scientists warmly. In 1986 Professor Joshua Jortner, president of the Israeli National Academy of Sciences, participated in a conference in Beijing. He succeeded in contacting the Chinese minister of science and asked him to permit Israeli scientists to attend conferences in China freely. The reply was positive. That year a Hebrew class was opened at Beijing University, and programs on Judaic and Israel studies were instituted in other locations in China.[280]

Global Jewish organizations also acted to promote relations between Israel and China through the academic channel. During the 1980s, Issi Liebler, vice president of the World Jewish Congress, visited China several times and met with leaders of Chinese Academy of Social Sciences. He encouraged them to organize a conference of Chinese and Jewish scholars

---

279 Yegar, *The Long Journey to Asia*, 264.
280 Ibid., 269.

(both Israeli and non-Israeli), which convened in Beijing in 1988 and addressed various aspects of Jewish studies.[281]

The development of academic relations was an encouraging process, but in the diplomatic arena things did not advance at the same pace. Reuven Merhav continued to promote diplomatic relations through the academic channel. He decided to focus on areas of Chinese interest—science, technology, and agriculture—whose development was part of the Chinese government's stated policy at the time. He succeeded in obtaining a declaration from the Chinese Academy of Sciences that it was interested in deepening ties with Israel. Around the same time, he arranged an unprecedented authorization by the China International Travel Service (CITS) that enabled groups of Israeli tourists to visit China on their Israeli passports. Further to Merhav's efforts, in a September 1988 meeting in New York between Foreign Minister Shimon Peres and Chinese Foreign Minister Qian Qichen, the leaders agreed that the Israel National Academy of Science would open a representational office in Beijing and that CITS would open an office in Tel Aviv. The Chinese office opened in 1989, while the Israeli academic representation opened soon after in 1990. Later, these offices became the basis for diplomatic representations between the two countries. On the economic aspect, the joint interface that Merhav initiated in 1986 with Copeco, a Chinese company that promoted economic ties between Israel and China, became the foundation for formal economic ties between the states.

In February 1991 the Chinese agreed to Merhav's request to add an Israeli diplomat to the Israeli academic representation. The diplomat's role would be to consult on political issues. After the Chinese side accepted this proposal, Merhav contacted Ze'ev Sufott and asked him to take the position. Shortly following, Sufott became the first Israeli ambassador in Beijing.

From 1989 on the relationship between the two states visibly warmed. Academic delegations traveled from Israel to China, and a Chinese delegation paid a reciprocal visit. Many of the senior Chinese who in the past had served as ambassadors in Arab states shared their impressions (mostly uncomplimentary) with the Israeli representatives of countries where they had served. They also clarified that China had no interest of its own in the Middle East beyond the desire for peace and security in the region. They expressed their sorrow over the delay in the Chinese–Israeli dialogue and

---

281 Ibid.

attributed this to historical circumstances. Meetings between the two sides were characterized by "the feeling of solidarity that is shared by a fraternity of pioneers," wrote Merhav.[282]

The Gulf War of January 1991 was also a significant precedent to the establishment of relations due to China's desire to establish a foothold in the international balance of powers. In mid-1991 the director of the Chinese Foreign Ministry's department of Western Asia and North Africa paid a secret visit to Israel and met with then Foreign Minister David Levy. In that year reciprocal visits of delegations on political issues became increasingly common. The regular participants in these meetings were representatives of the Chinese Ministry of Tourism and the Israeli academic representation. Usually the Chinese asked the Israelis to maintain confidentiality. Despite leaks to the Israeli press, which angered the Chinese side, Foreign Minister David Levy was invited to the ceremony for signature on the establishment of diplomatic relations between the two countries. The ceremony took place in Beijing on January 24, 1992, four days before the Moscow meeting of the Committee on Peace in the Middle East.

In October 1993 Israeli Prime Minister Yitzhak Rabin went to China, accompanied by the director of the Mossad. This was the visit that made history: the first visit to China by an Israeli prime minister. The visit was planned to strengthen cooperation between the two countries, with an emphasis on the fields of security and trade. Apparently, at this early stage, Israel made a preliminary attempt to prevent the Chinese from transferring nuclear know-how to Teheran, particularly knowledge that would enable transforming uranium into a gas—a necessary stage in the process of uranium enrichment. But Rabin's attempt was unsuccessful. The Chinese were very pragmatic, and their reasons were based on their need to purchase fuel from Iran as well as the aspiration to promote exports to that state.

China–Israel Relations since 1992

After embassies were opened in Beijing and Tel Aviv, trade and economic connections broadened, first at a moderate pace and then with increasing momentum. Israel exported technologies to China in fields such as high technology, chemical industries, communications, agriculture, and medical equipment. The volume of trade between the two states gradually swelled,

---

282 Merhav, "Dream of the Red Palaces," 577.

and China became one of Israel's leading trade partners.[283] Although this trade was affected by the economic crisis of 2008, in 2009 it declined by only 17 percent (to $4.5 billion, including diamonds). Rapid recovery began the very next year with growth of 48 percent, reaching $6.78 billion. In 2011 the growth trend continued for trade volume, which stood at over seven billion dollars, and in 2017 trade volume was measured at eleven billion dollars. Israeli exports to China were valued at over three billion dollars while imports from China rose to over seven billion dollars.[284] Still, Israeli exports to China are in highly focused areas. Over 70 percent of exports are concentrated in three categories: electronic components, chemicals, and minerals. Intel and Israel Chemicals Ltd. have logged impressive achievements in these fields. But as with other countries, entry into the Chinese market has not always been easy for Israeli companies. Many have lost large sums of money in China over the years, although the exact amounts are not known. The number of Israeli exporters that succeed in penetrating the Chinese market is small. Given appropriate government encouragement, possible open markets are the fields of water and environmental technology, medical equipment, and consumer products.

Trade with Hong Kong is not included in the data above. We must also recall that the information from past years does not include sales of Israeli weapons and military equipment to China. According to foreign sources, in the 1970s and early 1980s these sales reached three- to four billion dollars but were stopped due to American pressure.[285] But to Israel's fortune, the Chinese are not only interested in military equipment. China is interested in a wide variety of imports from Israel, and apparently it will continue to purchase and aspire to obtain access to the most advanced Israeli technologies, especially in the fields of agriculture, solar energy, communications, and defense.

The Chinese army has experienced severe difficulties due to its lack of access to advanced equipment and data collection technologies. For certain periods, Israel was China's second-largest weapons supplier (after Russia),

---

283 Magen, "China Will Be the Biggest Business Partner." http://www.israeldefense.co.il/he/node/28371 (retrieved November 30, 2017).

284 http://www.export.gov.il/files/publications/chinazoomin2017.pdf?redirect=no http://www.israeltrade.org.cn; http://www.tamas.gov.il; http://www.cbs.gov.il/hodaot2014n/16_14_017mazUSD.pdf;

285 Trade between Israel and China from January to April 2009 declined by 18 percent in comparison to the same period in 2008. Website of the Israel Export Institute, retrieved July 7, 2011.

providing a variety of weapons, including optical equipment, airplanes, missiles, and electronic components for tank communications. Aside from the financial profit, Israel hoped that these sales would ensure Beijing's agreement not to sell certain weapons to Israel's enemies in the Middle East. But this hope was rapidly shelved as China continued and continues to supply military equipment to Israel's neighbors. Furthermore, Israel's close ties with China have created tension in Israel's relationship with the United States. Since 1992 the American government has expressed increasing concern over China's acquisition of Israeli military technology and, by extension, American military technology that has been transferred to Israel at any point in time. This concern has been expressed especially regarding the Patriot missile system, the Lavi fighter planes, and the Phalcon and Harpy (Si'on) systems.[286] The American suspicions regarding the Patriot missile system were never proven, and Israel has consistently and forcefully denied them.

In the mid-1990s Israel agreed to sell China the Phalcon, a sophisticated airborne early warning and control (AEW&C) system. The Phalcon is an airborne radar picket system designed to detect aircraft, ships, and vehicles at long ranges and enable command and control of the battlespace in an air engagement by directing fighter and attack aircraft strikes. This Israeli-developed system also enabled sophisticated intelligence gathering. Its price tag was $250 million. But Israel's decision to sell the Phalcon to China triggered grave concerns at the Pentagon. At first the Clinton administration pressured Israel to cancel shipment of the system, which was installed on Soviet-manufactured Ilyushin IL-76 aircraft, and to cease the sale of other weapons to the Chinese military. Later, the United States put even heavier pressure on Israel. Finally, in July 2000, despite the reassurances of then Prime Minister Ehud Barak that the deal would go through, Israel cancelled the sale. The announcement of the cancellation was publicized after Jiang Zemin's visit to Israel in April 2000. Not surprisingly, the fact that Israel broke its promise and the humiliation that Jiang suffered as a result almost caused a diplomatic rupture between the two countries.

The Phalcon incident provoked an incendiary debate within Israel. Official Israeli entities asserted that the United States had not been clear enough in its objection to the deal, causing a misunderstanding with the

---

286 For more on this issue see Goldstein, "A Quadrilteral Relationship: Israel, China, Taiwan and the United States since 1992," and Shai, "China and Israel."

American government. In the end, Israel paid the Chinese $319 million, which included a refund for China's down payment as well as compensation for cancellation of the deal. As additional compensation, the Israelis also threw in the Ilyushin aircraft onto which the AEW&C system was to be installed. According to unofficial reports, the Chinese demanded another $630 million for additional expenses as well as $630 million in compensation—a total of $1.26 billion, an improbable sum for Israel. Undoubtedly, this situation ended with an enormous loss for Israel.[287]

Individuals involved in the deal still maintain that if Israel's minister of defense had been more sensitive to the Chinese way of thinking, more considerate of the foreign culture, and more willing to consult with China experts who were well-versed in the mysterious ways of the Chinese, Israel would not have reached this crisis with the Eastern power. In addition, wiser, more modest handling of the situation with the United States could have improved the atmosphere in all spheres and might have led Washington to agree to the sale of at least one Israeli system with the desired equipment. But as in the cases of the companies that lost money in China, once more negotiations failed due to the sin of pride, the sense of "me and only me," and unwillingness to consult with experts.[288]

The disturbing question in this incident is to what extent the negotiators, including military representatives, were sensitive to the impact of their words. For example, instead of using the English word "terminate" to inform the Chinese that Israel had to violate or cancel the agreement, the Israeli government could have used different terminology and tone—it could have humbly indicated the difficult constraints it was under.

One of the individuals involved emphasized that had Ehud Barak made a reciprocal visit to Beijing after Jiang Zemin's extended visit to Israel, this might have saved the situation somewhat. Furthermore, after Barak

---

287 Based on my knowledge of modern Chinese history, I contacted Yekutiel (Kuti) Mor, who was the person responsible at Israel's ministry of defense for contact with the Chinese on this issue. I suggested that he might learn a lesson from events following the Boxer Rebellion, and how China managed to meet the enormous payments levied on it by the global powers. According to this concept, Israel should propose that the Chinese divide the debt over many years. Israel could commit to providing China goods and services and deduct their value from the debt. In this manner, Israeli exports to China would increase, and along the way, a lasting connection would be created between the states based on a mutual trade foundation. But soon afterward, we realized that there was no need for creative techniques to solve the conflict, as it was solved by agreement on a reasonable sum.

288 See also, Haim, *Between the Cobra and the Dragon*, 52, 178.

offended then US Secretary of Defense William Cohen in the matter,[289] some argued that Defense Department officials turned the affair into a personal settling of accounts, and this was what eventually prevented the sale of the Phalcon. As said, we may assume that use of a different tone or even more precise English in formal and informal discussions would have assisted the Israeli representatives in convincing the Americans to change their position and enable completion of the deal, or at least part of it. Indeed, in the 1980s the United States sold AEW&C aircraft, a system similar to the Phalcon, to Saudi Arabia, and reequipped them in 2001 and 2002 with advanced hardware and software. In 2009 the United States authorized Israel to sell the Phalcon system to India in a massive deal of $1.1 billion.[290]

Like the Phalcon, the Harpy drone (or Disposable Unmanned Combat Aerial Vehicle—UCAV) was the product of exclusive Israeli development. It was more precious than gold to China in light of its unstable relationship with the government of Taiwan. In this professional field, both American and Chinese technology lagged far behind Israeli know-how. In 1994 Israel sold Harpy drones to China, and in 2004 and 2005 Israel made commitments to supply China with repair services and replacement parts. Subsequently, China sent the drones or their main components to Israel for maintenance, repair, and upgrade.

The Pentagon objected to this connection although it was part of a signed contract between Israel and China. The Americans suspected Israel of planning to perform not only maintenance and repairs but also to upgrade the drones significantly. Israel's denials were ineffective. In late 2004 State Councilor Tang Jiaxuan visited Israel. This visit of a senior Chinese official, the first of its type since the Phalcon incident, intensified American suspicions and incited powerful objections to the Harpy deal.

Undoubtedly, the United States' primary concern was for Taiwan's security. The Americans insisted that the Israelis refuse to send the Harpy drones (or their components) back to China, even though they belonged to Beijing. One way or another, Israel agreed to pay compensation to China for failure to meet the conditions of the agreement. Furthermore, in early September 2005, Amos Yaron, director of the Ministry of Defense, was forced to resign from his position under American pressure over this affair.

---

289 Jim Garamone, "Cohen, Barak Reaffirm US–Israeli Bonds, Discuss Contentions," US Department of Defense, http://www.defense.gov//News/NewsArticle.aspx?ID=45098, April 3, 2000.

290 Ron Ben-Yishai, "Weapons Deal: The First Israeli Phalcon Lands in India," Ynet, http://www.ynet.co.il/articles/0,7340,L-3721379,00.html, May 25, 2009.

Even though Israel's foreign minister at the time expressed regret over the events, the Harpy incident dragged US–Israel relations to a low point unknown since the imprisonment of Jonathan Pollard (a US Navy intelligence analyst who admitted to spying for Israel and was sentenced in 1987 to life in prison) twenty years earlier.

Since then clear rules have been set, or rather dictated by the United States regarding transfer of technology to China. The Americans also placed limits on Israeli exports to China, particularly for dual use components, which can be used for both military and civilian purposes. According to Chinese sources, these new rules have delayed and seriously damaged exports to China because the Americans required that all products be checked at least twice before they are sent to China. Despite attempts to satisfy both sides, Israel was unable to ensure that it could fully honor its commitments and the contracts it had signed with China. Even worse, China indicated that it would levy sanctions against Israeli companies not just inside China but in Hong Kong as well. China's vice premier visited Israel in late December 2004 along with Tang Jiaxuan, former minister of foreign affairs, to deliver this harsh message.[291] Israel feared that its exports would suffer a severe blow both to China and to other locations, as other countries might feel insecurity due to Israeli capitulation to American dictates and draw their own conclusions.

Improvement of relations between China and Israel did not prevent Beijing from continuing to produce weapons for countries such as Iran that threatened Israel. This practice still continues today. In many ways and for a long time, China even exploited the continuous conflicts among the Gulf States. After the Second Lebanon War, China took on a different role in the Middle East. It made significant advancements in the level of its military technology. Israel suspected that China might sell advanced weapons to several organizations. This was demonstrated at the beginning of the Second Lebanon War on July 14, 2006,[292] when Hezbollah shot a missile that hit an Israeli Navy boat and killed four IDF soldiers. The missile shot was a C-802 Silkworm, which was produced in China and sold to Iran a decade earlier. Possibly, Hezbollah shot the missile after receiving training from Iranian soldiers.

---

291 China's Vice Premier: Return the Drones, Or Else We'll Start Hurting Israeli Companies Operating in China," *Tik Debka*, December 26, 2004.
292 Israel Ministry of Foreign Affairs. http://www.mfa.gov.il/MFA/Terrorism. July 15, 2006.

Concerns about China's technological and military progress continued to disturb many and were expressed at a conference on military history held in Sofia, Bulgaria in 2012. The director of the Chinese association of military history, General Ren Haiquan, noted that the possessor of more advanced technology may not necessarily become the winner. In keeping with Mao's philosophy, he emphasized that sometimes the side that boasts the highest morale among soldiers and society will win despite being at a technological disadvantage. For example, while the Japanese and the Guomindang held many technological advantages over the Chinese Communists, the Communists won the battle. Thus technology is not necessarily the most important factor. The fighters must adapt their existing technology to the manner of waging the war—in other words, tactics and strategy. He also stated that in pivotal moments during their war against China, the Japanese became objects of ridicule, as did the UN forces under McArthur. Technology may offer a chance at victory, but the human element is the deciding factor.

The general's theory was based on the concept of the "people's war": in the history of nations, farmers and slaves have often been able to overcome enemies that were physically stronger. The general cited Mao's most famous motto: "When the enemy attacks, we retreat. When he hesitates, we wait, and when he retreats, we attack." The two revolutionary armies, the New Fourth Army and the Eighth Route Army, followed this approach, but they were also able to fight frontally in the traditional manner when necessary and when the conditions were ripe. This flexibility compensated for their lack of advanced equipment and technology. The more innovative the technology, the more the army is required to adapt its tactics and strategy to the new reality. This was the case in Korea, when Chinese forces operated on the peninsula at night just as they would in a daytime frontal battle. According to the general, in the future the Chinese army will be victorious again, even if its technology is inferior to the enemy, as long as it upholds the characteristics of the "people's war."

But it seems that times have changed. After all, since 1964 China has possessed nuclear capabilities, and since the 1980s, following the Open Door Policy, China boasts impressive financial resources that are constantly improving. China has evolved to the point where it can carve its own path both technologically and militarily. This is certainly true when we examine China's capabilities at the end of the second decade of the present century. Fueled by decades of rapid economic growth and a desire to ensure its security interests, China has embarked on a large-scale modernization of its military. Extensive military reforms have been instituted aimed at streamlining command structures and improving Chinese military strength. China now boasts its second aircraft carrier (inaugurated in April 2017), a credible fleet of both diesel and nuclear missile submarines, one of the largest air forces in the world, and over fifty intercontinental ballistic missiles. China has successfully translated its impressive economic leverage into military power on a global scale.

Despite All, a Relationship

Parallel to the slowdown and retreat in China–Israel relations, there were some successes: the Israeli Philharmonic visited Beijing in 1995, and the Israel Museum of Jerusalem displayed an exhibit on traditional China for four months in 2001. The original displays were brought over from China and were unprecedented in scope. Simultaneously, Israel hosted a festival of Chinese opera and performances of acrobatics and dance as well as a variety of traditional Chinese works of art.

In the fall of 2000, five cities in China were scheduled to host an exhibit on the life of Albert Einstein. However, this exhibit was cancelled after the Chinese Ministry of Culture insisted on removing three facts about the famous physicist's life from the captions: first, that he was a Jew; second, that he supported the establishment of a Jewish state; and third, that David Ben Gurion had invited him to serve as the State of Israel's second president. Due to the rising tension in Israel's relations with the Arab world, China had no desire to be exposed to criticism for supporting an exhibit that highlighted Einstein's connections with the Jewish state.

Despite tensions, China and Israel remained committed to technological cooperation. Around the time of the cancellation of the Phalcon deal and the incident with the Einstein exhibit, China signed an agreement similar in value to the Phalcon deal to purchase the Israeli-manufactured satellites HK1 and HK2. These were intended for broadcasting the Olympic Games that took place in Beijing in 2008. This agreement was an example of the line that Beijing drew between economic and diplomatic issues. Understanding this policy and mentality of China can aid in comprehending the contrasts that exist in bilateral relations: China may voice harsh criticism against Israel on the Palestinian issue, but at the same time it signs contracts of an impressive scope with Israeli high-tech companies.

Between 2002 and the Harpy affair in 2005, relations between the two countries proceeded without notable incident. An Israeli military delegation visited China, and a Chinese delegation paid a reciprocal visit to Israel. The Chinese vice premier came to Israel, and Israeli members of Knesset visited China. Joint research projects were carried out and continue actively to the present day.

Academic ties between the states have proven beneficial to both sides. Chinese students study and carry out research at universities in Israel. At Tel Aviv University Israelis study traditional and modern China, while Israeli students at schools and universities study the Chinese language. A growing number of Israeli students travel to China to study Chinese and gain expertise in fields such as Chinese culture (for purposes of tourism, for example) and traditional medicine. In addition, the student exchange programs between the states have been fruitful. At Tel Aviv University, as at many universities worldwide, a Confucius Institute was established, enabling breakthroughs in understanding and learning from Chinese culture. An increasing number of books on Chinese philosophy and Chinese literary works are translated into Hebrew. Similarly, books on Judaism, the history of the Jewish people, the Holocaust, the Middle East, and even modern Israeli literature are translated into Chinese and studied in Chinese academic institutions. An increasing number of websites on Israel and the Israeli–Arab conflict appear in the Chinese language and web space.

In the political arena, in 2010 senior Israeli officials began to renew advances toward China. Bank of Israel Governor Stanley Fisher and Minister of Strategic Affairs Moshe (Bogie) Ya'alon paid a joint visit to Beijing.[293] Their visit was mainly intended to discuss the issue of Iranian nuclear power while attempting to convince China to support sanctions against Iran. The director of IDF intelligence, Major General Amos Yadlin, and the director of the IDF planning department, Major General Amir Eshel, also visited China. Finance Minister Yuval Steinitz traveled to China and Hong Kong,[294] and the highlight of his trip was opening the Israeli booth at Expo 2010. Joining him were Finance Ministry Director Haim Shani, Minister of Environmental Protection Gilad Erdan, and a delegation of some twenty Israeli businessmen.

---

293 Bengal, "Governor Stanley Fisher Joins the Struggle against Iran."
294 Weisman, "Steinetz Leaves on a Trip to China and Hong Kong."

By the summer of 2011 a definite improvement was apparent in relations between the two countries with regard to military and security issues. In June Defense Minister Ehud Barak went to China in the first such visit in over a decade. This represented a breakthrough in China–Israel relations since 2000. During his visit, Barak met with his Chinese equivalent, China's chief of staff, and the vice premier, and he also visited military installations. Three weeks after the visit the announcement was made that Israeli companies would participate in a tender for a factory to produce an executive jet in Chengdu, the capital of Sichuan province. Aside from Israeli companies, Canadian and American companies participated in this tender, which was issued by the Aviation Industry Corporation of China (AVIC). Participation of the Israeli companies in the tender was approved by the authorized entities in Israel as well as the US Federal Aviation Administration (FAA).[295]

On August 14, 2011, General Chen Bingde, China's chief of general staff, came to Israel, where he met with then President Shimon Peres, Prime Minister Benjamin Netanyahu, Defense Minister Ehud Barak, and Chief of Staff Benny Gantz.[296] Apparently, the issues at the top of the agenda were strategic affairs, cooperative ventures in military technology, and China's international tender for producing executive jets. In late 2011 Netanyahu accepted the invitation of China's ambassador to Israel and planned a state visit to Beijing for 2012. During that visit he intended to announce the continued improvement of bilateral relations. The invitation to Netanyahu was repeated during the celebrations in Israel and China marking the twenty-year anniversary of the establishment of diplomatic relations.

The improvement in relations was surprising, as we might have assumed that the Phalcon and Harpy affairs would continue to cast a dark cloud for many years. Furthermore, it seemed that the United States would not give up its tireless efforts to place obstacles in the path of improved strategic ties between Jerusalem and Beijing.

Signs multiplied that connections on the strategic plane were tightening. One of these was the August 2012 visit to Haifa port of a Chinese naval fleet, following a friendly visit to nearby Turkey. The arrival of three war ships was surprising to many who never dared to dream of such an exceptional gesture. The flotilla included the Qingdao, a missile-carrying

---

295 Sikuler, "Thaw in China–Israel Relations."
296 Yaakov Katz, "Chinese Army Chief Due in Israel Next Week," *The Jerusalem Post*, http://www.jpost.com/Defense/Article.aspx?id=232878, August 8, 2011.

destroyer; the Yantai, a frigate; and the Wei Shang Hu, a large, multi-purpose supply ship. This was the first visit to Israel of the Chinese Navy. On August 16 a large reception was held on the deck of the Qingdao destroyer, and officials gave moving speeches about the close relations between the two states.

Relations had begun to thaw somewhat earlier, with the official inauguration of five Israel studies programs in China in 2011. As part of these programs, the Communist Party expressed open interest in Israeli political representatives. Knesset member Yuli Edelstein, representing the majority party, was invited to participate in an academic-political "think-tank" conference in China. For its part, Beijing sent representatives to the first seminar on strategy and security in China–Israel relations held at the Herzliya Interdisciplinary Center.[297] In addition to these gestures, Chinese delegations regularly visited the Center for Strategic Studies at Tel Aviv University. Political contact under the umbrella of academia was a successful means of pursuing rapprochement. Since then dozens of Chinese academic delegations have visited Israel with the goal of strengthening ties with Israeli universities. They are sending academic interns in many fields.

In October 2013 Liu Qibao visited Tel Aviv University. Liu was a senior official in the Chinese government and in the Community Party who had considerable influence on Chinese policy. This was an official state visit, during which Liu and his accompanying delegation met with President Shimon Peres in his residence as well as with Prime Minister Benjamin Netanyahu. At Tel Aviv University the delegation visited the Confucius Institute and participated in a symposium with senior Israeli–China experts. The visit went well, and promises were made regarding future aid and cooperative ventures. In addition, the visit was reported in the Israeli and Chinese media.[298]

The thawing of relations also had impressive economic results. In 2011 ChemChina purchased a 60 percent controlling interest in the Israeli company Makhteshim-Agan, based on a company value of $2.4 billion. Makhteshim-Agan was an Israeli manufacturer and distributor of crop protection products including herbicides, insecticides, and fungicides. This was the biggest deal ever signed between the Chinese government and an Israeli company, and it was also the first major deal in which China became an investor in an Israeli company. Public stockholders received $1.272 billion,

---

297 Witte, "A Quiet Transformation in China's Approach to Israel."

298 "Senior Chinese Officials Arrive for State Visit to Israel," *Israel Hayom* website (October 21, 2013): http://www.israelhayom.co.il/article/125749

Koor received $1.128 billion, and they were expected to register net profit of up to NIS 674 million for the deal.

This deal had less heartwarming political ramifications at home. When Prime Minister Benjamin Netanyahu congratulated businessman Nochi Dankner (who held the controlling interest in IDB Group and Makhteshim-Agan) on the deal, saying that it proved "the State of Israel's economic power," leftist political entities cast a critical eye. For example, the chairman of the Labor Party, MK Shelly Yachimovich, said that "Netanyahu's congratulations to Dankner for the profit he pocketed from the sale of Makhteshim-Agan in the Negev to ChemChina are outrageous and inappropriate. This is not the time for congratulations, but rather deep sorrow, and the realization that this is a sophisticated, large Israeli factory that gave an income to thousands of families in the Negev. Due to failed management and the transfer into Chinese hands, it is doomed to close after a tortuous process of downsizing. The prime minister must understand that without successful blue and white industry, there will be no income in Israel for workers no scientific development or growth for the economy."[299] However, the Israeli Consul General in Shanghai, Jackie Eldan, continued in the official vein and emphasized the broad strategic significance of the deal, beyond the business facet. "Makhteshim-Agan will remain in Israel, and suddenly China has a very important anchor in Israel," he said. "The Chinese are very interested in green technologies, and China will be a key player in this field. The Chinese are looking here for new energy technologies. As for the question of whether ChemChina is planning to close Makhteshim-Agan, I think this is a process that will take several years, and in the meantime, a Chinese connection will be created."[300] Indeed, in 2018 the company (rebranded in 2014 as ADAMA Agricultural Solutions Ltd.) continues functioning as in the past.

The Carmel Tunnels marked another major economic partnership between the two countries. Digging commenced in 2007 and was completed in 2009. It was performed by China Civil Engineering Construction Corporation (CCECC) in cooperation with Y. Lehrer Engineering of Israel. Originally the Chinese company was supposed to be the only contractor on the project. But due to a financial dispute and disagreement between the project franchisee (Carmelton) and Israel's Ministry of Economy, Industry,

299 Hazani, "The Deal Is Closed."
300 Koren, "As Long as China Is Growing."

and Labor regarding hiring additional foreign workers, the Israeli company was added to the project. Still, individuals involved in the project emphasized that the Chinese company performed high-quality, efficient work and even finished ahead of the deadline set for it, while the Israeli company fell behind the deadlines.[301]

In early and mid-2014, the possibility was raised multiple times that the Chinese government would purchase Tnuva, an Israeli food processing cooperative (co-op) historically specializing in milk and dairy products. Tnuva for decades had symbolized the rebirth of Zionism in the State of Israel (although a portion of Tnuva was purchased in 2007 by Apax, a British company).[302] Strident objections were voiced to this deal. Some public figures also objected to rumors that Chinese companies might be involved in constructing the railroad to the southern port of Eilat, purchasing Clal Insurance Company and other financial firms, or constructing and operating two private ports to be built in Haifa and Ashdod. The issue raised broad, fundamental strategic questions: what national resources can be handed over to a foreign entity, in one way or another? What inalienable assets should Israel refuse to give up for any price? Foreign investments were certainly desirable—but what was their limit, beyond which the nation's freedom was likely to be harmed?

In May 2014 the Chinese company Bright Food signed an agreement to purchase the controlling interest in Tnuva.[303] Avishai Braverman, member of Knesset and chairman of the Economic Committee, and Efraim Halevi, former director of the Mossad, scathingly criticized the deal, saying it was harmful to Israel's national interests.[304]

However, the opposite view asserted that the Chinese did not intend this as a casual "walk in the park" but rather as a strategic investment, like its other investments in Israel and elsewhere. Food security is one of the three central issues at the top of the Chinese government's agenda, and therefore the Chinese intend to remain in control of the company long-term and continue to develop it. Furthermore, if we consider the issues surrounding the deal, for example the potential benefits for the Israeli dairy market, including sale of cows, know-how related to milk yield, dairy farming technology, and other related fields, the Israeli economy stands to benefit

---

301 Baron and Udi, "The Conflict Intensifies."
302 On this issue, see, for example, Rolnick, "Who Profits and Who Loses."
303 Gavison, "Apax Expected to Give Bright Food a Discount."
304 Shai, *The Evolution*, 6–55; Interview with Halevi, June 15, 2015.

from the deal. As it happened, the Tnuva deal, which was highly profitable for the sellers—Apax Partners and Mivtach Shamir—continues to emerge as problematic, to say the least, for the buyer: Bright Food. A steep decline in the value of the dairy products company forced Bright Food to inject capital into the firm. One element in its focus on food security is the scarcity of clean water. This lies behind China's interest in importing agricultural products that contain a high proportion of water, as well as poultry, beef, and pork.

According to some estimates, within the coming decade the Chinese stand to acquire control of other major Israeli companies, perhaps even Teva, the pharmaceutical giant. It is likely to become involved in many additional ventures on top of existing projects like the Akko-Karmiel railway (the Gilon tunnel), and the Tel Aviv light train. One of the hottest issues debated in knowledgeable Israeli circles focuses on China's involvement in the Israeli economy and technology, asking to what extent China might benefit from local know-how and even copy local patents.

For decades, Egypt has had the potential to isolate Israel and damage its international trade by closing the Suez Canal to Israeli shipping or to ships bringing merchandise to Israel. Construction of a fast, modern railroad that connects Eilat Port and the Mediterranean ports of Ashdod and Haifa (Red-Med Line) seems to be a viable solution to this threat, enabling Israel to circumvent the Canal and render it unnecessary in a rapid, inexpensive manner.[305] The Israeli government decided that China would be permitted to construct only one port, the private port at Ashdod. The franchisee was China Harbor, a subsidiary of the infrastructure consortium China Communications Construction Co. (CCCC). In fall 2014 the possibility was raised that this Chinese company would also be involved in constructing the railway to Eilat. Regarding the franchise for operating and maintaining the new Haifa deep-water private port for twenty-five years, in 2015 the Israeli government awarded the tender to Shanghai International Port Group (SPIG) [306] of China.

In 2013 China proposed the Silk Road Economic Belt and the Twenty-first Century Silk Road, better known as the One Belt One Road or Belt and Road Initiative. This development strategy focuses on connectivity

---

305 Ibid.

306 Shamir and Bar-Eli, "The Private Port at Ashdod Sets Sail"; Port Strategy, "SPIG Nets Haifa Concession," March 25, 2015. See also: Gideon Elazar, "China in the Red Sea," BESA, Bar-Ilan University, August 23, 2017.

and cooperation between Eurasian countries, primarily aiming to expand China's role in global affairs and create a China-centered trading network. As of 2018 the focus of attention has been infrastructure investments such as railways, highways, and the power grid. As part of this initiative, China is slowly establishing what the Americans call "A String of Pearls." This refers to the network of Chinese military and commercial stations or strongholds along the maritime Silk Road from the Chinese mainland to Port Sudan and further up the Red Sea. The sea lanes run through several major maritime straits, such as the Strait of Mandeb, the Strait of Malacca, the Strait of Hormuz, Hambantota Port in Sri Lanka (recently leased to China for ninety-nine years) as well as other strategic maritime locations in Pakistan, Bangladesh, the Maldives, and Somalia. Furthermore, in the summer of 2017 the Chinese established their first ever military base outside of the Asia-Pacific region, in Djibouti, thus expanding its influence in regions near Israel.

On the whole, China is investing in Israel's high-tech, agriculture, food, water, med-tech, and biotech sectors. In 2015 its total investments in Israel reached more than half a billion dollars. It is involved in various innovative enterprises. Also, new Israeli tech incubators in China, new investments, joint ventures, trade conferences, and delegations are announced on an almost daily basis.

In 2015 the Ministry of Finance decided to open Israel's cheese import industry to competition by issuing the necessary authorizations, shattering the foundations of Israel's dairy monopoly. Tnuva filed suit against a rival importer whose packaging recalled the design for Tnuva's Emek cheese package. Apparently, instead of trying to compete, the monopoly preferred to try to push the competitor out of the market. Tnuva managers have committed to supplying substantial returns to their Chinese investors. Undoubtedly this point adds a new thread to the complex fabric discussed above. To put it simply, today Israeli managers have obligations toward their new owners—the Chinese. The government seems unlikely to bend over backwards to continue pressuring the monopoly. This distinction illustrates the consequences of placing Tnuva into foreign hands. In the past the government could navigate economic matters based on official directives or economic dictates, for better or for worse. From now on, however, decision-makers in Israel will have their hands tied by complex diplomatic and political considerations. This is particularly true when the company involved is no longer an international corporation managed by a diverse group of investors led by a British company, but rather a very national company, even nationalist, under the control of the Chinese government and the Communist Party.[307]

As we recall, in 2011 Prime Minister Netanyahu was invited with great ceremony to China, but the visit did not take place in 2012. In late 2012 the Chinese began to demonstrate their agreement with the new European diplomacy, which was characterized by increasing pressure on the Netanyahu government in the wake of expansion of settlements and blatant disregard for the protests of international and national organizations. Operation Pillar of Defense in Gaza in November 2012 exacerbated the situation. Beijing denounced Israel in harsh condemnatory tones. Once again the pendulum of the relationship swung back in the other direction, and a bitter wind blew from Beijing in its policy toward Israel.

Prime Minister Netanyahu finally made his visit to China in early May 2013, and a certain change was evident in the tenor of relations. Netanyahu arrived in Shanghai on May 6 and then traveled to the capital. The importance of the visit was that it actually took place, and not in its results, which were marginal. This was the first visit by an Israeli prime minister since Ehud Olmert's trip in 2007. The invitation from the Chinese was made over a year earlier, but at that time the visit was postponed due to Netanyahu's participation in the conference of Jewish Federations in the United States. The Chinese were offended by this preference and thus delayed sending a new invitation.

Some noted that another difficulty arose on the way to implementing the visit.[308] The Chinese government threatened to cancel the invitation if the Israeli government proceeded with its intention to present documents and testimony harmful to China in a US legal case. An Israeli security establishment representative was supposed to testify in a New York federal court against the Bank of China for aiding in money laundering activities for Hamas and Islamic Jihad, which were defined as terror organizations by the United States and Israel. In 2005 Bank of China in Guangzhou was accused of maintaining a live channel for transferring funds from Syria to Hamas and Islamic Jihad terrorists in Gaza. In the sophisticated operation, clothes and toys manufactured in China were sent to Gaza, but instead of being donated to preschools they were sold in public auctions. The profits

---

307 Meirav Arlozorov, "The Chinese Will Profit: Israel's Government Fortifies Tnuva's Monopoly Forever," *The Marker*, April 1, 2015.

308 Nachum Barnea and Shimon Shiffer, "Commentary," *Yediot Aharonot*, July 12, 2013.

were transferred to the two terror organizations and designated for military purposes—in short, money laundering through commerce. The Chinese demanded that Netanyahu prevent the testimony, which interrupted the trial and damaged the global battle against terror and its funding.

The Chinese government thus succeeded in dissuading Israel's government from taking a significant step to help block the money pipeline that was nourishing terror.

In late July 2013, protocols revealed in the New York court documented regular meetings for security coordination between China and Israel in which the Israeli representatives warned about money laundering for Islamic Jihad through Bank of China. In the coming months and into 2014, additional details were revealed in the case, and it became clear that China had tried to hide the existence of these discussions. The affair was discovered following an investigation carried out in the death of Daniel Waltz, a Jewish-American youth who was murdered in a terrorist attack in Tel Aviv in 2006. The victim's family filed a lawsuit against Bank of China, arguing that the Chinese had helped fund the suicide terrorist.[309] According to documents of the Israel Security Agency (Shabak) that were revealed in late 2013, money laundering for Hamas in China continued for years after the Bank of China affair, and apparently it continued for a while.[310]

When Netanyahu's visit finally took place, the timing was not ideal for potential media attention. At the time the headlines in Israel were reporting the IDF's air attacks against weapons caches in Syria. Also on the local agenda was the controversial budget implemented by Yair Lapid, the new finance minister. Before Netanyahu left Israel, the director of IDF military intelligence, Major General Aviv Kochavi, held secret talks in Beijing with his Chinese colleagues to discuss the Iranian nuclear program and the civil war in Syria. Kochavi presented current intelligence on the Iranians' nuclear progress and warned against the dangers of sending advanced weapons, some made in China, to Syria, as these were likely to wind up in Hezbollah hands.[311] About ten days later, Netanyahu traveled to China.

---

309 See, for example, Harel Zota, "The Connection between the Biggest Bank in China and the Terror Attack in Tel Aviv."

310 "Shin Bet Probe Reveals Scope of Hamas Money Laundering Through Chinese Banks" *Ha'Aretz*, September 29, 2013.

311 Ravid, "Reaching Iran through China."

As researcher Sam Chester noted,[312] Netanyahu arrived just several days after the visit of Mahmoud Abbas (Abu Mazen), chairman of the Palestinian Authority. The Chinese had planned this timing with brilliant consideration for the challenging diplomatic dilemmas involved. Now they were holding the rope at both ends—on one hand they ascribed great importance to the Israeli leader's visit, while on the other they adeptly appeased public opinion in the Arab-Palestinian world, as Abbas arrived in Beijing before Netanyahu. Abbas' visit was defined as an official state visit while Netanyahu's was defined as "formal." Some thought that the combination of visits was designed to present China as involved in the political process in the Middle East no less than in the international diplomatic arena. But the question was whether Beijing was ready to take on the role of mediator in full. In the meantime it seemed that China aspired to gain as much as possible from Israel (it had very little to gain from the Palestinian Authority). Perhaps Beijing was searching for an easy path to the hearts of the Arab states, who severely criticized China's support of Syrian leader Bashar al-Assad. Possibly, Abbas' visit was a diplomatic fig leaf for Netanyahu's more important visit, which was accompanied by dozens of businessmen and was covered more widely in the Chinese press. Netanyahu also received special honors not granted to every foreign leader, such as an invitation to speak at the main school of the Communist Party, the institution that trains China's future leaders.

Freshly inaugurated President Xi Jinping presented to Abu Mazen his "four-point program" for solving the Israeli–Palestinian conflict. The program included support for the two states plan; the requirement that Israel return to the 1967 borders; the complete cessation of building in the settlements; and adoption of the general principle of "land for peace." In parallel, Xi also mentioned that Israel's honor must be upheld, and that Israel had a right to exist and a legitimate right to maintain its security. Both Premier Li Keqiang and President Xi Jinping mentioned to Netanyahu the need to create appropriate conditions for reestablishing the Israeli–Palestinian negotiations. Their argument was that solving this conflict was the key to peace in the entire Middle East. But the discussions with the Israeli prime minister touched only lightly on political affairs. Instead, China was interested in strategic dialogue with Israel, in commerce between the two countries, and in Israeli technologies. In fact, despite certain criticisms leveled

---

312 Chester, "Why Netanyahu and Abbas went to China".

against Israel's policies, China was still very interested in interaction with the Jewish state.

Netanyahu's visit was primarily of an economic character. He came to promote deals and open new channels, aware that for his trip to be considered an achievement in Israel, he had to assist the Israeli manufacturers and exporters in breaking down the wall of Chinese bureaucracy; some reported that Netanyahu tried to promote a free trade agreement with China that would benefit Israeli exporters and grant their products an exemption from tax, but the Chinese refused to sign the agreement unless Israel granted work permits to thousands of Chinese laborers.[313] In his meeting with Netanyahu, Li Keqiang emphasized the importance of economic cooperation with Israel and demonstrated his willingness to make strides in this direction. For his part, Netanyahu stressed the potential that lay in integrating Chinese and Israeli abilities. The two leaders decided to establish two working groups tasked with studying and improving economic and social relations between China and Israel, focusing on the fields of technology and agriculture.[314] At the opening of the cabinet meeting following Netanyahu's return to Israel, he announced the establishment of the Israeli committee to be chaired by himself as prime minister and directed by Professor Eugene Kendall. Netanyahu also expressed the hope that China would take a similar step.[315] In this respect Israel will continue to face obstacles to commerce with China and advance trade in relatively narrow, well-defined fields: electronics, minerals, and chemicals.

In Israel Netanyahu's visit provoked criticism for several reasons. Many found it distasteful that the prime minister's entire family accompanied him on the trip and enjoyed VIP flights and accommodations. They attacked Netanyahu for enjoying the luxuries reserved for high-placed persons of influence without making sincere efforts on the critical issues.

---

313 Bardenstein, "Netanyahu is trying to promote a free trade agreement. As of the summer of 2015, the issue of bringing Chinese laborers to Israel had yet to be solved. In a change from their previous policy, the Chinese government refused to permit its citizens to be employed over the Green Line. Beijing also had preconditions regarding commissions." Cited by Meirav Arlozorov, "China Demands that Chinese Construction Workers Not Be Employed in the Settlements," *The Marker*, June 7, 2015. Netanyahu brought this issue up again during his 2017 visit to China.

314 Li and Cheng, "China, Israel Boost Cooperation."

315 "PM Netanyahu's Opening Remarks at Cabinet Meeting," Youtube (May 19, 2013): http://www.youtube.com/watch?v=-BpjmQNIuZ4&feature=youtu.be

More condemnation was aimed at Netanyahu's speech, in which he proposed "pushing the plug into the socket" as a metaphor for Israel–China relations. The expression was interpreted as arrogant since it portrayed the Israelis as the side offering initiative, intelligence, and vision while the Chinese provided nothing more than cheap, experienced labor.[316] The Israelis had already learned a thing or two about China since relations were established, and they knew that the worst thing for the Chinese was public humiliation, even unintentional. It is unclear how Netanyahu's metaphor was received on the Chinese side. At any rate, in hindsight Netanyahu's visit to China could be considered a watershed in bilateral relations. From then on relations took off with substantial momentum.[317]

Proof of this was offered during President Shimon Peres' visit to China from April 8 to 11 in 2014. During this visit the parties discussed the lengthy negotiations initiated by John Kerry, then US Secretary of State, on the Israeli–Palestinian conflict, which seemed to have failed. They also discussed the Iranian nuclear threat, which Israel hoped China would help block. Xi Jinping, Peres' host, called for Israel to take daring steps at decisive stages of the discussions with the Palestinians. He emphasized that China would continue to play a constructive role in the Middle East peace process. Bilaterally, the president of China called to push forward on issues of economic, technological, and agricultural cooperation between the countries in the fields of energy, environment, education, health, and innovation.[318]

China's rising interest in the Middle East and particularly in Israel was recognizable in the visit of Chinese Foreign Minister Wang Yi in December 2013. Netanyahu and his guest again tried to bolster ties between the countries, but they faced the obstacle of disagreement on several significant issues. Heading the list was Iran, followed by the continued debate on the Palestinian issue, settlements, and other topics. Thus it was understandable that more public attention was paid to the economic field and not the political arena. Again using a mildly paternalistic tone, Netanyahu repeated the refrain that each country's strengths complemented the other's. "China has massive global and industrial

---

316 See, for example, Peretz, "Syria Can Wait"; Melamed, "The Chinese Disgrace"; Blumenkranz, "El Al Named the Price."

317 Shai, *The Evolution*.

318 "President Peres on state visit to China," *Israel Ministry of Foreign Affairs—Press Room*, 8; *South China Morning Post and China Daily*, Beijing, April 9, 2014.

achievements; Israel has know-how and expertise in all high-tech fields," he stated. Aside from high-tech, he also mentioned agriculture, water, global transportation, and health. Netanyahu emphasized the importance of maintaining a decisive, firm position against Iranian nuclear power. Iran must not be permitted to manufacture nuclear weapons, he said, and it must follow the decisions of the UN Security Council on this issue. Iran must stop uranium enrichment, dismantle the centrifuges, destroy its enriched uranium reserves, and dismantle the heavy water reactor in Arak so that it will not be able to produce plutonium. The Chinese minister addressed bilateral agreements that called for the establishment of a task force for amplifying economic growth.[319]

The Chinese minister's visit made very modest waves in the Israeli media—unlike the attention paid to each and every visit of US Secretary of State John Kerry. Apparently, the Israelis seem to be less interested in the visits by Chinese high officials to the Holy Land than in visits by their American or European counterparts.

At the end of March 2016, Liu Yandong, vice premier of China, visited Israel with an impressive delegation to lay the foundation for a Free Trade Agreement. This would obviate entry visas for Israeli and Chinese citizens traveling between the two countries. According to estimates, this agreement could increase the number of Chinese tourists who visit Israel (now at eighty thousand) and would more than double the number of Israelis visiting China (now at seventy thousand). Hainan Airlines has inaugurated a direct service from Tel Aviv to Beijing, as has Cathay Pacific, with flight rates dropping steadily.

The inauguration of Donald Trump as the 45th President of the United States on January 20, 2017 seems to have heralded a quiet yet substantial transformation in the international arena. His controversial statements on many topics both before and after the official ceremony cannot leave Jerusalem and Beijing indifferent. After all, Sino–Israeli relations are an integral part of a sophisticated and complex triangle in which Washington plays a major role.

---

319 *Yahoo News*, December 18, 2013. The following parts, covering Netanyahu's second visit to China and the relations through the end of 2017 are based, for example, on: https://besacenter.org/perspectives-papers/netanyahus-china-visit, https://www.reuters.com/article/us-israel-china-business/as-part-of-asia-pivot-netanyahu-pushes-israeli-hi-tech-in-china-idUSKBN16R1AV, https://www.jta.org/2017/03/22/news-opinion/israel-middle-east/netanyahu-praises-china-upon-completing-state-visit-there (retrieved December 7, 2017), and INSS report March 29, 2017.

Netanyahu's second visit to China as prime minister of Israel in March 2017 was momentous, even historic. Netanyahu lauded the comprehensive innovation partnership between China and Israel and praised China's capabilities, its position on the world stage, and in history. He noted Israel's potential as a junior yet perfect partner for China in the development of technologies that "change the way we live, how long we live, how healthy we live, the water we drink, the food we eat and the milk that we drink— affecting every area." He hoped that China would approve Israel's request to be exempt from a new Chinese policy barring some investments in foreign countries. Indeed, just prior to Netanyahu's visit, in a bid to boost its domestic economy, Beijing decided to restrict Chinese capital spent abroad, causing much distress among businessmen worldwide. China expressed obvious interest in Israeli technology while Israel needed Chinese capital for its much-lauded innovation. Also, Israel expected China to reduce its regulatory burdens so that its technology would reach the Chinese market more easily.

Once a country like China has established basic infrastructure— roads, utilities, and factories—the only way to sustain growth is by consistently adding value to its products and services. Beyond a certain point, the only way to do this is with the addition of technology. During his visit Netanyahu emphasized that Israeli technology had the potential to improve the lives of the 1.3 billion people in China dramatically. He gave the example of China's one hundred million cars, which cause traffic jams, accidents, and heavy pollution. All these problems could be dramatically improved with new technology originating from Israel. Netanyahu referred to Mobileye, a Jerusalem-based company that was recently bought by computer chip giant Intel for the staggering amount of fifteen billion dollars, and Waze, a crowd-sourced navigation cellphone application that was acquired by Google in 2013. In his view China was a classic example, perhaps the preeminent one, of a country that could apply these technologies to benefit its citizens, resulting in fewer road accidents and less pollution. In addition, drivers would reach their destinations more quickly, avoiding the exorbitant expenses of running cars that are often idle. The Israeli delegates with Netanyahu also promoted digital health technologies. For example, the medical records of all Chinese citizens could be computerized so that whenever people visit different hospitals, they would not have to go through an entire battery of tests to establish their medical records. Health care databases could improve the relevant services and save time and money.

In response, President Xi Jingping praised Israel as a "world-renowned innovative country" and said that promoting innovation-driven development was a "priority for our cooperation." During the visit the Israelis signed a series of agreements with China, ranging from granting visas for twenty thousand Chinese construction workers to opening joint research centers in both countries and developing applications for artificial intelligence technology. They also held talks about various joint ventures, particularly in desalination.

In total, the Israeli members of Netanyahu's delegation to China signed twenty-five official agreements. Another twenty agreements were signed between private Israeli companies and individual Chinese firms in fields such as agriculture, medical equipment, and high-tech for a total value of over one hundred million dollars. Also, the two states held further talks on the establishment of a free trade zone between them. Further, Netanyahu met with heads of giant companies such as Alibaba, Novo, and Baidu, who control together over one hundred billion dollars in value.

Israel and China also discussed the possibility of trilateral cooperation involving third countries as well, specifically in Africa. The two countries would use their mutual expertise to aid African countries.

On March 21, 2017, President Xi Jinping called for peace between Israel and an independent Palestine "as soon as possible." He reiterated that "a peaceful, stable and developing Middle East is the common interest of all parties . . . . China appreciates that the Israeli side will continue to tackle the Israeli–Palestinian issue on the basis of the 'two-state solution.'" Netanyahu asserted Israel's willingness to see China play a bigger role in Middle East affairs. However, he was not specific on this point and seemed to feel much more comfortable discussing innovation, economic, and financial matters than relating to the controversial political issues.

One fact remained quite clear. China continues to vote almost consistently against Israel at the UN and in various other international forums and organizations. Its basic stance on the Israeli–Palestinian conflict and the Iranian nuclear agreement remains almost unchanged. Currently, when speaking of the Belt and Road Initiative, Israel is considered an important hub located at the meeting point of three continents. The Chinese make regular "pilgrimages" to the "Start-Up Nation" while carrying on their traditional diplomatic practice of lip service to the Arab world.

Recalling the 1973 Yom Kippur War (when Israel was attacked by surprise and needed immediate supplies which were flown in by an American air train), Israel cannot risk losing Washington's support. Today Israel is limited by constraints imposed by the American administration following the Phalcon and Harpy affairs as well as recent developments in the geopolitical arena. In general Israel must continue to accede to American requests and demands. This is particularly true considering President Trump's exceptional support of Netanyahu's right-wing government. In particular, on December 6, 2017, Trump declared US recognition of Jerusalem as Israel's capital. As expected, Netanyahu welcomed the announcement, calling it a "historic day," but Palestinian President Mahmoud Abbas declared that the United States could no longer act as a mediator between Israel and the Palestinians. China and many European countries criticized Trump's initiative. It remains to be seen whether Beijing will limit or at least pretend to scale back some of its initiatives relating to Israel.

From the Chinese viewpoint, improved relations with Israel and the Jewish people at large risks focusing world attention on China's conflicts with its Muslim minority. Robust Sino–Israeli relations are likely to jeopardize China's relations with the greater Muslim world and hamper its growing dependence on Middle Eastern oil producers. On the other hand, closer China–Israel links could perhaps benefit Sino–American relations as well, which are turning sour due to geopolitical and diplomatic confrontations. At any rate, bilateral Sino–Israeli talks on strategic matters indicate a change for the better.

Chapter Eight

China, Israel, and Other Spheres

China, the Palestinians, and the Middle East

At the April 1955 Bandung conference, China was fully exposed to the depth of the Arab–Israeli conflict. The Arab delegates and Ahmad Al-Shukeiri, then assistant secretary-general of the Arab League (later chairman of the PLO), asked to place the Palestinian issue on the agenda conference. China was strongly influenced by the Soviet Union's stance on the Middle East. While expressing sympathy to the Palestinian cause, China followed Moscow in valuing Israel as a socialist state, and so China did not call for Israel's destruction. Rather, it expressed the hope that the two rivals would resolve the conflict and live together. In 1964 the Palestinian Liberation Organization (PLO) was formed and China recognized the Palestinian people as a nation. It also granted Palestine full diplomatic recognition.

Twenty years later the PLO's office in Beijing was upgraded to the status of an embassy. Beijing's support of various Palestinian organizations and its recognition of Arab and Muslim countries were compatible with its emerging status as leader of the Third World, particularly the Afro-Asian countries, which were seen as victims of colonialism. Still lacking diplomatic relations with Israel, China supported the Israeli Communist Party (ICP), which supported the cause of the Palestinian Arabs, particularly those residing within the boundaries of the state of Israel.

In March 1965, during the PLO chairman's visit to China, Zhou Enlai pledged and delivered light arms to the PLO. This strengthened the status of the PLO worldwide. The 1967 defeat of three Arab states by Israel convinced the Palestinians that the Chinese doctrine of "people's war" was more applicable to their conflict with Israel than traditional, conventional war. In the ensuing conflict with Jordan, China provided arms shipments to the Palestinians through Syria, Lebanon, and Iraq. Diplomatically, China criticized American and Soviet peace initiatives, branding them unacceptable, as the rivals themselves—Arabs and Israelis—were excluded from the process. After the People's Republic of China was admitted to the United Nations in 1971 and assumed a permanent seat at the Security Council, the Palestinians had an advocate in the international organization.

But gradually, during the Cultural Revolution and following the death of Mao Zedong, China under Deng Xiaoping became a status quo nation concerned more with economic development and reconstruction, and less with revolutionary change and ethos. Chinese–American rapprochement and the improvement of relations with Israel influenced China's level of cooperation with the PLO. In the late 1970s and following the war with Vietnam, China began to realize Israel's importance and its potential to China's economic, academic, military, and scientific success. Israel had much to contribute in agriculture, technology, high-tech, industry, information technology, and many other advanced fields. Here the Arab states, and especially the Palestinians, could offer very little.

Palestinian setbacks in Jordan and later in Lebanon, the fragmentation of the Arab countries regarding the Arab–Israeli conflict (mainly the peace treaties signed between Israel, Egypt, and Jordan), among other developments in the Middle East, convinced Beijing that the path to peace based on UN resolutions was far more viable than revolutionary guerilla warfare. Still, in 1988 Beijing recognized the declaration of independence of the state of Palestine.

As Olimat explains in his book, following Operation Desert Storm (1991), the United States pursued a process aimed at resolving the Arab–Israeli conflict. Simultaneously, an interesting and fruitful process started in Oslo which led to the mutual acceptance of the Declaration of Principles on Interim Self-Government Arrangements. The Palestinians and Israelis accepted each other and their respective right to exist. At the same time the fragmentation among the Palestinian factions, namely between Hamas and Fatah (the Palestinian nationalist political party and the largest faction of the confederated multi-party Palestine Liberation Organization), contributed to the weakness of the position of the Palestinians in the peace process. Fatah denounced in principle violence, while Hamas (who controlled Gaza since 2006) continued to hold tight to the resistance option.

China has and still supports international efforts to end Israel's blockade to Gaza. Yet on the whole, in the post-Arab Spring (2010 to 2013) world, the Palestinian situation seemed quite bleak, and Israel's position vis-à-vis China became stronger and more solid. It was conceived as a rock-hard, stable, and reliable island in the stormy Middle East.

In December 2017 China's Foreign Minister Wang Yi reiterated China's willingness to bring Israeli and Palestinian representatives together as soon as possible. The offer came just a month after China's special envoy on Middle East affairs, Gong Xiaosheng, concluded a visit to Israel and Palestine and said both parties welcomed China's involvement in the peace talks and were ready to work with China to find a solution. China had proposed a trilateral dialogue with Palestine and Israel back in July, following separate visits by Palestinian President Mahmoud Abbas and Israeli Prime Minister Benjamin Netanyahu to Beijing. At times it seems that China is trying to fill the vacuum caused by President Donald Trump's decision to move the US embassy in Israel to Jerusalem, reversing decades of careful American diplomatic policy. It remains to be seen whether the United States has essentially disqualified itself from its leadership role in the quest for Middle East peace and will allow China, as President Xi Jinping put it at the 19th Party Congress in October, to move closer to the center of the stage.

As in the rest of the world, the Chinese government was alert to the dangers of terror when in September 2000, the Second Intifada (a Palestinian uprising against the Israeli occupation of the West Bank and Gaza) erupted in Israel. And despite the Chinese government's tendency to favor the Palestinians, it could hardly ignore the parallel between the Israeli–Palestinian conflict and the clashes between the ethnic Han Chinese and the Uyghurs, an ethnic Muslim group living in Xinjiang Province.[320] In early July 2009, violent clashes had broken out among the Uyghurs, the Han Chinese, and police forces in Ürümqi, the capital of Xinjiang, causing two hundred deaths and the wounding of 180. Following the clashes, the Chinese government imposed a curfew on the province and blocked access to the internet and the cellular network.

---

320 The section on China and the Palestinians is based on various sources such as Yitzhak Shichor, *The Middle East in China's Foreign Policy 1949–1977* (London, 1979) and Muhamad S. Olimat, *China and the Middle East Since World War II*, chapter 10 (London, 2014). For more on Xinjiang, see for example, Mackerras, "Xinjiang and the War against Terrorism."

Even before the outbreak of this violence, some Palestinian circles made statements in which they referred to Xinjiang as "occupied territory." But the use of this term was hardly helpful to the Palestinian cause—if anything, it was likely to lead to serious problems with the Chinese. If China continued to criticize Israel and support self-determination for the Palestinians and even for Arab Israelis, Palestinian identification with the Uyghur minority could prove to be a double-edged sword. China considered Xinjiang and also Tibet to be problematic, rebellious regions that aspired to disengage from the motherland. If China amplified its critique of Israel for refusing to enable Palestinian independence, what would prevent other countries from criticizing China for similar behavior toward the Uyghur and Tibetan minorities within its territory?

On July 25, 2006, during the Second Lebanon War, a Chinese UN officer named Du Zhaoyu and three UN observers from Austria, Finland, and Canada were killed when an Israeli shell hit their bunker. China condemned the incident and demanded that Israel carry out a comprehensive investigation and apologize to the Chinese government and the victims' families. The Chinese ambassador to the UN called for a ceasefire in Lebanon and demanded that the UN denounce Israel's actions there and carry out its own investigation of the incident. The United States vetoed both demands, thus blocking an anti-Israel process.

Still, in early 2006 China seemed to moderate its stance on this issue, following a Hamas victory in elections for the Palestinian Authority and increasing concern in China regarding Iran's mounting nuclear power. Although China demonstrated sympathy for Hamas leaders and the Iranian leadership, it simultaneously showed signs of willingness to be more involved in the Israel–Arab–Palestine conflict and even sent observers to Lebanon. In 2007 China held talks with Iran regarding the situation in Lebanon. Its membership in the UN Security Council enabled it to take on a significant role in problematic global arenas—including the Gaza Strip and Lebanon.

Another example of China's policy in the Middle East could be seen during the visit of Chinese Foreign Minister Yang Jiechi to Israel in April 2009, where he was met by a protest of Falun Gong practitioners.[321] In discussions with several Israeli officials, including President Shimon Peres, he encouraged Israel and the Palestinian Authority to return to the negotiating

---

321 See note 4, above.

table through "trust-building steps taken by all involved parties." He called for progress in the Middle East peace process and expressed the hope of holding talks as soon as possible between Israel on one side and Lebanon and Syria on the other.[322] Yang expressed this position at the press conference he held with Mahmoud Abbas (Abu Mazen) and repeated it when he met with Netanyahu. He expressed China's willingness to assist in advancing the peace process and to serve as an influential power on the Middle East issue. In reaction, Netanyahu explained Israel's position on the topic and emphasized that Israel placed significant emphasis on deepening its relationship with China and expanding cooperation with it.[323]

In April 2009, while visiting Damascus, Yang publicized a five-point plan for advancing the peace process. First, both sides had to continue the peace talks and cooperate with international proposals and solutions, including UN decisions, the principle of land for peace, the "road map," and the Arab peace initiative. Second, both sides had to take trust-building steps to create comfortable conditions and a positive atmosphere for advancing the peace process. Third, he expressly stated that China supported the two-state solution for both peoples. He called for the establishment of an independent Palestinian state alongside Israel, a step that would "ensure peace and security in the Middle East." Fourth, the international community had to continue to work on the Palestinian issue, including internal Palestinian issues such as politics and the economy. Fifth, the negotiation channels—Palestinian, Syrian, and Lebanese—must coordinate with each other to advance the peace process in the entire Middle East. In addition, he noted that "China, as a permanent member of the UN Security Council, will continue to support communication and coordination between the sides, and will play a significant role on the path to achieving a solution that is comprehensive, just, and sustainable, for the problems in the Middle East."[324]

Yang also expressed esteem for China's relations with the four Middle Eastern states that he visited on that trip and emphasized the importance of cooperation, trust, and mutual political coordination on

---

322 "Israeli President Meets with Foreign Minister Yang," *Chinese Mission to the UN Website* (April 23, 2009): http://www.china-un.ch/eng/xwdt/t558942.htm

323 "Chinese FM Urges Resumption of Israeli-Palestinian Peace Talks," *Xinhua* (April 23, 2009): http://news.xinhuanet.com/english/2009-04/23/content_11238582.htm

324 "Foreign Minister Yang Jiechi Makes Five-Point Proposal to Promote Mideast Peace Process," Chinese Ministry of Foreign Affairs Website: http://www.mfa.gov.cn/eng/wjb/wjbz/2467/t559690.htm.

international and regional issues. Regarding the global economic crisis, Yang emphasized China's activities to improve the situation and expressed hope that out of crisis, new economic initiatives would rise in fields such as commerce, investment, energy, infrastructure, and human resources development.[325]

Still, despite these declarations and the sending of a special envoy to the region, China's presence in the Middle East was barely felt. The United States and other Quartet members remained the main diplomatic players on this stage. The central challenge that Israel's government faced in its relationship with China was to advance Israel's own agenda and convince China of its justification.

China's fundamentally pro-Arab stance largely derives from interests related to energy and Third World nations. The amount of oil that China imports from the Middle East rose from 1.15 million tons during the 1990s to forty-five million tons in 2004. In 2005 China imported 58 percent of its oil from the Middle East, 13.6 percent of this from Iran. Since the economic crisis of 2008, imports of oil from the Middle East have declined. After the Chinese government located other sources to supply its energy needs, China's oil imports from the Middle East declined further, to 40 percent of the total.[326] Still, China remains very dependent on oil from the Middle East. According to the forecast of the US Energy Information Administration, the increase in the Chinese demand for oil will soon represent over 35 percent of the total increase in demand worldwide. Unsurprisingly, then, China has adopted a sympathetic policy toward Iran and the Arab world. Some even might say that China's geopolitical power will be increasingly dependent on its access to oil sources in the Middle East. Additionally, many states in Africa and the Middle East that supply oil or sell drilling rights to China purchase weapons and military equipment made in China. This commerce gives China a foothold in the region and, in practice, represents a strategic step on China's part to develop long-term ties with these states, which will ensure the supply for China's ever-increasing energy needs.[327]

---

325 Ibid.

326 China Daily, http://www.chinadaily.com.cn. The Middle East accounted for just under half of China's crude oil imports in 2016: see http://www.tankershipping.com/news/view,china-looks-beyond-the-middle-east-for-its-crude-oil-fix_48954.htm (retrieved December 14, 2017).

327 Pentland, "Did the US Invade Iraq to Contain China?"

The "Arab Spring," the wave of social protests that broke out in many Arab states in late 2010 and continued until 2013, borrowed its name from the collapse of old European regimes in 1848 known as the "Spring of Nations." Revolutions began in Tunisia, Egypt, Libya, Bahrain, Syria, and Yemen, making waves in other states in the region. Beijing suffered losses from the collapse of their initiatives in many of these states. In Libya, for example, following the fall of Muammar Khaddafi, China lost some twenty billion dollars. Official China was embarrassed. It preferred stability in the Arab world, even if this did not fit the profile of a regime that was representative, democratic, or even semi-democratic. The fall of established leaders with whom China had enjoyed a positive, strong relationship posed challenging dilemmas to Beijing policy-makers. The continued revolution in Syria, for example, was diplomatically destructive to China. China assisted by sending military and civilian aid, but developments on that front disappointed Beijing, especially in light of the appearance of Islamist fighters from Xinjiang (east Turkistan) on the side of the rebels. [328]

Instability in the Middle East did not prevent China from pressuring Israel and voicing criticism against it at the encouragement of Arab states. The Center for Middle Eastern Studies at Shanghai Jiao Tong University developed a new model for more assertive Chinese diplomatic involvement in the Middle East and North Africa, according to which China will adopt a proactive diplomatic stance. Beijing seems to gradually be exchanging the policy of non-involvement for a strategy that contributes to development and stability in these regions, both through political and business channels as well as with the assistance of non-government organizations. Thus in February 2012, a delegation of thirty Chinese businesspeople and academics visited Israel and the Palestinian Authority, aiming to gather information and identify targets for investment and development.[329]

The civil war in Syria from 2012 to date has created a new dilemma for policy-makers in Beijing. On one hand, China continues its obligation to Assad's regime. On the other, the seemingly endless state of war, with its cruel acts of violence toward innocent civilians, no longer permits China to maintain an apathetic, indifferent policy.

---

328 For more on this issue, see Evron, "Patterns of Chinese Involvement in the Middle East"; Wu Sike, "The Upheaval in West Asia and North Africa," and *Ynet*, Yaron Friedman, December 3, 2017 (retrieved December 14, 2017).

329 Witte, "A Quiet Transformation."

Discussions I held at the China Institute of International Studies revealed that both China and Israel are facing an uneasy crossroads with regard to Syria. Despite the uncomfortable tenor of the situation, both would prefer that Assad's regime remain in power to promise stability and quiet in the region. In September 2013 the US government refrained from attacking Syria by sea even after Syria used chemical weapons against the rebel forces, and this served to strengthen Russia's position in the Middle East and beyond. Suddenly it seemed that the unipolar system led by Washington had disappeared, replaced by the bipolar model of the Cold War—the United States versus Russia. Understandably, then, US Secretary of State John Kerry was quick to beg China to abandon its passive stance and adopt a constructive, positive role in decisions regarding the Syrian crisis. If the international community preferred a diplomatic solution even against the will of President Obama, Washington preferred that China take on a significant role in the newly evolving arrangement.[330]

Aside from these issues, some see China as an active and motivated candidate to replace the United States in involvement in the Middle East. Commerce between China and Middle Eastern countries, including Israel, is accelerated as opposed to American trade with countries in this region. Because Chinese interest in this region is still deeply interconnected with Iranian oil, greater cooperation between China and the United States could take place. Indeed, China is largely dependent on American military protection of oil shipments from the region. Still, it refuses to conform to the US position regarding foreign policy in the region in general, and toward Iran in particular.[331]

Iran–China–Israel

In addition to the United States, Russia, France, Germany, and Great Britain, China is one of the P5+1 states that holds discussions with Iran. The value of trade transactions between Iran and China from January to August 2017 reached $24.17 billion, showing a 24 percent increase compared to the same period in 2016. Between January and October of 2017, China's commodity turnover with Iran was $30.5 billion—22 percent higher

---

330 French News Agency, as cited in *Ynet*, September 19, 2013.
331 Paul Rivlin, "Will China Replace the US in the Middle East?" Iqtisadi, Moshe Dayan Center, vol. 4, no. 3, March 25, 2014.

than the previous year.[332] This value is expected to increase dramatically.[333] In May 2009 Chinese ministers participated in an economic conference in Tehran. Later that year a senior Iranian official noted that the increasing scope of commerce between these countries had transformed China into Iran's largest trade partner in Asia.[334] In 2011, 10 percent of China's oil imports came from Iran (a decline compared to six years previously), and some 80 percent of China's total imports from Iran were of oil. Today, China is investing in development and modernization of this field in Iran to ensure continued convenient access to this precious resource.[335] The China National Petroleum Corporation signed an eighty-five million dollar contract to drill nineteen wells in natural gas fields in southern Iran, and a similar contract for thirteen million dollars.[336] Alongside its cooperation with Iran, China is well-aware of objections from Israel and other countries to Iran's nuclear program.

In 2010 the UN Security Council passed Resolution No. 1929, which levied a fourth round of sanctions against Iran in response to its nuclear enrichment program. At first China objected to the decision, but later, and despite its connections with Iran, it was forced to support it. Israel explained to China the scenario of a preventive strike against Iran and the effect this would have on the global oil supply, and by extension China.[337] In December 2013, just before the renewal of talks between Iran and the major world powers, Prime Minister Benjamin Netanyahu spoke with Chinese Foreign Minister Wang Yi, who was visiting Israel on the Iranian nuclear issue. In Wang's statement to the media during the visit, he made no mention of Iran.[338]

The discussions on this issue began well before the present Netanyahu government. In his visit to China in 2007, Prime Minister Ehud Olmert

---

332 See http://theiranproject.com/blog/2017/10/22/iran-china-bilateral-trade-surpasses-24-bln-8-months-report, and https://eadaily.com/en/news/2017/12/06/iran-china-pragmatic-partnership-despite-us-sanctions (retrieved December 15, 2017).

333 "Iran–China Trade Value to Increase to $70b in 5 Yrs: Iranian Envoy," *Tehran Times*, http://tehrantimes.com/politics/100518-iran-china-trade-value-to-increase-to-70b-in-5-yrs-iranian-envoy, August 12, 2012.

334 Farrar-Wellman and Frasco, "China–Iran Foreign Relations."

335 Simpson, "Russian and Chinese Support for Tehran."

336 Dorraj and Currier, "Lubricated with Oil."

337 Jacobs, "Israel Makes Case to China."

338 "Netanyahu Warns Chinese Foreign Minister against Nuclear Iran": AFP, http://news.yahoo.com/netanyahu-warns-chinese-foreign-minister-against-nuclear-iran-202605078.html, December 18, 2013.

clarified that as a permanent member of the UN Security Council, China was expected to respond to Iran's efforts to arm itself with nuclear weapons. He expressed his appreciation for China's vote on Security Council Resolution 1737 of December 2006, which had levied sanctions against Iran. Still, he emphasized that from the Israeli viewpoint this step was insufficient. Israel expected broader cooperation from China regarding sanctions against Iran.

In October 2007 Israeli Foreign Minister Tsipi Livni met with Chinese Prime Minister Wen Jibao and Foreign Minister Yang Jiechi in Beijing and pressed them to assist in pushing a UN decision on sanctions against Iran. The Chinese reaction was diplomatic and polite. They praised the agricultural assistance that Israel was giving to Chinese farms, but they did not commit to any change in their policy toward Iran. Thus despite the impression that Olmert and Livni attempted to create, the Chinese did not deviate from their usual stance: the Iranian nuclear program must be stopped, but the actions taken should be part of what they called a "balanced policy." Olmert's visit to China had been preceded by a visit from Ali Larijani, secretary of the Supreme Council for National Security in Iran and the chief negotiator on the nuclear issue. During his visit the Iranian representative warned that if Iran felt threatened, it was liable to develop a nuclear program not only for civilian purposes, but for military use as well.

Following Olmert's and Livni's visits, China continued to maintain a delicate balance in its diplomatic approach. It refused (and still refuses) to ignore the major economic dimension of its relations with Iran. China's stance did not change even after Netanyahu's visit there in May 2013. Apparently, on this issue China has adopted a long-term strategic policy based on its fundamentally pragmatic approach to this topic. In June 2014 Sun Jiazheng, a member of China's political advisory committee and president of the NGO system, replied to Efraim Halevi's question of whether there was any chance that China might block Iran's nuclear program, as the Israeli government hoped. Jiazheng insisted that his government had no influence on Iran, contrary to what Westerners might think. He also asserted that China's influence on North Korea was also quite restricted.[339] Beyond pointing to the confines of China's power, these statements seemed to indicate its limited willingness to brake nuclear development in the two rogue states.

---

339 Interview with Efraim Halevi, June 15, 2015.

Undoubtedly this issue is interwoven with the fact that 60 percent of the oil imported to China passes through the Hormuz Straits, which are under Iranian control. Although China can purchase the oil it needs from other sources in a crisis, such as Saudi Arabia, it always prefers to rely on the broadest possible range of suppliers. For its part, Iran purchases significant quantities of Chinese products, an important consideration when calculating the Chinese balance of trade.

In general, we must recall that Iran has become a nuclear threshold nation with the assistance of China, which supplies it not only technology and uranium but also an international umbrella that prevents punishment by organizations in which China is a member.[340] China's peacemaking "harmony" policy in the global arena means that it avoids any possible conflict with Iran. China believes that this policy is efficient, and it hopes to reach diplomatic arrangements gradually and through mutual understanding. Decision-makers within Israel are perhaps gradually internalizing this reality, which means they will not be able to convince China to adopt an approach that conforms to their desires. China has interests that do not overlap with the United States and Israel—it has its own unique priorities.[341]

Farhad Ibrahimov has claimed that the Americans were not happy to observe the developing relations between Iran and China. Under Obama they "tried to improve their relations with the Iranians by lifting some of their sanctions. The Iranians responded with certain concessions on their nuclear program, but they were pragmatic enough not to stop the program at all. They kept the examples of Iraq and Libya in mind and did not trust the Americans." In January 2016 the United States lifted some of the anti-Iranian sanctions. However, President Trump called Obama's agreements shameful and renewed the US sanctions policy against Iran. He accused Iran of breaking its obligations concerning its nuclear program and supporting terrorists and extremists in the Middle East. Once again the Iranians concluded that they could not trust the Americans. Both China and Iran believe that the world should not be unipolar. China gives Iran strategic priority in the Middle East and will continue to strengthen its ties

---

340 Shiffer, "Former Mossad Chief."

341 For more on Iran's attitude toward Muslims in China, see "Iran Voices Support for Rights of Chinese Muslims: 'Xinjiang Incidents Had Nothing to Do with Religion,'" Press TV Online, July 9, 2009. See also: "China-Iran Foreign Relations," Mehr News Agency, July 23, 2009. https://eadaily.com/en/news/2017/12/06/iran-china-pragmatic-partnership-despite-us-sanctions (Farhad Ibrahimov for EADaily).

with that country. Iran considers China a great power that wields a weighty opinion on global issues, particularly Syria. Like Iran, China supports the Bashar al-Assad regime. One of the key projects of Iranian–Chinese cooperation is the Belt and Road Initiative. In 2014 China and Iran signed a military cooperation agreement and soon after that they agreed to cooperate in combating terrorism. In this respect, Israel finds itself quite alienated from these two countries.

China's Relations with North Korea

China aspires to create stability and quiet in the region. It has no desire for a nuclear Korea that will distract its military attention from the issue of Taiwan and the China Sea, which are more important to it. China does not support the North Korean policy of "walking on the edge" and its provocative behavior (especially under the regime of the young Kim Jong-un). It continues to play the role of mediator between the West and North Korea.

From Israel's viewpoint the question is whether China will be able to prevent military and strategic exports from North Korea to Syria and Iran. Will assisting Pyongyang grant Beijing the diplomatic leverage to serve as a moderating influence? Clearly, as in the past, Beijing cannot adopt a harsh stance toward North Korea—the two regimes have been connected at the umbilical cord for over six decades. China also fears that a severe crisis or dissolution of the North Korean regime will lead many Koreans to flee from the North into Chinese-governed territory. According to current estimates, between one hundred and three hundred thousand North Koreans have already entered China illegally. China wants to prevent this extreme scenario. This issue stands in contrast to the American demand for "complete, irreversible, and verifiable dismantling" of the nuclear reactors in Korea. Israel's possibilities on the China–Korea–US question are negligible. Can it be argued that Jerusalem erred in 1992 when it adopted the viewpoint of the Defense Ministry and the Mossad (against the position of the Foreign Ministry) and refused a momentary North Korean initiative for limited cooperation?[342] In April 2013 the situation on the Korean Peninsula intensified. North Korea made declarations of war and even sev-

---

342 See Efraim Halevi, Man in the Shade, 55–57, and interview with him, June 15, 2015 and Aron Shai, "North Korea and Israel: A Missed Opportunity"? *Israel Journal of Foreign Affairs*, vol. 10, 2016. Evelyn Cheng, https://www.cnbc.com/2017/08/29/north-koreas-missile-launch-a-real-test-for-china.html (retrieved December 16, 2017).

ered its loose, symbolic ties with the regime in South Korea. North Korea amplified its militaristic rhetoric and directed it against the United States and Japan. China found itself in the eye of a storm that it had never before experienced—would it be able to exploit its influence over Pyongyang, or would it be forced to concede defeat? Beijing hinted more than once that it could not force its will on Pyongyang.

North Korea's 2017 missile launch over Japan made China's job much harder. Pyongyang seemed to change the rules of the game and raise the stakes. It demonstrated that it had the range to reach Guam. Again all eyes turned to Beijing. The feeling was that it could do more to restrain the North Koreans as two-thirds of that country's trade is with China. Subsequently, China suspended coal imports from North Korea and banned North Korean individuals and enterprises from doing business in China. But in the key area of energy supply, Beijing has done little. It refused to agree on sanctions because these could destabilize the North Korean regime. As in the past, Beijing called for restraint and dialogue. In March 2018 President Donald Trump agreed to meet with North Korean leader Kim Jong-un by May, setting the scene for an unprecedented encounter between two nations that had threatened to wipe each other out. They met on June 12. It seemed that Pyongyang was willing to put its nuclear and missile program on the table.

Relations between Israel and Taiwan (Nationalist China)

Ties between Israel and Taiwan began after Chiang Kai-shek, the defeated leader of Nationalist China, abandoned the continent and fled to the island of Taiwan (Formosa) after the Communist victory.[343] Previously, when the State of Israel was founded in 1948, Nationalist China and Israel had diplomatic ties, and these continued until Israel recognized the revolutionary Chinese regime, the People's Republic of China, in January 1950.

Historian Jonathan Goldsmith divides Israel–Taiwan relations into five stages, beginning even before the establishment of the two states: 1) 1917 to 1945—Nationalist China actively supports the Zionist movement; 2) 1945

---

343 The Republic of China was established in 1912 under Sun Yat-sen, who was followed by Chiang Kai-shek. Nationalist China was ruled by the Guomindang, known as the "Nationalist Party." Following the defeat of the Nationalist Chinese government by the Communists, its leaders and supporters retreated to Taiwan. The term "Nationalist China" referred to Chiang Kai-shek's regime and his successors on Taiwan, but eventually the state came to be known informally as "Taiwan." Its formal name remains "the Republic of China."

to 1949—Nationalist China abstains from the UN vote to establish the State of Israel; 3) 1949—Nationalist China recognizes Israel, permits opening an honorary Israeli consul in Shanghai, and votes in favor of accepting Israel into the UN; 4) January 1950 to January 1992 (following the Communist success in mainland China)—Israel and Taiwan maintain limited, informal ties, including several weapons deals; 5) January 24, 1992 onward (following the establishment of diplomatic ties between the People's Republic of China and Israel)—Israel–Taiwan relations are based on a unique, informal footing.[344]

In December 1948, Moshe Yuval, then serving as Israel's vice consul in New York, was sent to Shanghai (then under the control of Nationalist China) as representative of the ministry of immigration to arrange the immigration of the Shanghai Jews to Israel. He remained in the cosmopolitan city for several weeks until early 1949. After some time, in May, Israel named a Yuval's replacement—Isador Magid, a respected Jew who had been born in Harbin and lived in China. He was given the title of honorary consul. Like his predecessor, he issued entry permits to Israel for any Jews who were interested.[345] During the initial period several thousand Jews emigrated to Israel from China. Yuval was not expected to carry out diplomacy with the Chinese government. The political and military situation in the city rapidly spiraled out of control (in May 1949 the city fell into Communist hands). But more importantly, the Nationalist Chinese government under Chiang Kai-shek recognized the State of Israel in March 1949. The change in China's approach toward Israel apparently stemmed from Israel and Egypt's signature on a ceasefire agreement one month earlier, which led to similar agreements with Jordan, Lebanon, and Syria. Nationalist China exchanged its indifferent approach to the Jewish state's aspirations for a positive attitude, which it expressed in discussions on accepting Israel as a member of the UN. As opposed to abstention from the critical vote on the partition plan for Palestine in 1947, Nationalist China's representatives voted in favor of accepting Israel as a member of the international body.[346] Some thought that following the unfriendly policy of the Republic of China (Taiwan), Israel repaid it equally when, as a UN member, Israel supported the popular regime that arose in Beijing.[347] But

---

344 Goldstein, "The Republic of China and Israel."
345 Magid, "I Was There," 43; see also Yegar, *The Long Journey to Asia*, 237–238.
346 Goldstein, 12–14.
347 Yegar, *The Long Journey to Asia*, 287.

apparently Jerusalem's reasons for supporting the Communist regime were more deeply thought out.

Magid remained in China until 1951, when he was replaced by Dr. D. Avish. As Israel was formally part of the UN coalition in the struggle then taking place in Korea, and in the absence of diplomatic relations between Jerusalem and Beijing and the almost complete disappearance of the Jewish community from Shanghai, there was no room for continuation of the informal activity of these two representatives of Israel. Even the final activities that Magid carried out to transfer some of the property of the city's Jewish community to the Israeli government proved hopeless, as when the Communist regime stabilized, it nationalized foreign property.[348]

In October 1949 the Communists declared victory and established the People's Republic of China. Chiang Kai-shek and his supporters fled to Taiwan, where they established the Republic of China. Ever since, two separate political entities have existed: Taiwan, which aspires to be an independent nation in all respects, and the People's Republic of China, which asserts that Taiwan is an inseparable part of itself, like Xinjiang and Tibet. The parallel existence of two opposing Chinese regimes has forced other global nations to take a stance on the question of which entity to recognize as the "official" state of China. In January 1950 Israel recognized the Communist regime in the People's Republic, a choice that tipped the balance of its relations with Taiwan. From that point on, Israel–Taiwan relations were always influenced by Israel's hope to complete the process of recognition and to establish formal diplomatic relations with the People's Republic of China. For example, in the votes over the seat reserved for China in the UN, Israel has tended to favor the People's Republic, but due to a few exceptions when Israel voted in favor of Taiwan, some have inferred an attempt to preserve a delicate balance.[349]

A significant turning point in relations came at the unlikely moment of the Cultural Revolution. In the early 1970s the violent stage of the revolution ended. China–US relations began to thaw, and with that, hope awakened in Israel for an improvement in ties with the People's Republic of China. A significant step in this direction took place in October 1971, when Israel expressed support for China's becoming a member of the UN—at

---

348 Goldstein, "The Republic of China and Israel," 15.

349 Yegar, *The Long Journey to Asia*, 287–288; author's interview with Mordechai Arbel on the votes of the Israeli delegation to the UN, June 2013.

Taiwan's expense. The Chinese leadership expressed appreciation for this process. Subsequently, Israel made the decision to open the Israeli consulate general in Hong Kong.[350]

Like many other countries, Taiwan shaped its policy toward Israel based on Israel's stance toward Beijing and on its own position toward the Arab states. It did not even consider the possibility of establishing true diplomatic relations with Israel. In most of its votes in the UN Taiwan adopted a pro-Arab stance, and due to its dependence on the Gulf Emirates for its oil supply, it avoided taking positive steps toward Israel.[351] This policy was mostly dictated by its close ties with Saudi Arabia. In the late 1970s the president of Taiwan made a joint declaration with Prince Fahd in which they both admonished Israel; called for immediate withdrawal from the occupied territories, including Jerusalem; and demanded that it grant independence and the right to self-determination to the Palestinian population.[352]

Still, over the years both sides managed to preserve shared interests, mainly economic, that have ensured the existence of informal ties. These interests primarily included mutual commercial ties, and on Taiwan's side learning about and purchasing Israeli-developed technologies.

In the 1960s Taiwanese officials had contact with representatives of the Israeli security establishment. Taiwan was especially interested in Israeli know-how in the field of nuclear research. Israel refused to cooperate on the nuclear issue but did not object to continued contacts in other fields of security and science. For example, in the late 1960s representatives of the Taiwan ministry of the economy visited Israel; a Taiwanese delegation came for training at the Weizmann Institute; and an informal delegation arrived to tour scientific institutions, defense establishment installations, and several factories. These groups mainly demonstrated interest in research in Israel and the possibility of knowledge exchange or purchasing knowledge from Israel. The central figure responsible for these contacts with Taiwan was the then chairman of Israel's atomic energy committee, Professor Ernst David Bergmann. Bergmann called for Israel to develop ties with Taiwan, whose importance was growing. This goal gained significance following Israel's impression that Taiwan viewed it as a path to liberating itself from dependence on the United States for know-how and defense.[353]

---

350 Merhav, "Dream of the Red Palaces," 567.
351 Yegar, *The Long Journey to Asia*, 288–289.
352 Goldstein, "The Republic of China and Israel," 18–19.
353 Yegar, *The Long Journey to Asia*, 288–289.

Despite this goodwill and the visiting delegations, the trend was not completely friendly, at least not with regard to open trade. Israeli companies were not awarded tenders in Taiwan, and the Taiwan Foreign Ministry prohibited importing Israeli goods. Israeli delegations that went to Taiwan in the late 1960s also faced defeat. For example, a meeting of the director of the Asian department in the Israel Foreign Ministry with the Taiwan ambassador to Tokyo was cancelled at the last minute by Taiwan, and an Israeli economic delegation that visited Taiwan was unable to meet with Taiwan Foreign Ministry officials regarding the trade restrictions.[354] But in this Taiwan was no different from many other countries around the world. Global opinion of Israel changed following victory in the Six Day War. As usual, the Arab states called for isolating and denouncing Israel. But other states began to view Israel as a regional power in the Middle East with a powerful army and advanced technology.

Accordingly, the 1970s were marked by tightening of Taiwan–Israel ties in the field of defense purchasing and commercial cooperation. Initially some deals fell through, such as the purchase of Gabriel and Gabriel 2 missiles, and Kfir aircraft. These were cancelled by Israel (fearing reaction from the People's Republic of China) or by the United States, as the Kfir aircraft carried American-manufactured components. But despite these failures, numerous deals were carried out. These included the sale of rifles, mortars, electronic equipment, and ammunition, and the transfer of technology for ground-to-ground missiles, short-range missiles, and anti-aircraft missiles. According to reports, by the end of the 1980s Israel had exported over five hundred missiles and seventy launchers to Taiwan as part of this cooperation. Other reports state that in the 1980s Israel supplied Taiwan with chemical materials, and in the 1990s deals were signed for selling Israeli manufactured Kfir aircraft, patrol speedboats, and missiles.[355] Another product of cooperation in these decades was that Israeli maritime company Zim opened a representative office in Taiwan.[356]

From the mid-1970s Ya'akov Lieberman served as mediator for Israeli sales to Taiwan on behalf of three major Israeli arms manufacturers. According to Lieberman, Israeli Aircraft Industries sold Gabriel sea-to-sea missiles to Taiwan for $180 million, Tadiran sold know-how and facilities for establishing a car battery factory as well as advanced communications

---

354 Ibid., 289.
355 Goldstein, "The Republic of China and Israel," 19.
356 Yegar, *The Long Journey to Asia*, 290–291.

equipment for over $130 million, and Elbit and Rafael sold electronic supervision and control equipment in a $150 million deal. Despite the impressive size of these deals, Lieberman qualified his words, adding that they were carried out due to the needs of the Taiwan defense system and not out of any honest desire for rapprochement with Israel. The deals did not document any change in Taiwan's stance toward Israel.[357]

A real change in Taiwan's cool attitude to Israel occurred in the 1990s, when it began to search for a thread that would lead to the creation of diplomatic ties with Israel. In late 1990 a representative of the Taiwan Foreign Ministry was sent to Israel to establish full diplomatic relations and to open mutual embassies, a consulate general, or a chamber of commerce if the first option proved not to be possible. Taiwan realized that it had erred in the past by avoiding ties with Israel, and that such ties would cause no real harm to its connections with Arab states.

But this significant change in Taiwan's approach was expressed at a problematic time from Israel's viewpoint, as it was then conducting negotiations with the People's Republic on the establishment of full diplomatic relations. Israel was not interested in taking any step that might endanger the emerging ties with China—and China objected outright to its friends having any diplomatic or political connection with Taiwan. Thus Israel tried to avoid Taiwan's attempts to create formal ties with it. However, Israel did not send the Taiwanese representative home empty-handed but expressed willingness to consider opening mutual chambers of commerce.[358]

Accordingly, after about two years of negotiations, in 1993 chambers of commerce were opened in Taiwan and Israel. During the discussions for this Israel carefully avoided arousing any objection on the part of the People's Republic and avoided damaging the ties with it. At the same time it followed the lead of many other states in tightening commercial ties with Taiwan. The Taiwan Chamber of Commerce opened in Tel Aviv in May 1993 under the name "Office of Economy and Commerce of Taipei." The Israeli office opened in August 1993 in Taipei, the capital of Taiwan.

Before that, Taiwan's deputy foreign minister visited Israel in 1992 to sign agreements on opening mutual chambers of commerce. Despite the objection of the Israeli Foreign Ministry a compromise was reached, and the senior Taiwan official was received in Israel as the guest of the Israel

---

357 Goldstein, "The Republic of China and Israel," 19–20.
358 Yegar, *The Long Journey to Asia*, 291.

Export Institute and not as an official guest of the Foreign Ministry. Clearly, at this point, and despite the rubber stamp that it gave to commercial ties between the two countries, Israel was not willing to grant the ties a diplomatic or political character. Israel understood that fulfilling the obligation not to engage in military, diplomatic, or political relations with Taiwan was a necessary condition to ensure the future of the still-fresh ties between Jerusalem and Beijing. Throughout that decade the Israeli Foreign Ministry continued to prevent formal visits of Taiwanese officials to Israel and turned away empty-handed those who desired to visit, such as Taiwan President Lee Teng-hui in 1995 and the deputy foreign minister in 1996.[359]

Despite the clear line that Israel drew in its diplomatic relations with Taiwan, ever since the tightening of commercial ties direct communication channels have been opened on issues of culture and economics, which until that point took place indirectly through Japanese mediation. For example, a tour guidebook for Israel was published in Taiwan; cooperative projects were initiated in music and art; and the scope of commerce grew, including Israeli exports to China. In 1995 bilateral trade reached four hundred million dollars, not including sales of weapons and diamonds.[360]

Fu-Kuo Liu identifies many similarities between Israel and Taiwan in the fields of economics, politics, society, diplomacy, and security.[361] On the aspect of diplomacy, he asserts, Israel and Taiwan are "islands of democracy and freedom" in regions where democracy is a rare commodity. Both have faced many obstacles in the attempt to take part in regional organizations, and neither can rely on continuous support from the UN. On the economic front, Fu declared, Israel and Taiwan have both developed at a rapid pace and are considered "economic miracles." They operate according to similar economic models and, as part of their development, place strong emphasis on education and human capital. In the field of defense both states face threats to their existence from larger neighbors, and their defense systems are based on advanced military technology and on special ties with the United States. Fu added that based on these similarities and shared values, the two countries have the potential for close friendship. Conceivably, Israel

---

359 Ibid., 292.

360 Goldstein, "The Republic of China and Israel," 20–21; Yegar, *The Long Journey to Asia*, 291.

361 "Taiwan–Israel Relations: Towards a New Partnership," Herzliya Conference Website (December 16–18, 2003): http://www.herzliyaconference.org/_Uploads/dbsAttachedFiles/1169Liu-taiwan.pdf

could place Taiwan in a high position on its list of friends in Asia.[362] This attitude is similar to that of Taiwan, which is searching for allies, including countries that have established formal relations with the People's Republic.

Today, more than a decade after the publication of Fu's research, we are left still wondering whether relations between the two countries are growing closer. The Taiwan issue was and remains extremely volatile in China's international relations. China views Taiwan's assertion of independence as the greatest threat to its hegemony and to peace in the region. China argues that it has the right to use force to "unite" with its "rebellious province." In March 2005, for example, China passed the Anti-Secession Law, which formalized this claim into law.

With regard to Taiwan the United States views itself as a protective, barrier entity, the power that guarantees peace for the island state. Thus it continues to sell defensive weapons to Taiwan—to China's frustration. Under certain circumstances, China is likely to adopt measures to prevent these actions, and we may assume that such initiatives will have far-reaching consequences not only in the Straits of Taiwan but elsewhere as well. During Obama's term tension between the United States and China flared surrounding the issues of Taiwan and Tibet. China's policy in the South China Sea also contributed to this escalation when it defined an air defense identification zone (ADIZ) for protection from Japanese and foreign aircraft.

As opposed to the United States, Israel continues to follow the line that China dictates. Still, to China's irritation, an Israel–Taiwan parliamentary friendship association is active in the Knesset, and Israeli members of Knesset visit Taiwan. Groups of Israeli Knesset members made two trips to Taiwan, causing serious diplomatic incidents with China.[363]

In 2010 and 2011 Taiwan was one of the five main markets for Israeli exports on the Asian continent. After several years of decline in exports between the two states, in 2013 trade reached $1.45 billion; by 2016 it had grown modestly to $1.48 billion ($655 million Israeli exports and $829 million imports).[364] Trade fields are mainly related to the electronics industry.

---

362 Fu-Kuo Liu, "Taiwan–Israel Relations."

363 See Amnon Mirenda and Ronen Bodoni, "MKs Visit to Taiwan Irks the Chinese," *Ynet*; and Ilan Marciano, "MKs Visited Taiwan and Shocked the Chinese," *Ynet*.

364 Israel Office of Economy and Culture in Taipei, "Israel-Taiwan Trade Data, April 2012." Website of the Israel Ministry of Economy, http://www.moital.gov.il/NR/rdonlyres/ FDA75C5B-9A66-42DD-BA4A-7CFC76D08490/0/israel_taiwan_trade_2012.pdf; and data from the Taiwan Office of Economy and Culture in Tel Aviv, in a letter from

Taiwan's investments in Israel are made directly or through third parties, mostly through Taiwan venture capital companies or as circular investments in Israeli high-tech companies traded on the US stock exchange.

Mutual trade agreements between Israel and Taiwan include the protocol on the cancellation of customs tax on marine products (June 1998); a cooperation agreement on standardization (March 1998); a protocol for actions on the issue of temporary transfer of merchandise (July 2003); a protocol for cooperation on agricultural produce (July 2004); a technological cooperation agreement (January 2006); a cooperation agreement on hygiene and medical treatments (July 2006); a cooperation agreement on arbitrage (January 2007); a sister port agreement between Keelung and Eilat (July 2007); a protocol for cooperation on computerization of citizen services (March 2008); a protocol for cooperation on small- and medium-sized new businesses (August 2008); and a protocol for cooperation on customs issues (May 2009). In addition, tourists and scholars from Taiwan frequently visited Israel.

China in the International Sphere

Before the global economic crisis in 2008, Chinese historians conducted a study of the rise and fall of world powers such as Spain, Great Britain, and even the United States. They presented this study to members of the Communist Party Politburo, and it was also made into a twelve-part television series. Indeed, China has suddenly become an empire (although without colonies). It is a major international power that has risen quietly and confidently, but world public opinion is only starting to internalize this development. For example, before 2011 China had accumulated foreign currency reserves of over three trillion dollars,[365] which subsequently grew to over $3.8 trillion (and then again in 2016 dropped to $3.011 trillion). Theoretically, if Beijing decides to transfer a sizeable portion of its investments from the dollar basket to the Euro basket, it could cause the

---

Susan C.I. Yang to Aron Shai, August 15, 2014. And information received from the Israeli office in Taipei, December 18, 2017.

365 People's Bank of China, pbc.gov.cn, March 31, 2011. China's foreign exchange reserves fell for a sixth straight month in December but by less than expected to the lowest since February 2011, as authorities stepped in to support the yuan ahead of US President-elect Donald Trump's inauguration. https://www.cnbc.com/2017/01/06/china-foreign-exchange-reserves-fall-in-december-to-lowest-since-february-2011.html (retrieved December 18, 2017).

American economy to crash. This threat means that China is one of the most influential entities on the fate of the greatest world power. By the end of 2014 China had invested ten billion dollars on many initiatives in the African continent. Some of these, such as quarries and oil drilling, are designed to extract raw materials, whether directly or indirectly.

After the Cold War, the international bipolar system pitting the United States against the Soviet Union disappeared. The United States became the only world power and enjoyed almost two decades of stable, uncontested hegemony. But this popular theory does not account for China's "quiet ascension" (*heping jueqi* 和平崛起), which came to the foreground in the context of the economic crisis of 2008.

What are the characteristics of this quiet ascension? In recent years a subtle but essential discussion has been taking place within China regarding its choices and strategy on global issues. On the pages of newspapers, magazines, and in numerous internal documents, senior Chinese officials and academics discuss the strategic possibility of translating their country's impressive economic success into achievements in the global political arena. From the Chinese point of view, adopting a "New Path" (*xin daolu* 新道路) does not mean entering conflicts with the United States or any other international power. On the contrary, it means showing the world that China intends to act to prevent possible conflicts. This process seems to fit China's policy of "harmony" (*he xie* 和谐), a national policy that aims to build an integrated society, combining progress and innovation with preservation of its rich cultural tradition. Quiet ascension means that China recognizes the challenges involved in its new historic role as the rising power in the international sphere. We may even say that this is an appropriate response for the argument of the "Chinese threat" frequently raised in the world's capitals. Indeed, the United States is concerned about the weapons and technology deals as well as the nuclear assistance that China is providing to rogue states, including Iran and Syria (which has a small Chinese-made reactor for research purposes).

There is one exception to China's role of "quiet ascension": the sensitive, even explosive issue of Taiwan. The recent Anti-Secession Law should be seen in this light.

Thus when determining its global priorities, Israel must consider China's economic achievements as well as the forecasts that are being realized regarding China's rise in the political arena. For example, China will undoubtedly play a significant role in the international arena, particularly in the Middle East and Israeli–Palestinian conflict. In broader terms, Israel must think "out of the box" and plan a long-term strategy. Under President Trump the United States will adopt a global role that differs from what Israel has been used to. Many lacunae will remain in which China may choose to act.

There are additional international issues that are connected to China–Israel relations, even if indirectly. China has attempted to achieve scientific and technological cooperative ventures and various arrangements with US allies in Asia, Central Asia, Europe, South America, Africa, and Canada. It also came to Russia's aid during the ruble crisis in late 2014.[366] These efforts do not have direct consequences for Israel or its relations with China, but they do have the potential to become severe points of contention between China and the United States. Only when the results of this situation are felt in the Middle East will these issues become imperative for Israel.

If China's appetite for natural resources grows, it is likely again to incite panic in Washington and lead to crucial decisions that have a domino effect on the Middle East. History has proven that conflicts between two powers based on the search for living space can lead to disastrous results. As already occurred in the Korean War, Israel might find itself at an uneasy junction for crucial decisions. In March and April 2018 it seemed that Donald Trump had embroiled the United States in a global trade war with China. The skirmish intensified after China imposed tit-for-tat import taxes on the United States and stock markets plunged. There are ways to make life quite harder for American companies in China that need not be formal or widely publicized. If the war spirals into a bigger conflict between the world's two biggest economies, it will be difficult to predict how the rules of the commercial, economic, and even the political arenas will develop.

The Future of Israel–China Relations

Israel has come a long way since the 1970s, when the Foreign Ministry decided to close its representations in Hong Kong and South Korea due to budget cuts. In those days Israel's Eurocentric tendency was so strong that appointing another diplomat to Paris or New York seemed more urgent than opening and maintaining representations in the young, emerging East Asian countries.

---

366 *The Marker*, December 23, 2014, Yediot Agencies.

Now we observe that Israel's conception has changed. The consulate general in Guangzhou was opened in March 2009. Its purpose is assisting and promoting cooperation between Israel and four important provinces in southeast China: Guangdong, Guangxi, Fujian, and Hainan, whose combined territory is thirty times the size of Israel and whose population is 220 million. During 2014 an Israeli consulate was opened in Chengdu, capital of Sichuan province. Undoubtedly this initiative will increase Israel's presence and influence in western China.

Aside from the diplomatic and economic channels, Israel is taking steps in other fields as well. In recent years new Israeli and Jewish nonprofit organizations have been established with a focus on understanding and improving Israel–China relations, and general organizations have opened departments to address this issue. We note for example the Sino–Israel Global Network and Academic Leadership institute (SIGNAL), the Schusterman Foundation, The Israel Project (TIP), and the Israel–Asia Center, which all work to promote understanding of Israel in China, mainly in the media and academia. Their projects bring delegations and students from China to Israel, design Israel studies programs for use in China, and organize joint seminars.[367]

Expanding cooperation in the fields of agriculture and technology and promoting tourism from China to Israel have the potential to double or even triple the scope of bilateral trade. These activities seem to be necessary in light of the American limitations on Israeli exports to China in other areas, mainly in the defense and security fields. These limitations may severely harm exports from Israel to other countries as well. Thus increasing the size of trade between China and Israel is not at all a guarantee. Still, in recent years business volume between the two states has reached an impressive level. The contracts for purchasing Makhteshim-Agan, Tnuva, and many more companies, as well as purchases and investments in high-tech, industry, and smartphone applications are perhaps an encouraging sign for the future. The guiding hand of the Chinese government seems to be pointing in a more lenient direction. Forecasts for the coming years estimate that business cooperation between the two countries will increase considerably.[368]

---

367 Tjong-Alvares, "The Geography of Sino–Israeli Relations," SIGNAL, 111–112.
368 Hagai Amit, "4 Billion NIS—2014 A Record Year for the Growing Business Between China and Israel," *The Marker*, March 9, 2015.

Certainly, any drastic change of course in the Israeli attitude toward China could be interpreted as a rushed, unwise step that might endanger the full support Israel enjoys from the United States. As for commerce, it is quite clear that following the strict limitations that the US government has placed on Israel after the Phalcon and Harpy incidents, Israel has been forced to accept American dictates. Still, the question remains: can Israel take more creative steps that will lead to a different reality vis-à-vis China?

From China's viewpoint, improved relations with Israel and Jewish organizations can exacerbate the Chinese regime's ties with the Muslim minority at home and the Muslim and Arab world abroad. China's ballooning oil needs are also likely to suffer. On the other hand, better relations with Israel are likely to improve China's relations with the United States.

Considering these points and despite the limitations noted, Israel must take significant steps to improve its relations with China and reap the anticipated fruits. It must dare to adopt a new policy toward China. This policy should be cautious, should consider the global changes that have taken place and continue to do so, and also must internalize the emerging reality in which not one power claims a foothold in our region but rather two (or even three).

Indeed, relations between the two countries are influenced by global changes in addition to the factors that affect only bilateral relations. Throughout the Arab Spring, China's rise as an economic power strengthened it as a balancing factor to the United States, with Israel only one consideration among many. Thus while China views the situation with detachment and realizes that Israel is just one of the countries in the Middle East, Israel pins its gaze on China through the narrower prism of what Israel stands to gain or lose from bilateral relations. Israel's interests in renewing military contact with China mainly focus on the possibility of intensifying pressure on Iran and deepening cooperation between China and Israel in the war on terror. Still, due to Israel's tight relationship with the United States, the horizon for strengthening Israel–China ties is limited. In the final analysis each country's interests will play the deciding role, as has been proved in the past.[369]

We conclude that the steps that Israel must take (and which it has already begun to take) are as follows: reevaluate its general policy toward China while examining probable future developments, identify obstacles

---

369 Evron, "The Rise of China from a Small State's Perspective."

to exports, and increase exports. Israel must assume that possibilities for activity in the field of defense exports remain low, as in the related field of dual use civilian-military products. This type of export will remain problematic. In addition Israel must take steps to strengthen the pro-Israeli stance among Chinese intellectuals and broader circles within the Chinese public and to create ties with individuals who are expected to become China's next leaders on the regional, national, and international levels, including the UN. Israel must also promote additional cooperative efforts in the neutral fields of science and academia, culture, and agriculture, strengthening informal ties in these areas.

Chapter Nine

Me, China, and Everyone Else

After the opening of the Chinese embassy in Israel in 1992 and the arrival of Chinese diplomats, I met on occasion with the ambassadors and embassy officials, mainly the cultural and higher education attachés. Within a relatively brief time, the Chinese became acquainted with some of the complexities of Israeli society and Israeli politics and diplomacy. The embassy's involvement in Israeli affairs has gradually increased. Alongside careful, highly professional diplomatic and consular work designed to promote bilateral ties in the economic, cultural, and educational realms, embassy officials have carefully followed events in the field of higher education. They were acquainted with the lecturers on Chinese studies and were aware of activities, classes, and lectures given on campuses, particularly those that addressed sensitive issues that deviated from Beijing's official policy, such as Tibet and the Falun Gong. As an example, embassy officials have attempted to foil the Dalai Lama's visits to Israel, or at least to minimize their significance and success.

For obvious political reasons Israel's official policy on this issue was to prohibit ministers and senior government officials from meeting the Dalai Lama. Israel also prohibited government representatives from having any contact with his retinue or with the Friends of Tibet Association, which was the main force behind bringing the Tibetan leader to Israel. During his last visit to Israel in 2006, the Chinese embassy tried to prevent the meeting with him held in the Smolarz Auditorium at Tel Aviv University. Ambassador Chen Yonglong called me and asked how we at Tel Aviv University, whom he considered friends of China, could permit such a visit. In response I contacted Professor Itamar Rabinovich, president of the university, and explained the dilemma of the Chinese and their request to the university. Rabinovich explained that Smolarz Auditorium functioned as an independent economic unit at the university and that anyone was permitted to rent it and use it for their purposes. "We cannot and do not wish to interfere in this issue," he asserted. When I explained this to the ambassador, he asked me to arrange a meeting with Rabinovich. As the president thought that the meeting should be short, we scheduled it for the fifteen minutes preceding the festive opening of the event—the first day of the Chinese New Year in February 2006.

In the meantime I made several inquiries and tried to discover what the Chinese ambassador might be after. I concluded that above all, he would consider it important to placate his government in Beijing. With this in mind I suggested that Rabinovich hand him an official letter stating that despite his position as head of the university, his hands were tied on the matter. At the meeting, which was held in the president's office, Rabinovich clarified his position diplomatically, and as per my suggestion he presented the letter to the ambassador. The ambassador was reasonably satisfied.

Another incident in which the ambassador tried to meddle in university affairs took place in 2004, about two years before the Dalai Lama incident. One of the secretaries at the Chinese embassy called me and asked whether a certain lecture on the Falun Gong was indeed planned to take place on our campus. At the time the Chinese government was conducting a comprehensive attack on this movement due to its teachings. The embassy representatives repeatedly emphasized to me that the movement was causing severe damage to its adherents and that many had even committed suicide due to the leaders' exhortations.

I clarified to the secretary that we did not teach this topic in the East Asian Studies Department and that we had no part in the event, but that possibly one of the students had initiated a lecture. Still, I emphasized that the university was a free and autonomous body and that we permitted a range of activities without overhead supervision.

Greater tension was caused following another initiative at the university related to the Falun Gong. In March 2008 the students' organization displayed an exhibit on the movement's activity at the entrance to the main library at the university. To be more exact, the exhibit was a graphic display of horrors allegedly perpetrated by the Chinese government against Falun Gong members, including torture and organ harvesting.

The students had received permission for the exhibit from the dean of students and China expert Professor Yoav Ariel. Regardless of whether Ariel investigated the origins of the exhibit and its implications, it was entitled "Truth, Compassion, Tolerance—An Art Exhibit." The first three terms were the official slogan of the Falun Gong. Possibly, the dean was misled into thinking the exhibit was about art or modern Chinese calligraphy.

At any rate, Chinese embassy officials found out about the exhibit the day after it opened. The Chinese educational attaché rushed to the office of the dean of students, and then to the vice rector's office. He protested the matter and demanded that the exhibit be removed at once. The vice rector tried to placate the attaché, asking him to explain the university's position to the ambassador. But soon afterward the attaché returned, apparently after being rebuked by the ambassador, and again insisted that the exhibit be removed.

In the meantime Ariel had words with the student representative. The dean of students demanded that the exhibit be removed due to the violent nature of the photographs. He felt that the students had misled him. In retrospect the university supported the dean's decision and the exhibit was closed. The news media got wind of the incident, and the students' organization threatened to sue the university and its directors for reneging on their promise to keep the exhibit up for two weeks, as it was removed after two days.

In dozens if not hundreds of interviews that I have given to the Israeli media, including newspapers, radio, and television, I have always been careful to uphold China's dignity. I have deep respect for the achievements of the Communist Revolution, as I am aware of the situation in China during the rule of Chiang Kai-Shek—hunger, malnourishment, corruption, and exploitation of workers and women. I have methodically avoided outspoken criticism of China on sensitive issues such as the Falun Gong, Tibet, Taiwan, human rights, organ harvesting, and the treatment of Muslims in the northwestern province Xinjiang. I believe that this avoidance stemmed from my love for the country and the recognition that I must prioritize the issues at the top of the list. Following the Falun Gong incident, I had the uncomfortable feeling that the Chinese were sticking their noses too deep into university affairs, and that they were blind to their own faults while free to criticize ours. I thus decided that I should adopt a slightly different stance. I clarified this in a discussion with the deputy ambassador with whom I occasionally conducted open discussions. I believe that she understood my position, but as an experienced diplomat who was faithful to her government and ambassador, she repeated the importance of not "embarrassing the Chinese." Meanwhile, I pointed out that the embassy had made several tactical errors. The embassy viewed cancelling the exhibition as a victory, but in Israel this might have the opposite result of increased publicity for the Falun Gong by propelling it into media headlines. In addition, if another exhibit were organized, hundreds of visitors would come to learn about the "inciteful" exhibit that the university had removed under pressure from the embassy.

A year passed, and the scenario I had predicted took place. The students sued the university administration for removing the exhibit. The issue was debated in the Tel Aviv district court before Judge Dr. Amiram Binyamini. The students argued that the exhibit had been removed prematurely and that the university had promised them it would remain open for two weeks. They demanded that the court compel the university to restore the exhibit. In addition, they asserted that the university's East Asian Studies Department had received financial support from the Chinese government through the Hanban, the office that administrated the branches of Confucius Institutes around the world, including at Tel Aviv University. They thus argued that the university had succumbed to unreasonable, inappropriate political pressure. The judge pressed this point and repeatedly warned Professor Yoav Ariel that if this were true, the university would be guilty of inappropriate management. Ironically, Ariel had been an opponent of establishing the Confucius Institute at Tel Aviv University, arguing that the Chinese would interfere in academic affairs. His fear was thus justified (in his defense, I add that he has continued to support an uncompromising position on this issue). The judge proposed a compromise: the exhibit would be restored, and Professor Ariel as dean would have the opportunity to choose the photos and avoid displaying the most violent ones. The university administration agreed to this compromise, but the students rejected it out of hand. In the resulting legal debate in late September 2009, the judge surprisingly ruled that the students would be permitted to display the exhibit again. He also awarded them NIS 45,000 for legal expenses. I relayed the news of this decision to the deputy ambassador and again noted to her that China had to digest the fact that as a world power, it would be the target of sharp criticism on similar issues.

Yoav Ariel was very hurt by the judge's remarks during the legal investigation. He again attempted to point out that he had objected to the establishment of the Confucius Institute at the university, but now he was being indirectly blamed for receiving favors from Beijing. He asserted that removal of the exhibit was his independent decision and that he had not been subject to pressure from the Chinese embassy on this issue.

A similar incident took place in March 2014. This time several students initiated a discussion on human organ harvesting in China. The university authorized the event, but when the embassy found out about it their representatives came to my office and demanded that I prevent it, in my position as rector. I repeated my stance and recalled the previous incident and the lessons learned. The embassy subsequently sent another delegation, this time to the university president. The Chinese demanded no less than a promise that such an event would not be repeated. The Beijing representatives once again demonstrated their resoluteness.

Around the time of the exhibit incident, I was invited by a certain dispatch company to give the keynote speech at a conference for customers of their transport services, held in the new office park at Airport City. About three hundred people were in attendance. After the new Chinese ambassador to Israel, Zhao Jun, gave the welcome speech and spoke about Israel–China trade relations, I went up to the podium and began my lecture. This was an academic lecture in which I presented issues and conflicting opinions on trade with China. I outlined China's unique economic achievements and noted that China had become the United States' strongest competitor in many areas, including the extraction of raw materials worldwide. Regarding possibilities for future growth in years to come, I added that success was not a given. China might experience setbacks due to local corruption or differences between regions and social classes. I outlined a kind of balance sheet between the positive and negative components in a manner that I thought was objective and comprehensive. In doing so, I relied on a variety of economic indicators and on studies by several researchers.

While I was speaking, the ambassador suddenly got up and left the auditorium. When the seminar was over, the organizers and a high-level clerk in the Israel Foreign Ministry informed me that the ambassador had been deeply offended by my statements and had walked out in fury. In the ensuing saga, Foreign Ministry officials apologized for my words—without my knowledge—attempting to repair relations and thaw the tension that had been created.

Shortly following this incident, I met with the educational affairs attaché at the Chinese embassy. He stated that he valued my friendship with China and my contribution to establishing the Confucius Institute at Tel Aviv University. I gave an in-depth explanation regarding my position on free expression. I then responded to the ambassador's complaint about two terms that he thought I had used, which turned out to be translation errors.

I had delivered my speech in Hebrew and two translators had translated my words into English. The ambassador said that I had used the derogatory expression "Chinamen" five times in my speech to refer to the Chinese. After the speech, when I realized there was a diplomatic problem, I spoke with the two translators, and one admitted that she had used the pejorative term "Chinamen" by mistake. The ambassador also complained about my use of the Hebrew expression *ha-mishtar ha-Sini*, which means "the Chinese government." The translator had rendered this expression "the Chinese regime," which the Chinese also interpreted as negative.

This diplomatic incident and the previous incidents that involved my contact with the embassy led me to reevaluate dealings with the Chinese. I had the impression that the Chinese were guilty of the sin of pride. This feeling only intensified as time went on, and we had to consider how to deal with this new psychological reality.

As one who had been involved with China–Israel relations for many years, during that period I felt for the first time that the relationship of the Israeli media to China had changed for the worse. International criticism against China on numerous issues, including human rights and Tibet, swept some Israeli intellectuals and journalists into a furor. Former minister Yossi Sarid published many articles in which he attacked China, the rising global power. His anti-Chinese approach reminded his readers of his critical position against Turkey on the Armenian genocide issue. Sarid was an independent politician and a top-tier intellectual who over the years became a virulent critic of the government even while he served in its ranks. He claimed to be guided only by his own conscience.

At the time, several journalists contacted me, and from their questions I realized just how noisy the criticism of the People's Republic had become. A journalist from *Globes* business newspaper contacted me under the pretense of hearing my impressions and understanding my position regarding China–Israel relations. But during the telephone interview I realized that she was digging for criticisms of China and its Tel Aviv embassy. She repeatedly asked about the removal of the students' association exhibit on the Falun Gong and insisted that China did not permit researchers from Israel to travel to Beijing and access its archives. She particularly noted the case of Yitzhak Shichor. Shichor was a Sinologist and an old friend of mine. Until recently, the Chinese embassy refused to grant him an entry visa to China (aside from Israeli Falun Gong activist Yishai Lamish, Shichor was the only Israeli who had been refused entry). Although the Chinese authorities have never explained the reason for their refusal, obviously they were disturbed by his research on the Uyghur Muslims of Xinjiang in northwest China. Shichor was connected with a group of American researchers who published their findings on this issue, and this acted as a thorn in the side of the Beijing government. All attempts by the Israeli Foreign Ministry and pleas from various entities to reverse the decision were in vain.

In my conversations with the deputy ambassador I frequently raised the prohibition against Shichor's entering China. I explained to her that on this issue, the embassy was acting against its own best interests. While the deputy ambassador indicated special concern for the issue, she hinted that the embassy had no influence in the matter. Over the next few years, no compromise appeared on the horizon. The Chinese considered that Shichor had been too outspoken in his criticism of the People's Republic, and in one conversation the deputy ambassador hinted to me that the chances were very low that her government would change its position against him. In at least one case the Chinese embassy refused to cooperate with an Israeli body that Shichor headed. Communication between the institutions was possible only after he was removed from the position. Recently, the Chinese authorities altered their stance on Shichor and now he visits China frequently. Again, no explanations have been given for the change of policy.

The Confucius Institute: Founding, Crises, and Return to Routine

In late 2007 a branch of the worldwide Confucius Institute was founded at Tel Aviv University. The Confucius Institutes are funded by the Hanban, a Chinese government office with the goal of teaching Chinese language and culture on campuses around the world. Its establishment at Tel Aviv University was preceded by burdensome, troubling internal discussions. Some colleagues were suspicious of a Chinese presence on campus. If the activity of the Confucius Institute resembled that of the Goethe Institute, Cervantes Institute, the British Council, and other similar bodies, then it should not, they asserted, be established on campus but rather outside the university walls. My colleagues feared that the Chinese would become overly involved in academic activity and that they would try to influence the university through the Institute. As one of the founders and the first director of the East Asian Studies Department, my opinion was that given the lack of other sources of funding for the department, we should open the Institute. This would enable us to promote the teaching of the Chinese language at the university and beyond as well as expand our research on issues related to China. I hoped that the funding we would receive would permit us to make breakthroughs in areas such as Israel–China relations and the Chinese Jews, as well as many other sinology topics. In the end, despite the objections I succeeded in convincing the president and rector of the university that we should open the Institute.

With the assistance of the university legal advisor, I wrote a document that would ensure the university's independence. The center began to function with Professor Meir Shahar as director. Since then our ties with the embassy have strengthened with regard to teaching Chinese language and culture. Naturally, China's critics continued to complain that the Institute's existence did not allow the university adequate room to maneuver beyond the reach of political pressure. "Did you remove the exhibit on the Falun Gong because of your obligations toward the Chinese? Can the Confucius Institute organize a conference on Tibetan issues?" Such questions were raised repeatedly. In fact, the Institute did pose a problem. My contacts with directors of other Confucius Institutes around the world revealed that they had second thoughts regarding the connection with Beijing—the Chinese issued too many directives and orders to the Institute researchers. Often, Institute members asked whether they had taken the right step in connecting with a Chinese government body. A Canadian branch of the Confucius Institute was closed in 2013 following intervention of the court, which argued that the Chinese demands regarding Institute employees contradicted the values of freedom of employment and worship.

My view was that the Institute was intended to promote cultural topics, and considering that members of the Institute steering committee were professors, I did not expect them to experience any real pressure from Beijing. One of the points that I made sure to include in the founding document covered the possibility of cancelling the relationship (with advance notice of six months).

The Confucius Institute at Tel Aviv University blossomed. We expanded activity and increased the number of schools where our students and graduates taught Chinese. The university hosted major international conferences on Chinese studies on diverse topics such as Chinese popular religion and China as a global economic power. In October 2009 the Institute hosted a symposium on "China, Israel and the World Economy" with the participation of Wang Chen, China's Minister of Information, and Stanley Fischer, Governor of the Bank of Israel.

Wang said that despite the brevity of their diplomatic relations, China and Israel had made notable progress in advancing bilateral ties. Political relations enjoyed sound development, and frequent high-level political contacts triggered cooperation in trade, science and technology, culture, agriculture, tourism, and the non-governmental sector, delivering tangible benefits to the two peoples. He asserted that cultural, educational, and youth exchanges served as an important bridge to enhancing mutual understanding and friendship, and as a major force driving the stable development of China–Israel relations. He then called on students and scholars in both countries to engage in more academic exchanges.

Stanley Fischer hailed China's rapid economic development of the previous thirty years, calling it a miracle in global economic history. He also underscored the Chinese government's efforts to avoid the global financial crisis by adopting a massive fiscal stimulus package in November 2008, noting that "the results of what China has done are to transform China's role in the world, the life of the Chinese people, and the global economy."

I presented my theory on Israel–China relations: considering the change in the balance of economic and trade power between China and the United States in favor of China, the Israeli government would have to rewrite its diplomatic policy toward China. Possibly, Israel should encourage Beijing to become more involved in the Middle East conflict while acquiring information about Israel's history and challenges.

One particular incident that drew my attention was the Chinese embassy's behavior in preparation for the minister's visit to the above conference. I noted the strict discipline that surrounded the arrival of the minister's delegation as well as the middle level officials' concern for satisfying the desires of the high echelons. At endless meetings with the Chinese, the visit was planned down to the tiniest detail, including the placement of the flags, length of the speeches, and position of the minister's seat. In addition, the embassy feared anti-China demonstrations and antagonism from television and other media. Throughout the planning process we emphasized that we would not tolerate any censorship or limitations on campus. This issue grew out of my position against embassy pressure, despite the presence of the Confucius Institute at the university. I insisted on our autonomy and would not agree to any attempt to dictate terms, even in the gentlest manner.

In early 2014, Liu Qibao, a member of the Politburo of the Chinese Communist Party, visited Tel Aviv University, and we experienced similar problems. The Chinese representatives in Israel nagged us endlessly with preparations that seemed odd and unnecessary to us. One of their requests was for our students to leave the classrooms and wave the Chinese flag at the entrance to Gilman Building, where Lui's speech was planned.

Running the Confucius Institute was quite challenging. For example, in summer 2011 we felt that the authorities in Beijing, both the Hanban and representatives of Renmin University, were obstructing our plans. No explanation was given for the change of heart on their part. However, we speculated that it could be a reaction to our refusal to appoint a Chinese representative as director of the Confucius Institute in parallel to the Israeli director. I maintained that Tel Aviv University could not appoint a foreign citizen who was not a professor as director of a TAU institute—this was against our university regulations. We concluded that appointing a Chinese representative as deputy director could be a solution to the emerging difficulties. A deputy director would pose no real problem to the Israeli director. Meanwhile the Chinese delayed their annual financial assistance for operation of the Institute. While past delays had caused us inconvenience and disrupted our work, the current crisis was particularly deep.

By August, shortly before the 2011 to 2012 academic year was scheduled to begin, the money had still not arrived. During an extended stay in Beijing, Meir Shahar attempted to discover the source of the problem, but without success. Fluent in Chinese and married to a Chinese woman who taught in the East Asian Studies Department at Tel Aviv University, Shahar could be expected to understand the convolutions of the Chinese officials' thinking—but when he called me from Beijing trying to explain the difficulties, he sounded hopeless. Would we be forced to cease all Institute activities? Shahar suggested that I travel to China to solve the problem. Israel's ambassador to China, Amos Nadai, was also of this opinion. But I was not willing to fly over there to beg. Ran Peleg, cultural attaché at the Israeli embassy, took the initiative and met with Hanban representatives in Beijing. When I received the report of their discussion, I was astonished. The Hanban had no less than five complaints against Tel Aviv University. While we replied to each assertion with an appropriate answer, I sensed something strange and nebulous in the atmosphere.

After a hearing process required by law, in which I explained that the Institute's budget had run out and we were running at a deficit, I informed the Institute employees that we were forced to terminate their contracts. Nevertheless, I tried to continue some operations with the limited funds at our disposal. We even began a program to train teachers to teach Chinese language in schools and continued to initiate conferences.

Meanwhile, Gao Yanping, China's new ambassador to Israel, visited Tel Aviv University.[370] She emphasized the importance of the existence of the Confucius Institute but was unwilling to explore the problems in depth. She merely noted in her conversation with the president that it was important to iron out all the difficulties regarding the functioning of the Confucius Institute. I was still wavering. In impressions I gathered in the United States and Europe, I realized there were fundamental problems with the Confucius Institutes and that under certain circumstances, we would have no choice but to give up the Institute's activity at Tel Aviv University.

Signs of Conciliation

In late January 2012 I received a visit from the first secretary of the Chinese embassy in Israel and the cultural attaché. Meir Shahar joined our discussion. The two Chinese visitors informed us that Renmin University was now willing to cooperate with us and that we should reinstate our former activity. It seemed obvious that the Hanban office in Beijing would not permit the crisis to grow. Closing the Confucius Institute in Israel was undesirable to the Chinese. I clarified that because the funding had been cut off, we had terminated the work of all Institute employees. We were convinced that the new ambassador had helped move matters forward, as she asked us to organize an event at Tel Aviv University honoring twenty years of China–Israel relations, and she emphasized that this was a priority for her.[371] Because this time the Chinese had approached us, we decided to resume our activities at the Institute.

At that time others around the world were also critical of Confucius Institute activities. For example, Nick Byron of the London School of Economics expressed dissatisfaction with the Hanban for dictating to universities outside China regarding their choice of a Chinese partner

---

370 "Biography of Ambassador Gao Yanping," Chinese Embassy in Israel Website (September 8, 2011): http://il.china-embassy.org/eng/sgxx/t857116.htm

371 For a summary article on the Confucius Institutes in general and in Israel in particular, expressing suspicion about their establishment and the long-term goals of the Chinese government and the Chinese Communist Party, see Eyal Levinter and Ben Kaminsky, "Has a Trojan Horse Penetrated Israeli Academia," *Epoch Times*, July 2014. In this article, Tel Aviv University was singled out for its independent stance toward the Confucius Institute administration in Beijing.

institution. A lecturer on modern China at Miami University said that the university could not address some issues due to the Chinese veto, such as the role of the Dalai Lama (nor could they invite him to visit, of course), Tibet, Taiwan, development of Chinese weaponry, or the Muslims in Xinjiang. Richard Saller, dean at Stanford University, illustrated this through the Hanban's suggestion to grant the university four million dollars to establish an institute there and to fund a professorship on the condition that they avoid the issue of Tibet. Stanford refused to meet the Chinese demands but the money was sent to the university anyway, and today Stanford maintains a Confucius Institute. Arthur Waldron, a professor at the University of Pennsylvania, noted that under the current structure the Institutes were connected to the Chinese Communist Party, which meant that the Party was behind the Institute's every step. "The Chinese government already keeps track of Chinese students through their embassies and consulates. Do we really want to bring their representatives to our campuses?" he asked.

Other lecturers from American universities that host Confucius Institutes preferred to voice their criticisms anonymously. They stated that they hesitated to express their opinions on political issues involving China, fearing that they would not receive tenure at their institutions. Another professor went further and said that the status quo in ties between the Institutes and the host academic institutions was maintained only because China's internal and foreign affairs were calm for the moment. For this reason, he said, the global network of Confucius Institutes is "a time bomb waiting for the next Tiananmen incident."[372] Towards the end of 2014 several Confucius Institutes in North America closed at the insistence of the academic staff—for example, at the University of Chicago.[373] In addition, Congressman Chris Smith demanded a hearing in the US House of Representatives on the question of whether the Chinese had too much influence on American university campuses.[374]

Undoubtedly the pendulum is showing sharp preliminary movement toward criticism and even condemnation of the Confucius Institutes. Interestingly though, despite the critique, interest in China and willingness to cooperate with it continue to grow. Under the norm that has developed, states are willing to absorb some dictates from the Chinese and bend their accepted practices.

---

372 Guttenplan, "Critics Worry about Influence of Chinese."
373 See *Inside Higher Ed.*, Sept. 26, 2014, http://www.insidehighered.com
374 Fischer, *Online Chronicle of Higher Education*, Dec. 3, 2014.

Between 2012 and 2017, Israeli academic activities involving China thrived. For example, a ceremony was held to mark signature of a contract between the Tel Aviv University business school and Nanjing authorities for a program for Chinese students on innovation and technology. In addition, an agreement was signed between Tel Aviv University and China's elite Tsinghua University for the foundation of the XIN ("Innovation Center") with Liu Yandong, China's vice premier, in attendance. The agreement was based on anticipated fundraising of three hundred million dollars and determined that the two institutions would focus on top-priority scientific fields such as nanotechnology, biotechnology, and renewable energy. Also, many delegations from China in a variety of fields have visited Tel Aviv and inquired about ties with the university.

On October 22 2018, China's Vice President, Wang Qishan, visited Israel, a clear indication of the increasingly warm ties between the two countries. Wang and Israeli Prime Minister Benjamin Netanyahu co-hosted a joint summit on innovation cooperation between the two countries and viewed an exhibition of Israeli technological start-ups. The visit proved once again that Israel and China have become close trade partners, with China showing particular interest in Israeli developments in agriculture, water, hi-tech, environmental technologies, electronics, information technology, modern medicine, and more. Israel has also become a popular destination for Chinese tourists.

Wang praised Israel as an innovation hub from which China hopes to learn as it modernizes its fast-growing economy. Indeed, China has become Israel's second largest trading partner. In 2017/8 Israel and China signed a breakthrough visa agreement, opened direct flights, and conducted hundreds of joint research projects. Netanyahu announced that next year the two countries will finalize a free trade agreement, and China plans to invest heavily in Israeli infrastructure, including new ports and a light rail.

Israeli defense experts have expressed concern that Chinese participation in huge national infrastructure projects may pose a security risk, given China's close relations with Israel's regional foes, such as Iran.

Thus as Parama Sinha Palit and Amitendu Palit asserted, the Chinese used "soft power" to promote their interests. This term refers to cultural diplomacy, public relations, economic assistance, and other similar means.[375] It is a strategic tool used to create and project a positive, soft,

---

375 Palit and Palit, "Strategic Influence of Soft Power."

benign image of China and its government, which is often criticized. The various expressions of soft power act as a gentle spearhead for aiding the breakthrough into new markets and for neutralizing critique of the Chinese government's human rights record. Its entire purpose is to improve China's image. The Chinese have acted and continue to act to change negative attitudes toward them around the world and particularly in Asian countries. They consciously utilize their rich cultural heritage toward this purpose. To date they have founded over five hundred Confucius Institutes in several countries and regions. Estimates hold that by 2020, some one hundred million individuals will have studied Chinese through the Institutes.[376] Still, the attempt to use soft power as a cultural weapon to achieve the goal of improving China's image has not always succeeded, as criticism of its record on human rights and freedom of expression remains high.

As early as 2007 Yossi Sarid wrote in his article "It Has No God"[377] that the international community had adopted the correct pedagogical approach toward China as a wayward child in deciding to reward it with the rare gift of hosting the Olympics. The Israeli representative was one of the supporters of this decision. Sarid saw this as giving the Chinese another chance despite their inappropriate behavior and argued that sports and politics should not be separated. Even Hitler "used a similar justification—sports were one thing, politics another. He stood in the balcony [at sports events], applauded and lauded the Germans' purity. Although the Chinese are not Nazis, many of their citizens would disagree with a more moderate description—especially those waiting in line for the firing squad. The same is true for the Tibetans, and the other ethnic and religious minorities throughout this rising power." These were harsh words from the far-left Israeli politician.

Disseminating the Chinese Language

Between one incident and the next, the Confucius Institute has achieved several important goals, such as the initiative of teaching Chinese in elementary schools. In spring 2011 Nitzanim elementary school in Ramat Aviv hosted a festive ceremony commemorating the adoption of the Chinese language into the Israeli educational system. In attendance were Chinese Deputy

---

376 "China's Confucius Institutes to Reach 500 Global Cities by 2020," *Xinhua*: http://news. xinhuanet.com/english/china/2013-03/11/c_132225228.htm, March 11, 2013

377 Sarid, "It Has No God," *Ha'Aretz*, October 5, 2007.

Education Minister Zheng Shushan, Israeli Education Minister Gideon Sa'ar, and myself. We watched in excitement as children in the third through sixth grades chattered and even sang in Chinese. The Chinese deputy minister was moved to invite a group of children to visit China in the summer. Sa'ar and Shlomo Alon, director of Chinese language education in Israel, spoke about their plans to promote instruction of the language in Israel, including authorizing it as a subject in the high school matriculation exams. Sa'ar indicated that a small group of students had already been granted permission to take the matriculation test in the subject of the Chinese language. Prior to this decision many discussions on this topic had been held with Sa'ar, who had emphasized the need for a continuous framework. He also arranged that children studying Chinese in one elementary school would be permitted to continue when they transferred to another school. By 2017 numerous schools in Israel were offering programs to teach the Chinese language.

More Questions, This Time from Guangzhou

On November 13 and 14, 2010, I attended a large meeting of university directors in Asia, held in Guangzhou. At the conference the Chinese Education Minister and his deputy spoke, as did top official Liu Yangdong, responsible for education on behalf of the State Council (the State Council is comprised of top officials, each responsible for several ministers and departments). Eventually she was appointed vice premier.

This conference emphasized the importance of higher education, including the program known to the Chinese as "211." The government's defined goal for the twenty-first century is to grant preference to one hundred universities out of the thousands existing in China and to provide them all the resources necessary to push them into the top global rankings. In general, I gained the impression that the Chinese government is doing everything in its capability to promote higher education, to connect universities and industry, and to create ties between its universities and other institutions worldwide in order to gain the advantages of inter-university cooperation.

In her keynote speech, Liu asserted that while Great Britain had dominated the nineteenth century and the United States the twentieth, the twenty-first would belong to Asia, particularly China.[378] She anticipated

---

378 See for example, her speech six months earlier in Nanjing: http://www.moe.edu.cn/ publicfiles/business/htmlfiles/moe/moe_2862/201008/96836.html

that in the field of education, especially at the university level, China would become the focal point and spearhead in the current century. China has close to twenty-five million students in various higher education institutions. The number of students has increased exponentially in the past decade. She emphasized the need for cooperation between universities in China and parallel institutions elsewhere in Asia and around the world. She also stressed the importance of research collaboration and of Chinese students leaving China to study abroad. She indicated the importance of technological innovation, research on energy conservation, and improving knowledge resources—textbooks and teacher quality. She committed to raising the universities' budget to ensure quality teaching, improve the level of research, and promote student and lecturer exchanges. In her words, universities bore the burden of advancing culture and civilization. The government was responsible for encouraging the universities to act as inter-cultural bridges, to promote understanding and appreciation for other cultures. She also noted that as part of prioritizing higher education, the government aimed to provide more opportunities for professors and academic committees to participate in the modernization of China. "If we have increased our investment in universities in the past two years by 50 percent, we will continue this trend and expand the population's access to higher education," she emphasized. I was very impressed by the vice premier's speech, and I envied the Chinese for having a woman of such stature and openness at the head of their educational system.

On the day of the conference I was escorted by a Guangzhou University of Agriculture staff member in an official university vehicle to the island of Hai Xin Sha in the Pearl River (Zhu Jiang). We walked along the northern bank of a spotless new promenade and enjoyed the view of the southern bank. The lights of recently constructed houses twinkled across from us while the stunning column of a television tower rose alongside—completed just before the conference, it was one of the tallest buildings in Asia. Parents and young children strolled alongside us, enjoying their outing. I thought—this is the new generation that never knew Mao. After over a dozen trips that I had made to China I was overcome by a distressing comparison to Israel. I had the general impression that we were falling behind in the academic field, in our global university ranking, and in many other fields in which we used to enjoy high status. Meanwhile the Chinese were sprinting forward. In fall 1989, during my first visit to China, I felt that I had arrived in the heart of the Third World, and I had pitied the Chinese for their harsh living conditions. In many areas I had seen ramshackle build-ings, dark alleys, and public toilets that served entire neighborhoods. The general feeling was of scarcity and misery. I recalled details of my research on the Sino–Japanese war, the hunger that raged in China, and even cases of cannibalism in distant provinces. I recalled the China of American author Pearl Buck. But now, everything was different.

In the 1960s I had viewed China as carving out a path between two superpowers (the United States and the Soviet Union). I had high hopes for its ability to serve as a beacon for the Third World. Today, however, I view it less as an ideological pioneer and more as a formidable achiever as a result of its Open Door Policy, which has led to impressive economic and strategic accomplishments. Paradoxically, the harsh regime that ruled the People's Republic of China in the first thirty years of its establishment was what enabled the openness and success of the subsequent forty years. After the Second World War and its own civil war, China deftly extricated itself from the brink of starvation into a new age. Although we can hardly envy those who were condemned to undergo the trying times of China's early days and its harsh, intolerant regime, it seems that these tribulations were necessary to weed out negative characteristics such as crime, addic-tion to opium and other drugs, slavery, prostitution, and exploitation of women. Only after these features were stamped out with an iron hand was China able to enter the new era of the Open Door. Still, as proven by the Tiananmen massacre, China has not opened its gates completely to permit what the Chinese call "the fifth modernization"—meaning democracy. It has permitted only "the four modernizations" in the fields of science and technology, military, industry, and agriculture. The fact that the state has maintained strict controls while preventing full democracy has effectively created a new state. For one who believes in the spirit of democracy and liberal policies, it is not easy to admit that restraining civil society and maintaining control in the hands of decision-makers has enabled China to "leap forward" and develop. Civil society in the West tends to distort the constructive intentions of decision-makers; thus, governments have diffi-culty constructing railroads, bridges, or overpasses in the face of constant resistance from environmental movements, neighborhood organizations, or other interest groups.

Israel's Consul General in Guangzhou shared the following story with me. A certain civil engineer in Israel came to Guangzhou and Shenzhen. Observing the upsurge of development there with his own eyes, he threw up his hands in despair and envy. On witnessing the stupendous successes there, he admitted to feeling failure and helplessness, and when asked about the plans for his own city he was unable to respond.

The opening of the Asia Games in Guangzhou reached above and beyond my expectations. Not only was I thrilled by the impressive display, which according to witnesses outranked the opening of the Beijing Olympics in 2008, but I was also taken aback by the astounding order that prevailed when tens of thousands of people gathered with polite discipline in the local stadium. Cleanliness and an overall feeling of patriotism permeated the event. It was like a fantasy film, displaying the satisfaction of sweet victory.

I also recalled courses I gave at New York University and Sciences Po in Paris while on sabbatical, in which I conducted a comparison of the contemporary histories of Israel and China. While preparing and teaching the courses, I identified many similarities between the Chinese and the Jewish national movements. I found something heartwarming in the formation of these movements, which led to the establishment of the renewed states.

As mentioned, in the case of Chinese history the nascent national movement attained exceptional achievements under the leadership of Sun Yat-sen. A similar process, albeit with different details, took place at the modern beginnings of the Jewish national movement founded by Theodor Herzl. These outstanding individuals of the same generation broke new ground with their original leadership and became symbolic figures.

On the eve of the First World War the two national movements faced similar challenges. The arrangements that took shape after the war deeply influenced both on their paths toward establishing old-new nations. The leaders of both movements expected fair compensation for their assistance to the Allies. In the case of Sun, he demanded that the architects of the Treaty of Versailles extricate China from imperialist exploitation, particularly on the part of the Japanese. The May Fourth Movement of 1919 represented a low point of shattered hopes. In the case of the Zionist movement, the Balfour Declaration of 1917 offered compensation to the Jewish national movement for service and support it had given during the war to the victorious powers, led by Great Britain.

In the inter-war period, we also recognize many similarities between the experiences of the two movements. China witnessed vicious civil war between two ideological factions after the Northern Expedition set out. In the British Mandate of Palestine, the riots of 1929 and of 1936 to 1939 were also a kind of civil war. The Nazi threat and the Holocaust took place at the same time as Japan's fascist aggressions against China.

Indeed, similarities are present throughout the Second World War and its upheavals. In its aftermath in 1948 and 1949, the two states were founded based on socialist ideology, and over time they metamorphosed from the collective approach to the worldview of self-actualization and individualization of society, with the accompanying economic privatization. While in China the Communist Party continues to act as a rigid framework, ensuring that the borders are not crossed, in Israel centers of authority were shattered and are still being deconstructed. The relative homogeneity of Israeli society prior to the 1967 Six Day War was damaged after that war—and even more so following the Yom Kippur War. A sort of "second republic" was created in Israel whose geographical borders are unclear and whose population is more divided. Occupation has resulted in alienation between communities, and the foundations of Zionism are frequently questioned.

Chapter Ten

Review So Far, and What's Next?

This book covers three axes: historical-political, economic-trade, and personal-communal (the Jews and Israelis in China). I have attempted to expose the reader to various layers of my fifty years of exposure to a unique country, culture, and way of thinking. Further, this book has woven a dynamic plot out of the relationship between the subjects of this story: China and Israel. Throughout the extended period surveyed here, significant changes have taken place in this relationship, within each of the two countries, and in the story-teller himself. Their study is expressed here from the viewpoint of a passenger on a moving train who is observing the movement of a passenger on another train speeding past him.

We first summarized the history of various Jewish communities that settled in China. Then we focused on the stories of two specific Jews who left their mark on China's history and earned the recognition of the Chinese: one an erratic adventurer, the other a dedicated physician who devoted his life to helping the Chinese and became a hero of the Communist Revolution. Before that we addressed the early years of attempts to create ties between Israel and China. These failed attempts focused our discussion on the "missed opportunity"—the effort to create official relations. We based our in-depth analysis on a broad range of documents, attempting to locate the turning point, that point of no return (as it then seemed) after which (almost) nothing remained to be done. The closure of this window of opportunity inspired the question: could adjustments in Jerusalem's diplomatic management during the early days of the state have resulted in a different, more positive reality? It seems that in the end, the question of creating bilateral relations with China in the early stages remained purely academic. Even had appropriate ties developed and reciprocal representations opened in both countries, we may assume that as soon as the Six Day War began, Beijing would have returned its representatives from Israel. At most, China might have permitted an insignificant representation to remain in Israel long-term.

Behind the scenes of the relationship between the two countries, which is more or less familiar, another battle was taking place in the informal field of relations between Israeli civil society and Chinese organizations (which were always inspired and supervised by the Communist Party). The book addresses these ties as well, presenting their history for the first time based on sources and interviews that have never been used before. The leftist parties and radical groups in Israel were the major players in this battle, but they were unsuccessful in breaking down the wall that separated Israel and China.

Between 1955 and 1978, when the two nations had no relations, even the Israeli Communist Party was unable to work miracles and embrace distant China. The pioneer in the breakthrough in bilateral relations during these complex years was Shaul Eisenberg. His full story is still shrouded in uncertainty, and systematic documentation appears to be unavailable. Relatives and friends are also unable or unwilling to provide information. Still, intensive data collection has led, we might hope, to noteworthy results. Eisenberg's story in the history of covert relations between Beijing and Jerusalem becomes increasingly clear. While Eisenberg was amazingly successful in increasing his personal wealth, this was not the case for other Israeli companies that tried their luck in China. We attempted to trace the fates of four major Israeli companies from the time they entered the heart of the Chinese market: Sano, Osem, DavidShield, and Kardan. These companies formed the tip of an important iceberg in the field of bilateral commerce. Naturally, not every company is willing to reveal its documentation or its managers' musings on the history of its dealings in China. Still, in analyzing their declared manner of management, we have made a preliminary attempt to explain the background of the failures of these major companies and, through these examples, to explore how and why foreigners lose money in China. These thoughts led to another question asked by many: to what extent do China experts (with quotation marks and without) play a role in the game played between the two countries? Is it perhaps enough to rely on commercial intuition with a dose of legal advice?

Undoubtedly, what is usually called "the final frontier in China–Israel relations" is not really the last stop. It does not mark the end of the saga addressed in this book. The chain of events will continue for many years. So what comes next?

Although it is impossible to predict the developments in store, we can certainly rely on the threads that we hold in our hands today to forecast several likely scenarios. For example, when we study the broad history of China from the Opium War to the inheritors of Mao Zedong, we see clearly that in the past eighteen decades China has undergone a fascinating process of transition. China has moved from a position of subjugation and humility against the Western powers into national resourcefulness, overweening pride, and even hubris—which in Greek mythology is a crime deserving of harsh punishment. The term "hubris" might sound too severe, but China's actions in the academic and cultural spheres and even in the global business sphere, including their use of soft power, may prove this harsh term apt. Furthermore, we now observe preliminary signs that China's economic power and its financial reserves are at the apex of a process of "translation" into the language of "hard power"—in other words, conventional power. We may assume that at least in the observable future, this process will not fade but rather intensify.

The chief conclusions reached here regarding China's powers indicate to policy-makers in Israel that they must reevaluate their long-standing policy toward China. They must abandon the traditional line that is satisfied with mere "maintenance" of relations with China. Instead, Israel must upgrade these ties and adopt a more assertive policy and perhaps even encourage China to engage in broader involvement in the Israeli–Palestinian conflict and in tensions between Israel and Iran and its neighbors.

Still, Israel must be wary of sharp turns and internalize the warnings of challenges awaiting those who blindly follow the Chinese lead. A red light has been lit by a Chinese company's purchase of Tnuva, the aim of Chinese companies to win the long-term contract for construction and operation of the railroad to Eilat, Chinese interest in purchase of insurance companies (which own pensions and savings plans of many Israeli employees), and Beijing's aspiration to win tenders for construction and operation of the two private ports in Ashdod and Haifa. Objections to these moves include broad strategic and fundamental questions on the very definition of national resources that must not be handed over to foreign entities. Where do we define our borders in the process of close cooperation with the Chinese?[379] As noted, in late 2014 Israel decided to permit China to construct just one port, the private one in Ashdod, and to operate the private port of Haifa once it is completed.

Alongside the need to work closely with China and deepen its involvement in Israeli and Middle Eastern affairs, we must avoid getting carried away. We will not be able to follow the desires of the Israeli government alone and focus only on economic aspects of relations with China with the intention of exploiting them to the maximum, meanwhile hoping that Beijing will ignore the political issues that are less desirable to Israel. We must also avoid the expectation that China will fulfill Israel's requests in the political arena (containing the Iranian threat, for example) while forgetting less pleasant issues of Jerusalem's choice.

In 1971 Uri Orlev published a fascinating story called "The Chinese" in which he simulated a situation like that in 1930s and 1940s Europe, but in twentieth-century Israel and with a surrealistic twist. Orlev ascribed the role of the cruel conqueror to the Chinese, with the Arabs in Israel in the role of the persecuted minority that is eventually wiped out. The central figures in this story are the members of a Jewish family, one of whom cooperates with the conqueror while the rest of them remain on the other side of the conflict and hide Arab children to save them from the clutches of the Chinese. Orlev creates an allegory that is hard to digest, to say the least.

Orlev begins the story with this speech:

On the day the Chinese army invaded, my brother came to live with us. He arrived just after the surrender, when we handed Jerusalem over to them. In fact, the surrender was only formal, because our army didn't even put up a fight after the Allies left. There was no reason to fight, and the Jews were promised home rule.[380]

Orlev describes the blind hatred of the Chinese for the Arabs, the rumors of the massacres of Arabs and other peoples in the Arab states, and the settlement of their own "yellow" citizens in their stead.

This imaginary and fantastic story is based on the past reality when interest in the global sphere was mainly focused on hard power, meaning the use of aircraft, tanks, and conventional weapons and ammunition. Today, in the second decade of the twenty-first century, when we speak

---

379 Interview with Efraim Halevy, June 15, 2015.
380 Orlev, The Chinese.

of China we relate increasingly to soft power. Even if we relegate Orlev's cruel fantasy to the back of the bookshelf, we ponder how China has gained control through soft power strategies such as economic diplomacy and investment in essential realms. One of the questions that disturb European, Latin American, and African states is to what extent China is obtaining a global foothold in peaceful ways, through economic propagation and gradual takeover, sometimes under cover of aid. Is this imperialism of the sort that recalls the American imperialism of the past, an imperialism that is not based on settlements and colonies but rather on economic deterrence and power?

As I have emphasized, in Israel we have entered the stage in which the Chinese have begun to create economic centers of power, which in time can be transformed into strategic and geopolitical centers of power. We may already distinguish this kind of development in other locations. China's soft power penetration into states such as Italy, Portugal, Spain, the African continent, and even Australia has long-term importance. Through these means the Chinese have gained powerful leverage, which has broad diplomatic and political implications even exceeding expectations. Behind every Chinese company, whether governmental or private, stands an efficient system that is well-aware of every detail and is backed by an effective, focused political party. Realistically, we must anticipate that in Israel as well as in the region that it occupies, China will have influence at a level that currently seems the stuff of fantasy.

Bibliography

Archives, Official Sources, and Sources without an Author

Hebrew and Chinese sources

"China's Vice Premier: Return the Drones, Or Else We'll Start Hurting Israeli Companies Operating in China," *Tik Debka*, December 26, 2004.

"Commentary," *Yedi'ot Aharonot*, July 12, 2013.

Conference on Business in China, Tel Aviv University, Business School, July 2013.

Data of the Taiwan office of Economy and Culture in Tel Aviv, August 15, 2014, Susan C.I. Yang to Aron Shai.

Files of Yehoshua N. Shai, "List of Special Cases," Immigration and Naturalization Services, n.d., estimated 1954.

Foreign Ministry of China Archives, January 14, 1950; January 16, 1950; January 29, 1950; May 31, 1950; June 27, 1950; September 10, 1951; December 8, 1953; December 31, 1953; March 25, 1954; April 7, 1954; August 29, 1954; December 8, 1954; December 24, 1954; December 31, 1954; January 26, 1955; February 4, 1955; February 26, 1955; July 17, 1955; August 11, 1955; September 2, 1955.

Foreign Ministry of Israel Archives, Folder 2391/32, in Yemima Rosental, ed. *Documents on the Foreign Policy of the State of Israel, 1949–1951* (Jerusalem: State Archives, 1980, 1988, 1991); Galia Lindenstrauss, *Israel–China Relations, 1950–1992 (1994)*, Appendices 2-12.

"Foreign Trade 2013," Israel Central Bureau of Statistics. http://www.cbs.gov.il/hodaot2014n/16_14_017mazUSD.pdf, 2014.

"He Fangshan," Yadvashem.org.il. http://www.yadvashem.org/yv/he/righteous/stories/ho.asp?WT.mc_id=wiki, retrieved September 2013.

Information on the high-tech industry in China and its commercial relations with Israel: http://www.knesset.gov.il/mmm/data/pdf/m03476.pdf.

ISA Documents: Hamas Continues to Launder Money in China." *Ha'Aretz*, September 29, 2013.

Israel Ministry of Economy and Culture in Taipei. "Israel–Taiwan Trade Data, April 2012," Israel Ministry of Industry, Trade and Labor website, http://www.moital.gov.il/NR/rdonlyres/FDA75C5B-9A66-42DD-BA4A-7CFC76D08490/0/israel_taiwan_trade_2012.pdf.

Kol Ha'am, July 18, 1954.

Letter send by the committee on September 24, 1954 to Moshe Sharett and the Israeli delegation to the UN General Council, Yad Tabenkin Archives, section 15, series Israel Comes to Judea, file 26d.

Prime Minister's Office Archives, 7/5565/C.

Protocol of the Meeting of the Secretariat of Kibbutz Ha'meu'had, June 13, 1954, Yad Tabenkin Archives, 2-4/11/3.

"Senior Chinese Arrive for a State Visit to Israel," Israelhayom.co.il, http://www.israelhayom.co.il/article/125749, October 21, 2013.

"Special Database Documenting Shanghai Jewry Arouses a Wave of Responses around the World," source at Israeli Consulate, Shanghai, June 2008.

"The Chinese Connection," television program on China with Prof. Shlomo Avineri, Dr. Meron Medzini, Abba Eban, David Hacohen, Ya'akov Shimoni, Meir De-Shalit, and Yosef Zarhin, Kol Yisrael Radio, 1975.

Yad Tabenkin Archives, 15-31/26/3, 15-36/3/1, 10-11/11/3.

English sources

Business Week, "The Business Empire of a Global Mystery Man," November 16, 1981.

"Biography of Ambassador Gao Yanping," Website of Chinese Embassy in Israel: http://il.china-embassy.org/eng/sgxx/t857116.htm, September 8, 2011.

"China's Confucius Institutes to Reach 500 Global Cities by 2020," *Xinhua*: http://news.xinhuanet.com/english/china/2013-03/11/c_132225228.htm, March 11, 2013.

"China Legislators Vote to End Labour Camps," *AFP*: http://news.yahoo.com/china-formalis e-reforms-one-child-policy-labour-camps-033439167.html, retrieved December 24, 2013.

"China Savings Rate World's Highest," *The People's Daily*: http://english.people.com.cn/90778/8040481.html, November 30, 2012.

"China Surpasses U.S as EU's Top Trade Partner," *Xinhua*: http://news.xinhuanet.com/english2010/china/2011-10/16/c_131194386.htm, October 16, 2011.

"Chinese FM Urges Resumption of Israeli-Palestinian Peace Talks," *Xinhua*: http://news.xinhuanet.com/english/2009-04/23/content_11238582.htm, April 23, 2009.

"Dr. Feng Shan Ho & Jewish Refugees—From Vienna to Shanghai," *Shanghai Jewish Refugee Museum Website*: http://www.shanghaijews.org.cn/english/article/?aid=64, retrieved August 26, 2011.

"Foreign Minister Yang Jiechi Makes Five-point Proposal to Promote Mideast Peace Process," *Chinese Ministry of Foreign Affairs Website*: http://www.mfa.gov.cn/eng/wjb/wjbz/2467/t559690.htm, retrieved October 2014.

"Full Text of Hu Jintao's Report at 18th Party Congress," *Xinhua*: http://news.xinhuanet.com/english/special/18cpcnc/2012-11/17/c_131981259.htm, November 17 2012.

"Iran and China to Expand Trade Relations," *Payvand*: http://www.payvand.com/news/12/apr/1001.html, 4 January 2012.

"Iran-China Trade Value to Increase to $70b in 5 Yrs: Iranian Envoy," *Tehran Times*: http://tehrantimes.com/politics/100518-iran-china-trade-value-to-increase-to-70b-in-5-yrs-iranian-envoy, August 12, 2012.

"Iran Voices Support for Rights of Chinese Muslims," *Press TV Online*, July 9, 2009.

International Monetary Fund: http://www.imf.org.

Israel Ministry of Economy Website: http://www.tamas.gov.il.

Israel Ministry of Foreign Affairs Website: http://www.mfa.gov.il/MFA/Terrorism. July 15, 2006.

"Israeli President Meets with Foreign Minister Yang," *Chinese Mission to the U.N. Website*: http://www.china-un.ch/eng/xwdt/t558942.htm, April 23, 2009.

Books and Periodicals (Hebrew)

Amit, Hagai. "4 Billion NIS—2014 was a Record Year for the Growing Business Between China and Israel." *The Marker*, March 9, 2015.

Arlozorov, Meirav. "The Chinese Will Profit: Israel's Government Fortifies Tnuva's Monopoly Forever," *The Marker*, April 1, 2015.

———. "China Demands that Chinese Construction Workers Not Be Employed in the Settlements," *The Marker*, June 7, 2015.

Avisar, Irit. "How is Kardan Group Trying to Breach the Great Wall of China?" *Globes.com*, http://www.globes.co.il/news/article.aspx?did=1000684884, retrieved September 22, 2011).

Bardenstein, Eli. "Netanyahu Tries to Promote Free Trade Agreement with China, Beijing Demands Work Permits for Thousands of Workers." *Ma'ariv*, May 7, 2013.

Barnea, Nachum and Shimon Shiffer. "Commentary." *Yediot Aharonot*, July 12, 2013.

Baron, Lior and Michel Udi. "The Conflict Intensifies: Carmelton Brought in an Israeli Contractor to Dig in the Carmel Tunnels Project." *Globes.co.il*. http://www.globes.co.il/news/article.aspx?did=1000381231. September 11, 2008.

Barzilai, Amnon. "That's How You Break Down a Wall." *Ha'Aretz* supplement, May 2, 1999.

———. "Weizmann Initiated Eisenberg's Involvement in the Arms Deal with China 20 Years Ago." *Ha'Aretz* supplement, February 3, 1999.

Bat-Rachel (Tarshish), Yocheved. "Impressions from Peking on May 1st." Yad Tabenkin Archives, 15-36/3/1.

———. *In the Path I Walked: Memoirs and Realms of Activity*. Efal: Tabenkin Institute for Research and Kibbutz Studies and United Kibbutz Movement Publishers, 5741/1981.

———. "On Chinese Soil, 1956." Yad Tabenkin Archives, 15-36/3/1.

———. "Trip to the Congress of the International Democratic Women's Federation." Yad Tabenkin Archives, 15-36/3/1.

Bat-Israel, Dvora. "With Leaders and Writers—Chronicles of a Journey in the People's Republic of China." Davar, Yad Tabenkin Archives, 15-138/10/09.

Beit-Aryeh, Rachel. "David Shield Enters China." *Calcalist.co.il.* http://www.calcalist.co.il/articles/0,7340,L-3359851,00.html, retrieved September 3, 2009.

Ben, Aluf. "The New Phalcon Rules." *Ha'Aretz* supplement, December 25, 2001.

Bengal, Mia. "Governor Stanley Fisher Joins the Struggle against Iran." *nrg.co.il.* http://www.nrg.co.il/online/1/ART2/064/556.html, February 21, 2010.

Ben-Yishai, Ron. "Weapons Deal: The First Israeli Phalcon Lands in India." *Ynet.* http://www.ynet.co.il/articles/0,7340,L-3721379,00.html, May 25, 2009.

Ben-Porat, Yishayahu. "I Nicked Vegetables So that I Could Eat." *Yediot Aharonot—Sukkot* supplement. September 25, 1988.

Bialer, Uri. "Ben Gurion and the Question of Israel's International Orientation, 1948–1956." *Katedra*, vol. 3 (Nissan 5747).

Blumencranz, Zohar. "El Al Set the Price and the State Paid $1.43 Million for Netanyahu's Flight to China." *The Marker*, May 21, 2013.

Confucius. *Analects.* Trans. Amira Katz. Jerusalem: Mossad Bialik, 2006.

Confucius. *Analects.* Trans. Daniel Lesley and Amatzia Porat. Jerusalem: Mossad Bialik, 5721/1960.

Eber, Irene. *Chinese and Jews: Cultural Encounters.* Jerusalem: Mossad Bialik, 2002.

Eitan, H. "Eisenberg: Money Breeds Money." *Yedi'ot Aharonot—7 Days*, January 25, 1980.

Evron, Yoram. "Patterns of China's Involvement in the Middle East." *INSS Strategy Update*, vol. 16, no. 3 (October 2013): 73–84.

Frustig, Na'ama. "Activity of the Jewish National Fund in China Between the World Wars." PhD diss., Tel Aviv University, 2009.

Gavizon, Yoram. "Apax is Expected to Give Bright Food a Discount." *The Marker*, September 29, 2014.

———. "Maalot: The Only Opportunity of Kardan NV—Quick Sale of Assets." *The Marker*, July 13, 2014.

Galili, Orit. "The Next Generation's Turn." *Ha'Aretz* supplement, October 10, 1997.

Gelber, Emmanuel, "The Yom Kippur War in the PRC Media." Emmanuel Gelber correspondence collection—Israeli Foreign Ministry, personal copy, November 26, 1973.

———. "Anti-Confucius Campaign." Emmanuel Gelber correspondence collection—Israeli Foreign Ministry, personal copy, December 27, 1973.

———. "China and Hong Kong." Emmanuel Gelber correspondence collection—Israeli Foreign Ministry, the author's personal copy, September 25, 1973.

———. "China and the War in the Middle East." Emmanuel Gelber correspondence collection—Israeli Foreign Ministry, personal copy, November 27, 1973.

———. "Chinese Foreign Minister is Replaced." Emmanuel Gelber correspondence collection—Israeli Foreign Ministry, personal copy, November 19, 1974.

———. "Energy Sources of the PRC." Emmanuel Gelber correspondence collection—Israeli Foreign Ministry, personal copy, October 16, 1974.

———. "Israel's Image in Communist China." Emmanuel Gelber correspondence collection—Israeli Foreign Ministry, personal copy, October 3, 1974.

———. "Replacement of Personnel in the Chinese Military." Emmanuel Gelber correspondence collection, Israeli Foreign Ministry, personal copy, January 16, 1974.

Golan, Avirma. "Thousands Attended Eisenberg's Funeral." *Ha'Aretz* supplement, March 31, 1997.

Gutman, Uri. General Consul in Shanghai, in a letter to Avner Shalev, Chairman of Yad Vashem Board of Directors. March 4, 2008.

Hacohen, David. *Burma Diary: Memoirs of a Diplomatic Mission, 1953–1955*. Tel Aviv: Am Oved, 1963.

Haim, Yehoyada. *Between the Cobra and the Dragon*. Tel Aviv: Yediot Books Publishing, 2008.

Halevi, Efraim. *Man in the Shadows*. Tel Aviv: Matar Publishing, 2006.

Harel, Amos and Ruti Zota. "The Connection between the Biggest Bank in China and the Terror Attack in Tel Aviv." *Ha'Aretz*, June 15, 2013.

Hazani, Golan. "The Deal is Closed: ChemChina Transferred $2.4 Billion for Merger with Makhteshim." Calcalist.co.il. http://www.calcalist.co.il/markets/articles/0,7340,L-3541904,00.html. October 17, 2011.

Immerglick, Shira. "The Chinese People's Hero Buried in Tel Aviv." *Ma'ariv*, January 18, 1995.

Katzir, Uri. "The Chinese General Moshe Cohen." Aplatonblog by Uri Katzir, May 1, 2012. http://www.aplaton.co.il/story_103, retrieved in October 2014.

Kaufmann, Teddy. *Harbin Jewry in My Heart*. Ed. Bat-Ami Melnick. Tel Aviv: Association of Former Residents of China, 2004.

Koren, Ora. "As Long as China is Growing 8% a Year, It Will Preserve its Economic Stability." TheMarker.com. http://www.themarker.com/wallstreet/asia/1.1623707, January 23, 2012.

Laskov, Shulamit. *Trumpeldor: His Life Story*. Jerusalem: Keter, 1982.

Lev-Ari, Shiri. "The Harbin Community: An Island of Tranquility in Jewish History." *Ha'Aretz*. http://www.haaretz.co.il/misc/1.1384952. February 8, 2007.

Levin, Eleazar. "All of Eisenberg's Men." *Ha'Aretz*, January 30, 1981.

———. "The Man Who Buys and Sells Everything." *Ha'Aretz*, January 6, 1978.

Levinter, Eyal and Ben Kaminsky. "Has a Trojan Horse Penetrated Israeli Academia?" *Epoch Times,* July 2014.

Levitsky, Naomi. "Shaul, King of China." *Hadashot* (newspaper) supplement, November 2, 1990.

Lifkin, David. "Started with $50 and Reached More Than a Billion." *Ma'ariv*, March 30, 1997.

Lubitz, Ruth. *I Chose to Live in Struggle*. Tel Aviv: Shachar Publishing, 1985.

Magen, Hadas. "China Will be Israel's Biggest Business Partner." *Globes*, December 11, 2011.

Melamed, Arianna. "The Chinese Humiliation." *Ynet*. http://ynet.co.il.d4p.net/articles/0,7340,L-4377598,00.html. May 8, 2013.

Merhav, Reuven. "Dream of the Red Palaces—From the Fragrant Port to the Forbidden City, From Hong Kong to Beijing." In: Moshe Yegar et al. (eds.), *The Foreign Ministry—The First 50 Years*. Jerusalem: Keter, 2002, 565–578.

Meshayoff, Meshual Meir. Memoirs. Private publication, Hagit Masser-Yaron Family, President of the Open University, undated.

Oren, Amir. "The Cutting Robber." *Ha'Aretz* supplement, October 13, 1995.

Orlev, Uri. "The Chinese." *Ha'Aretz*, August 13, 1971.

Peretz, Gad. "The Heir is Already Apparent." *Ha'Aretz* supplement, March 30, 1997.

Peretz, Samy. "Syria Can Wait—Netanyahu is Hungry for Business Opportunities in China." *The Marker*, May 7, 2013.

Ravid, Barak. "Reaching Iran Through China." *Ha'Aretz*, May 5, 2013.

Rolnick, Guy. "Who Profits and Who Loses from the Sale of Tnuva to the Chinese." *The Marker*, May 23, 2014.

Rosen, Rami. "When I Whistle, My Employees Come Running." *Ha'Aretz* supplement, December 26, 1997.

Sacks, Ofer. "China Doesn't Welcome Israeli Exports." *The Marker*, May 23, 2013.

Sarid, Yossi. "It Has No God." *Ha'Aretz*, October 5, 2007.

Senor, Dan and Shaul Singer. *Start-Up Nation: The Story of Israel's Economic Miracle*. Tel Aviv: Zemora Bitan and Matar, 5771/2011.

Shai, Aron. *China in the Twentieth Century*. Tel Aviv: Ministry of Defense Publishing Department, Broadcast University, 1998.

———. *From the Opium War to Mao's Inheritors: China in the International Arena, 1840–1990*. Tel Aviv: Zmora-Bitan, 5750/1990.

Shai, Aron. *Zhang Xueliang—The General Who Never Fought*. Or Yehuda: Zmora-Bitan, 2008.

Shamir, Daniel and Avi Bar-Eli. "The Private Port in Ashdod Sets Sail." *The Marker*, September 22, 2014.

Shiffer, Shimon. "The Former Mossad Chief: We Didn't Get What We Wanted." *Yedi'ot Aharonot*, November 24, 2013.

Sicolar, Na'ama. "China–Israel Relations Warm Up: IAI is on the Way to Establishing a Factory in China." *Calcalist*, July 3, 2011.

Stein, Ron and Eran Parr. "The Phoenix Expands: Offered to Purchase 50% of David Shield Agency." *Globes.co.il*. http://www.globes.co.il/news/article.aspx?did=1000588533, September 14, 2010.

Steinberg, Robbie. "Agreement between Eisenberg Group and the Chinese Government: They Will Construct a Potassium Plant for 450 Million." *Ha'Aretz* supplement, May 14, 1998.

Sufott, Ze'ev. "Chinese Policy toward Israel, 1950–1992." In: Moshe Yegar et al. (eds.), *The Foreign Ministry—The First 50 Years*. Jerusalem: Keter, 2002, 583–585.

Urbach, Noam. "Kaifeng Jews—Between Revival and Obliteration," *Zmanim* 85 (winter 2003–2004), 38–53.

Vagman, Avraham. "Agricultural Reform in China—Chronicles of a Visit." Davar, Yad Tabenkin Archives, 15-138/10/09.

Weissman, Lilach. "Steinetz Goes to Visit China and Hong Kong with 25 Businessmen." *Globes.co.il*. http://www.globes.co.il/news/article.aspx?did=1000556262&fid=2. May 2, 2010.

Yegar, Moshe. *The Long Journey to Asia: A Chapter in Israel's Diplomatic History*. Haifa: Haifa University Publishing, 2004.

Zaban, Yair. "Confucianizing of Marx?" *Ha'Aretz*, 1971.

Zigmund, Shmuel and Gertrude Hirschberg. From Berlin to Shanghai—Letters to the Land of Israel. Jerusalem: Yad Vashem, 2013.

Books and Periodicals (English and Chinese)

Barr, Michael. *Who's Afraid of China?—The Challenge of Chinese Soft Power*. London: Zed Books Ltd., September 2011.

Bialer, Uri. *Between East and West—Israel's Foreign Policy Orientation 1948–1956*. Cambridge: Cambridge University Press, 1990.

Blanchard, Ben and Yao, Kevin. "China Unveils Boldest Reforms in Decades, Shows Xi in Command," *Reuters*: http://www.reuters.com/article/2013/11/15/us-china-reform-idUSBRE9AE0BL20131115, November 15, 2013.

Brecher, Michael. *Israel, the Korean War and China*. Jerusalem: Academic Press, 1974.

Chang, Gordon G. *The Coming Collapse of China*. New York: Random House, July 2001.

Chang, Jung, and Halliday, Jon. *Mao: The unknown story*. Random House, 2012.

Chester, Sam. "Why Netanyahu and Abbas Went to China," *Tablet*: http://www.tabletmag.com/scroll/132220/why-netanyahu-and-abbas-went-to-china, May 13, 2013.

Cochran, Sherman. *Big Business in China: Sino–Foreign Rivaling in the Cigarette Industry 1890–1930*. Harvard University Press, 1980.

Dorraj, Manochehr and Carrie L. Currier, "Lubricated with Oil: Iran–China Relations in a Changing World," *Middle East Policy* 15, no. 2 (Summer 2008).

Drage, Charles. *Two Gun Cohen*. London: Jonathan Cape, 1954.

Elazar, Gideon, "China in the Red Sea," BESA, Bar-Ilan University, August 23, 2017.

Evron, Yoram. "The Rise of China from a Small States' Perspective: The Case of the Sino–Israeli Military Relations," *The 11th Annual Conference of Asia Studies in Israel*, Tel Aviv University, May 2012.

———. "Chinese Involvement in the Middle East: The Libyan and Syrian Crises," *INSS*, October 3, 2013.

Fang, Jianchang 房建昌。"房建昌。内蒙古，辽宁·天津· 及青岛犹太人史 (1911–1949年) (History of Jews in Inner Mongolia, Liaoning, Beijing, Tianjin and Qingdao [1911–1949])," in: Malek, Roman (ed.), *From Kaifeng—to Shanghai: Jews in China*. Joint Publication of Monumenta Serica Institute and the China-Zentrum. Nettetal: Steyler, 2000.

Farrar-Wellman, Ariel and Robert Frasco. "China–Iran Foreign Relations," *American Enterprise Institute for Public Policy Research,* http://www.irantracker.org/foreign-relations/china-iran-foreign-relations, July 13, 2010.

Fischer, Karin. "House Panel Plans to Scrutinize US Universities' Ties with China," *Online Chronicle of Higher Education* (Washington, D.C.), December 3, 2014.

Gao, Qiufu, He, Beijian and Zhenxian Yao (ed.), *You and Us—Stories of China and Israel Friendships*. Translation: Ego. Beijing: China Intercontinental Press, 2014.

Garamone, Jim. "Cohen, Barak Reaffirm US–Israeli Bonds, Discuss Contentions," US Department of Defense, http://www.defense.gov//News/NewsArticle. aspx?ID=45098, April 3, 2000.

Goodstadt, Leo. "The Middle East Backlash," *Far Eastern Economic Review*, vol. 82, November 12, 1973.

Goldstein, Jonathan. "China Honors Its Holocaust Rescuer," *Times Georgian*, Carrollton, Georgia, USA, April 13, 2002.

———. "A Quadrilateral Relationship: Israel, China, Taiwan and the United States since 1992," *American Journal of Chinese Studies*, October 2005.

———. "The Republic of China and Israel," in: Jonathan Goldstein (ed.), *China and Israel, 1948–1998*. London: Praeger, 1999.

———. (ed.). *China and Israel, 1948–1998: A Fifty Year Retrospective*. Westport: Praeger Publishers, 1999.

Guttenplan, D. D. "Critics Worry about Influence of Chinese Institutes on US Campuses," *The New York Times*, March 4, 2012.

Herbert Franke. "Der Weg nach Osten. Jüdische Niederlassungen im Alten China (The Way Eastward. Jewish Settlements in Old China)," in: Malek, Roman (ed.). *From Kaifeng—to Shanghai: Jews in China*. Joint Publication of Monumenta Serica Institute and the China-Zentrum. Nettetal: Steyler, 2000.

Ho, Feng-Shan. *My Forty Years as a Diplomat*. Trans. and ed. Monto Ho. Pennsylvania: Dorrance Publishing, 2010.

Jacobs, Andrew. "Israel Makes Case to China for Iran Sanctions," *The New York Times*, June 8, 2010.

Jacques, Martin. "Welcome to China's Millennium," *The Guardian*: http://www.guardian.co.uk/commentisfree/2009/jun/23/china-martin-jacques-economics, June 23, 2009.

Johnson, Stephen. "Balancing China's Growing Influence in Latin America," *The Heritage Foundation*: http://www.heritage.org/research/latinamerica/bg1888.cfm, October 24, 2005.

Kaminski, Gerd. *General Luo Genannt Langnase; das abenteuerliche Leben des Dr med Jakob Rosenfeld*. Wien: REMA print, 1993.

King, Joe. "Two-Gun Cohen; Chinese Spy Master and a second Moishe," *The Museum of the Jewish Soldier in World War II Website*: http://www.jwmww2.org/vf/ib_items/1480/Two%20Gun%20Cohen.pdf, undated.

Kissinger, Henry. *On China*. London: Penguin Books, April 2012.

Kranzler, David. "Jewish Refugee Community of Shanghai 1938–1949," in: Malek, Roman (ed.), *From Kaifeng—to Shanghai: Jews in China*. Joint Publication of Monumenta Serica Institute and the China-Zentrum. Nettetal: Steyler, 2000.

Krasno, Rena. "History of Russian Jews in Shanghai," in: Malek, Roman (ed.), *From Kaifeng—to Shanghai: Jews in China*. Joint Publication of Monumenta Serica Institute and the China-Zentrum. Nettetal: Steyler, 2000.

Leslie, Donald D. "Integration, Assimilation and Survival of Minorities in China: The Case of the Kaifeng Jews," in: Malek, Roman (ed.), *From Kaifeng—to Shanghai: Jews in China*. Joint Publication of Monumenta Serica Institute and the China-Zentrum. Nettetal: Steyler, 2000.

Levinter, Eyal and Ben Kaminsky. "Has a Trojan Horse Penetrated Israeli Academia," *Epoch Times*, July 2014.

Levy, Daniel S. *Two-Gun Cohen: A Biography*. New York: St. Martin's Press, 1997.

Li, Xiaokun and Guangjin Cheng. "China, Israel Boost Cooperation," *China Daily*: http://www.chinadaily.com.cn/china/2013-05/09/content_16486378.htm, May 9, 2013.

Liu, Fu-Kuo. *Taiwan-Israel Relations: Towards a New Partnership*, paper presented at the Fourth Annual Conference of The Balance of Israel's National Security, Hertzlia, Israel, December 16–18, 2003.

Mackerras, Colin. "Xinjiang and the War against Terrorism," in: Shen, Simon (ed.), *China and Antiterrorism*. New York: Nova Science Publishers, 2007.

Madhukar, Shukla. "A World Deceived by Numbers/Facts," in *Alternative Perspective Newsletter*, August 11, 2005.

Magid, Isador A. "I Was there: The Viewpoint of an Honorary Israeli Consul in Shanghai 1949–1951," in Goldstein, Jonathan (ed.), *China and Israel, 1948–1998*. London: Praeger, 1999.

Ma'Oz, Moshe. *Soviet and Chinese Relations with the Palestinian Guerrilla Organizations*. Jerusalem: Hebrew University Press, 1974.

Meyer, Maisie J. "The Sephardi Jewish Community of Shanghai and the Question of Identity," in Malek, Roman (ed.), *From Kaifeng—to Shanghai: Jews in China*. Joint Publication of Monumenta Serica Institute and the China-Zentrum. Nettetal: Steyler, 2000.

———. *From the Rivers of Babylon to the Whangpoo: A Century of Sephardi Jewish Life in Shanghai*. Lanham, Md.: University Press of America, 2003.

Olimat, Muhamad S. *China and the Middle East Since World War II*, chapter 10. London, 2014.

Palit, P. S. and A. Palit, "Strategic Influence of Soft Power: Inferences for India from Chinese Engagement of South and Southeast Asia," *ICRIER* Policy Series, no. 3, August 2011.

Pan, Guang. *China and Israel: Analysis on Bilateral Relations, 1948–1992*. New York: The American Jewish Committee, 1999.

Pentland, William. "Did the US Invade Iraq to Contain China?," *blogs.forbes.com*: http://www.forbes.com/sites/williampentland/2011/01/07/did-the-u-s-invade-iraq-to-contain-china/, July 1, 2011.

Pollak, Michael. *Mandarins, Jews, and Missionaries: the Jewish Experience in the Chinese Empire*. Philadelphia: Jewish Publication Society of America, 1980.

———. "The Manuscripts and Artifacts of the Synagogue of Kaifeng: Their Peregrinations and Present Whereabouts." In Malek, Roman (ed.), *From Kaifeng—to Shanghai: Jews in China*. Joint Publication of Monumenta Serica Institute and the China-Zentrum. Nettetal: Steyler, 2000.

Portman, Julian and Kipfer, Jean. *Shadow over China*. New York: Paperjacks, Redux Books, 1988.

Rivlin, Paul. "The Economic Melt-Down (1): America," *Tel Aviv Notes*, October 28, 2008.

———. "Will China Replace the US in the Middle East?" Iqtisadi, Moshe Dayan Center, vol. 4, no. 3, March 25, 2014.

Roubini, Nouriel. "China's Bad Growth Bet," *Project Syndicate*: http://www.project-syndicate.org/commentary/roubini37/English, April 14, 2011.

Sadeh, Shuki. "Yosef Greenfeld's Battle for Survival," *The Marker*, April 24, 2015.

Schurmann, Franz. *Ideology and Organization in Communist China*. Berkeley: University of California Press, 1968.

Shai, Aron. *Origins of the War in the East: Britain, China, Japan 1937–1939*. London: Croom Helm, 1976.

———. *Britain and China 1941–1947: Imperial Momentum*. London: Macmillan, St. Antony's College, Oxford and St. Martin's Press, New York, 1984.

———. *The Fate of British and French Firms in China 1949–1954: Imperialism Imprisoned*. Houndmills, Basingstoke: Macmillan in association with St. Antony's College, Oxford, 1996.

———. "Israeli Communist Party and PRC, 1949–1998," in Goldstein, Jonathan (ed.), *China and Israel, 1948–1998—A Fifty Year Retrospective*. London: Praeger, 1999.

———. "China and Israel—Strange Bedfellows 1948–2006," in Shen, Simon (ed.), *China and Antiterrorism*. New York: Nova Science Publishers, 2007.

———. *Sino–Israeli Relations: Current Reality and Future Prospects (memorandum)*. Tel Aviv: Institute for National Security Studies, 2009.

———. *The Evolution of Israeli–Chinese Friendship*. Tel Aviv: The S. Daniel Abraham Center and Confucius Institute, 2014.

Shatzman-Steinhardt, Nancy. "The Synagogue at Kaifeng: Sino–Judaic Architechture of the Diaspora," in: Goldstein, Jonathan. *The Jews of China*. Armonk, N.Y: M.E Sharpe, 1999.

Shen, Simon (ed.). *China and Antiterrorism*. New York: Nova Science Publishers, 2007.

Shichor, Yitzhak. *The Middle East in China's Foreign Policy 1949–1977*. London, 1979.

———. "Israel's Military Transfers to China and Taiwan," *Survival* 40, no. 1 (Spring 1998): 68–91.

———. "Ethno-Diplomacy: The Uyghur Hitch in Sino–Turkish Relations," *Policy Studies* 53, East-West Center, Honolulu, 2009.

Simpson, L. George Jr. "Russian and Chinese Support for Tehran," *Middle East Quarterly*, no. 17–2 (Spring 2010): 63.

Sufott, Zev. *A China Diary*. London: Frank Cass, 1997.

Tjong-Alvares, Benjamin. "The Geography of Sino–Isreali Relations," *SIGNAL* http://jcpa. org/wp-content/uploads/2013/05/V24_3_6.pdf, May 2013.

Urbanek, Vladimir. "China's Foreign Exchange Reserves at the End of 2012 Grew to 3.3 Trillion, from +700% L.04," *KurzyCZ*: http://news.kurzy.cz/347840-chinas-foreign-excha nge-reserves-at-the-end-of-2012-grew-to-3-3-trillion-from-700-l-04/, March 4, 2013.

Wallerstein, Immanuel. "The United States and Israel: The Approaching Separation," *Mita'am* 12 (December 2007): 89–99.

Walter, E. Carl and Fraser J. T. Howie. *Red Capitalism, the Fragile Financial Foundation of China's Extraordinary Rise*. Singapore: Wiley, 2011.

Witte, Carice. "A Quiet Transformation in China's Approach to Israel," *SIGNAL* 12, no. 6: http://jcpa.org/article/a-quiet-transformation-in-chinas-approach-to-israel/, April 2, 2012.

Wu, Sike. "The Upheaval in West Asia and North Africa: A Constructed New Viewpoint of World Security," *Journal of Middle Eastern and Islamic Studies (in Asia)* 7, no. 1 (2013): 1–16.

Xu, Xin. "On the Religious Life of the Kaifeng Jewish Community in the 15th–17th Centuries," in: Roman Malek (ed.), *From Kaifeng—to Shanghai: Jews in China*. Joint Publication of Monumenta Serica Institute and the China-Zentrum. Nettetal: Steyler, 2000.

———. *Holocaust Education in China—Discussion Paper*. The Holocaust and the United Nations Outreach Programme, 2012.

Interviews

Yigal Alon. Interview by Reudor Manor, Kibbutz Ginosar, August 26, 1979, on behalf of the Davis Institute of International Relations, Hebrew University of Jerusalem.

Iris Arbel. Interview by Or Biron, Tel Aviv, July 18, 2013.

The following interviews were conducted by the author:

David (Sasha) Hanin, Tel Aviv, July 17, 1995.

Meir Vilner, Chinese ambassador's residence, Savion, September 2, 1995.

Gabriel Gidor, Tel Aviv, 2004.

Horacio Furman, Europe House, Shaul Hamelech Ave., Tel Aviv, January 26, 2004.

Amos Yudan, Tel Aviv University, July 21, 2004.

Dr. Ze'ev Suffot, Jerusalem, September 6, 2004.

Yair Zaban, Tel Aviv University, July 6, 2011.

Bruno and Alex Landesberg, Hod Hasharon, July 17, 2011.

Gad Propper, Tel Aviv, August 14, 2011.

Mordechai Arbel, by phone, Tel Aviv, June 2013.

Dr. Ze'ev Suffot, by phone, Tel Aviv, December 10, 2013.

Alon Shlank, Kardan offices, Tel Aviv, May 7, 2014.

Alon Ketzef, David Shield offices, Netanya, August 3, 2014.

Efraim Halevi, Tel Aviv University, June 15 and August 12, 2015.

Index